London

DIRECTIONS

WRITTEN AND RESEARCHED BY

Rob Humphreys

ROUGH
GUIDES

NEW YORK • LONDON • DELHI
www.roughguides.com

Contents

Introduction to

London

London is a very big city. In fact, it's one of Europe's largest capitals, stretching for more than thirty miles on either side of the River Thames, and with a population of just under eight million. Ethnically and linguistically, it's also Europe's most diverse metropolis, offering cultural and culinary delights from right across the globe. Londoners tend to cope with all this by compartmentalizing the city, identifying with the neighbourhoods in which they work or live, and just making occasional forays "into town" or "up West", to the West End, London's shopping and entertainment heartland.

◄ Lion, Trafalgar Square

With no single predominant focus of interest, the city can seem bewilderingly amorphous to newcomers. The key to enjoying London is not to try and do everything in a single visit – concentrate on one or two areas and you'll get a lot more out of the place. London has always been an enthralling city, and the capital's traditional sights – Big Ben, Westminster Abbey,

When to visit

Despite the temperateness of the English climate, it's impossible to say with any degree of certainty that the weather will be pleasant in any given month. With average daily temperatures of around 22°C, English summers rarely get unbearably hot, while the winters (average daily temperature 6–10°C) don't get very cold – though they're often wet. However, whenever you come, be prepared for all eventualities: it has been known to snow at Easter and occasionally approach 40°C on very hot summer days. As far as crowds go, tourists stream into London pretty much all year round, with peak season from Easter to October, and the biggest crush in July and August, when you'll need to book your accommodation well in advance.

Buckingham Palace, St Paul's Cathedral and the Tower of London – continue to draw in millions of tourists every year. Things change fast, though, and the regular emergence of new attractions ensures that there's plenty to do even for those who've visited before. In the last decade, virtually all of London's world-class museums, galleries and institutions have been reinvented, from the Royal Opera House to the British Museum. And with Tate Modern and the London Eye, the city can now boast the

▲ St James's Park

world's largest modern art gallery and Ferris wheel, as well as the Millennium Bridge, the first new Thames-crossing for over a hundred years.

Monuments from the capital's glorious past are everywhere, from medieval banqueting halls and the great churches of Christopher Wren to the eclectic Victorian architecture of the triumphalist British Empire. There's also much enjoyment to be had

from the city's quiet Georgian squares, the narrow alleyways of the City of London, the riverside walks, and the assorted quirks of what is still identifiably a collection of villages. And London is offset by surprisingly large expanses of greenery, with several public parks right in the centre as well as wilder spaces on the outskirts.

You could spend days just shopping in London, too, mixing with the upper classes

▼ Sunset over the Thames

in the "tiara triangle" around Harrods, or sampling the off-beat weekend markets of Portobello Road, Camden and Greenwich. The music, clubbing and gay/lesbian scenes are second to none, and mainstream arts are no less exciting, with regular opportunities to catch first-rate theatre companies, dance troupes, exhibitions and opera. The city's pubs have always had heaps of atmosphere, but its restaurants are now an attraction too, with everything from three-star Michelin establishments to low-cost, high-quality Chinese restaurants and Indian curry houses.

▲ London door

▼ Columbia Road market

London
AT A GLANCE

WESTMINSTER

Home to the Houses of Parliament, Big Ben and the striking Abbey and Cathedral, Westminster easily justifies its status as one of London's busiest tourist honeypots.

▼ Westminster Abbey and Big Ben

SOHO

The headquarters of hedonistic London, Soho is the heart of the West End entertainment district, with the city's largest concentration of theatres, cinemas, clubs, bars, cafés and restaurants.

GREENWICH

Well worth the boat or train journey from central London, Greenwich makes the most of its riverside setting, with heaps of maritime sights, a royal park, a bustling weekend market and the famous Greenwich Meridian.

COVENT GARDEN

With its big covered market hall, cobbled piazza and fantastic range

▼ Neal's Yard, Covent Garden

of shops, pedestrian-friendly Covent Garden is justifiably many visitors' favourite slice of central London.

BANKSIDE AND SOUTHWARK

The traffic-free riverside path takes you past Tate Modern, Shakespeare's Globe Theatre and several more sights in neighbouring Southwark, while dishing out great views over the water to St Paul's Cathedral.

▼ *Golden Hinde*, Bankside and Southwark

SOUTH KENSINGTON

A fashionably smart part of London in its own right, South Kensington is also home to the city's most impressive trio of free museums:

the Natural History, Science, and Victoria & Albert.

▼ Natural History Museum

HAMPSTEAD

Although buzzing with cosmopolitan life, Hampstead has managed to retain a more village-like feel than any other London suburb and boasts the wild open space of the Heath as well as a clutch of intriguing small museums.

▼ Hampstead Heath

Ideas

The big six

London has lots of hidden gems, but amongst the well-known sights, the "big six" really do live up to their hype. Westminster Abbey and the Tower of London have justifiably been pulling in the crowds for centuries; the British Museum and the National Gallery have grown in popularity over the last hundred years or so; while the elegance of the London Eye and the stunning collection housed in the Tate Modern have captured the imagination of today's visitors like no other sights.

▲ British Museum

London's most popular museum, worth a visit for its glazed-over Great Court and magnificent Round Reading Room alone.

P.104 ▸ BLOOMSBURY

▼ National Gallery

The vast range of work here, from Giotto to Picasso, ensures that there's something for everyone.

P.67 ▸ TRAFALGAR SQUARE AND WHITEHALL

▶ Westminster Abbey

Venue for every coronation since William the Conqueror and resting place of countless kings and queens, the abbey is an essential stop on any London tour.

P.75 ▸ WESTMINSTER

▼ London Eye

The world's largest Ferris wheel is already an iconic addition to the London skyline.

P.154 ▸ SOUTH BANK AND AROUND

▲ Tower of London

England's most perfectly preserved medieval fortress, site of some of the goriest events in the nation's history and somewhere everyone should visit at least once.

P.145 ▸ THE TOWER AND DOCKLANDS

▼ Tate Modern

Austere former power station that's now an awesome cathedral to modern art.

P.159 ▸ BANKSIDE AND SOUTHWARK

London outdoors

Summer can be unpredictable, and the winter a little damp, but Londoners get out and enjoy the great outdoors whatever the weather. Temporary outdoor ice rinks are a regular feature of the winter season, boats ply up and down the Thames throughout the year, and in the summer there are several little-known spots where you can enjoy an alfresco dip.

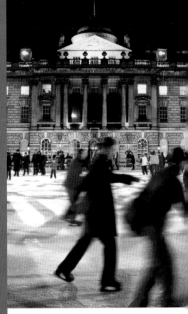

▲ Somerset House ice rink

Set up each winter in the eighteenth-century courtyard of Somerset House, this is London's most picturesque place to skate.

P.114 ▶ ESSENTIALS

▲ Westminster Abbey College Gardens

Hidden behind the abbey, this secret oasis of green is great for picnics, croquet matches and brass-band concerts.

P.75 ▶ WESTMINSTER

▶ Portobello Road Market

London's best street market offers brilliant retro clothes, bric-a-brac, antiques, and fruit and veg.

P.181 ▶ HIGH STREET KENSINGTON TO NOTTING HILL

▲ Boat trip on the Thames

Zig-zag your way from pier to pier on the central section of the Thames, or take longer trips downriver to Greenwich or upstream to Kew and Richmond.

P.234 ▶ ESSENTIALS

▼ Hampstead Ponds

Tucked amidst woodland, the Heath's natural ponds are extremely popular for alfresco swimming.

P.194 ▶ HAMPSTEAD AND HIGHGATE

What to eat

London is an exciting – though often expensive – place in which to eat out. You can sample pretty much every kind of cuisine here, from traditional and modern British food to Georgian and Peruvian. Indeed, London can boast some of the best Cantonese restaurants in the whole of Europe, is a noted centre for Indian and Bangladeshi food, and has some very good French, Greek, Italian, Japanese, Spanish and Thai eateries.

▲ Pie and mash

London's most peculiar culinary speciality: minced beef and gravy pie, mashed potatoes and "liquor" (parsley sauce).

P.127 ▸ CLERKENWELL

▼ Dim Sum

This bargain spread of dumplings and other little morsels is a Cantonese lunchtime ritual.

P.98 ▸ SOHO

▶ Haute cuisine

The capital now boasts an impressive array of restaurants serving top-notch, Michelin-starred haute cuisine.

P.135 ▶ THE CITY

◀ Curry

Attracting top-notch chefs from Bangladesh, Nepal, Sri Lanka and Pakistan as well as all the Indian regions, London is now one of the curry capitals of the world.

P.142 ▶ HOXTON AND
SPITALFIELDS

▼ Fish and chips

The national dish – fish in batter with deep-fried potato chips – remains as popular and tasty as ever.

P.183 ▶ HIGH STREET KENSINGTON
TO NOTTING HILL

▼ Vegetarian

London has a vast range of exclusively veggie eating places, ranging from small, wholesome, informal cafés to smart à la carte restaurants.

P.116 ▶ COVENT GARDEN

Gourmet London

From champagne to chocolates, you'll find all the luxury goods you'd expect in London; seafood – particularly oysters – remains very popular; and there's been a renewed interest in gourmet British food: cheese, smoked fish, beer and even wine. As well as being sold in deluxe emporia, top-quality produce is a main feature of London's increasingly popular farmers' markets.

▲ Neal's Yard Dairy

Experienced, helpful staff encourage customers to sample the outstanding variety of British cheeses piled high on the counters.

`P.116` ▸ COVENT GARDEN

▼ Charbonnel et Walker

If it ain't broke, don't fix it – Her Majesty's chocolatier sticks to its 1875 recipes.

`P.89` ▸ PICCADILLY AND MAYFAIR

◀ **Borough Market**

Stalls at this weekly gourmet food market sell the very best of British produce.

P.162 ▶ BANKSIDE AND SOUTHWARK

▶ **Paul**

Long-established Parisian café-boulangerie, selling authentic and delicious French breads and pastries.

P.116 ▶ COVENT GARDEN

◀ **Fortnum & Mason**

Piccadilly's most famous food emporium, renowned for its picnic hampers, sumptuous food hall and pukka tearoom.

P.89 ▶ PICCADILLY AND MAYFAIR

▶ **Harrods Food Hall**

The Arts and Crafts food hall of the ultimate Knightsbridge department store is a feast for the eyes as well as the stomach.

P.176 ▶ SOUTH KENSINGTON, KNIGHTSBRIDGE AND CHELSEA

Afternoon tea

One of London's most accessible indulgent rituals is taking afternoon tea in a luxury hotel. At a cost of around £30 a head, this is no quick cuppa, but a high-cholesterol feast that kicks off with sandwiches, moves on to scones slathered with clotted cream and jam, and finishes up with assorted cakes, all washed down with innumerable pots of tea.

▼ Claridge's

Tasteful and terribly English Art Deco hotel that's perfect for a champagne tea.

P.91 ▸ PICCADILLY AND MAYFAIR

▼ The Lanesborough

Exclusive and very plush venue in a converted hospital on Hyde Park Corner, where tea is served in the glass-roofed conservatory.

P.89 ▸ PICCADILLY AND MAYFAIR

▲ Savoy

Superb Art Deco hotel, originally managed by César Ritz, and where Guccio Gucci started out as a dishwasher.

P.89 ▸ PICCADILLY AND MAYFAIR

◀ Ritz

The Palm Court here has been a favourite spot to take tea since the hotel first wowed Edwardian society in 1906.

P.89 ▸ PICCADILLY AND MAYFAIR

▼ The Dorchester

Wildly over-the-top gilded and mirrored Hollywood decor is the Dorchester's hallmark.

P.91 ▸ PICCADILLY AND MAYFAIR

London pubs

One of the country's most enduring social institutions, pubs remain the focal point of London's communities, offering the prospect of fringe theatre, alternative comedy and live music as well as a pint. The city's great period of pub building took place in the Victorian era, and though many pubs merely pay homage to that period, there are also plenty of genuine, evocative late nineteenth-century interiors, boasting etched glass partitions and lots of authentic polished wood and brass fittings.

▲ **Salisbury**

Flamboyant late-Victorian pub a stone's throw from Trafalgar Square, replete with bronze nymphs and etched glasswork.

P.102 ▶ SOHO

▲ **Ye Olde Cheshire Cheese**

A dark, snug seventeenth-century tavern hidden down an alleyway off Fleet Street – look out for the sign.

P.123 ▶ HOLBORN

▶ Anchor

Ancient riverside inn near the Tate Modern, where Pepys watched London burn, and Dr Johnson worked on his dictionary.

▲ The Lamb

Classic, beautifully preserved Victorian pub serving London's own Young's beers.

▼ Dog and Duck

Victorian Soho pub with real character, real ales and original tiled and mosaiced decor.

Club-bars

The last decade and a half has seen the inexorable rise of the club-bar. Catering for a clubby crowd, with resident DJs, late opening hours and, more often than not, free (or very cheap) entry, club-bars came about as part of the backlash against London's "superclubs", where entrance fees were climbing ever higher and door-policies becoming increasingly draconian. These days, club-bars are ubiquitous, and are ideal if you fancy a laid-back night on the tiles.

▲ Dragon

Low-key bar popular with a mixed clientele of laid-back locals who like to party on down to the resident DJs.

P.144 ▶ HOXTON AND SPITALFIELDS

▲ Cherry Jam

Great west London cocktail bar whose DJ line-ups attract a trendy young crowd.

P.184 ▶ HIGH STREET KENSINGTON TO NOTTING HILL

▲ AKA

A minimalist adjunct to The End night-club, this central venue's regular DJ nights pull in a crowd of good-time clubbers.

P.117 ▸ COVENT GARDEN

▼ Big Chill Bar

Buzzing, busy DJ venue situated off Brick Lane with large comfy sofas inside and tables outside in the summer.

P.143 ▸ HOXTON AND SPITALFIELDS

▶ The Social

Industrial club-bar run by the Heavenly record label with excellent DJs playing to a relaxed and music-savvy crowd.

P.103 ▸ SOHO

Gay and lesbian

London's lesbian and gay scene is huge, diverse and well established. Pink power has given rise to the pink pound, gay liberation to gay lifestyle, and ever-expanding Soho – now firmly established as the homo heart of the city – is vibrant, self-assured and unashamedly commercial. As a result of all this high-profile activity, straight Londoners tend to be a fairly homo-savvy bunch and, on the whole, happy to embrace and sometimes dip into the city's queer offerings.

▲ Old Compton Street

Lined with upfront bars and cafés, and some rather risqué shops, this Soho drag is Gay London's main street.

P.98 ▶ SOHO

▲ G.A.Y.

Huge, unpretentious and fun-loving dance night at the Astoria where the young crowd gather on Mon, Thurs, Fri & Sat.

P.103 ▶ SOHO

▲ Candy Bar

Central London's hottest girl-bar is a cruisey, upbeat spot that's open until the early hours on the weekend.

P.102 ▶ SOHO

▶ Chariots Roman Baths

London's largest and most fabulous gay sauna features everything you could wish for in the way of hot and sweaty nights indoors.

P.239 ▶ ESSENTIALS

▼ First Out

The West End's original gay café-bar still draws in the crowds, and runs a popular weekly pre-club session for women each Friday.

P.118 ▶ COVENT GARDEN

Diverse London

With around three hundred languages spoken in its confines, all the major religions represented, and with immigrants making up over thirty percent of the population, London is Europe's most ethnically diverse city. As well as improving the local cuisine immeasurably, London's immigrants have provided a vast workforce, had a profound impact on the arts and music scene, and are responsible for the Notting Hill Carnival, the country's biggest street party.

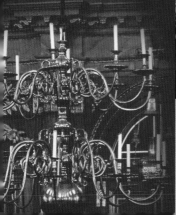

▲ Bevis Marks Synagogue

Built in 1701 in the City, this Sephardi synagogue is the country's oldest, and a favourite venue for candlelit Jewish weddings.

P.134 ▶ THE CITY

▲ Brixton market

Brixton's upfront African-Caribbean consciousness is especially evident around the wonderful market, with its outdoor produce stalls and network of indoor arcades.

P.238 ▶ ESSENTIALS

▲ Brick Lane

This East End street is the spiritual heart of London's Bangladeshi community, and is best known for its inexpensive curry houses.

P.140 ▸ HOXTON AND SPITALFIELDS

▶ London Central Mosque

Thousands of worshippers congregate for Friday prayers at this striking modern mosque in Regent's Park.

P.186 ▸ REGENT'S PARK AND CAMDEN

▼ Chinatown

London's most distinct and popular ethnic enclave, characterized by its bewildering array of cafés and restaurants.

P.98 ▸ SOHO

Art galleries

The astute taste and financial muscle of London's collectors over the centuries has endowed the capital with some wonderful art galleries, many of which offer free entry. The National boasts both quality and quantity, stretching from the Italian Renaissance to the Impressionists, while Tate Modern is London's magnificent repository of modern art. In addition, there are several smaller galleries, where the quality is comparable but the collections more manageable.

▲ Tate Modern

A wonderful hotchpotch of wild and wacky art, from video installations to gargantuan pieces that fill the vastness of the turbine hall.

P.159 ▸ BANKSIDE AND SOUTHWARK

▼ Kenwood House

Small but perfectly formed gallery of seventeenth- and eighteenth-century paintings, including works by Gainsborough, Reynolds, Rembrandt and Vermeer.

P.196 ▸ HAMPSTEAD AND HIGHGATE

▶ Wallace Collection

Exquisite miniature eighteenth-century chateau close to Oxford Street, housing period furniture and masterpieces by the likes of Rembrandt, Van Dyck, Hals, Fragonard and Watteau.

P.92 ▶ MARYLEBONE

◀ Tate Britain

The history of British painting from Holbein and Hogarth to Hockney and Hirst, plus copious pre-Raphaelites and lots of Turners.

P.77 ▶ WESTMINSTER

▼ Courtauld Institute

Quality, not quantity, is the hallmark of this gallery, best known for its superlative collection of Impressionist masterpieces.

P.115 ▶ COVENT GARDEN

▼ National Gallery

A comprehensive overview of the history of Western painting, from Renaissance classics in the airy Sainsbury Wing to works from fin-de-siècle Paris.

P.67 ▶ TRAFALGAR SQUARE AND WHITEHALL

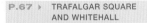

Museums

London has a fantastic number and variety of museums, but some stand head and shoulders above the rest. The British Museum and the Victoria and Albert are both world-class repositories of art treasures. For a balanced view of human conflict, head for the Imperial War Museum, but for exemplary modern, interactive museums, choose the National Maritime Museum or the Science Museum. All these are giants compared with Sir John Soane's Museum, a hidden gem with totally unique, treasure-trove atmosphere.

▲ British Museum

Roman and Greek art, Egyptian and Assyrian artefacts, fabulous treasures from Anglo-Saxon, Roman and Medieval Britain, and vast ethnographic collections from all over the world.

P.104 ▸ BLOOMSBURY

▼ V&A

The world's greatest applied arts museum, with something for everyone, whether you're into the history of dress, musical instruments, silver, Indian and Islamic art or modern mass-produced design.

P.175 ▸ SOUTH KENSINGTON,
KNIGHTSBRIDGE AND
CHELSEA

▶ National Maritime Museum

Encompassing the old Royal Observatory as well as the nautical exhibits, this imaginatively designed complex will appeal to all ages..

◀ Sir John Soane's Museum

This early nineteenth-century home-cum-studio of the idiosyncratic architect of the Bank of England is crammed with paintings and antique sculpture.

▼ Science Museum

The great new interactive galleries and the daily demonstrations are the most impressive aspects of this enormous complex, covering every conceivable area of science.

▼ Imperial War Museum

The capital's finest military museum puts on fascinating talks and events, houses a huge art collection and gives a sober account of the horrors of war.

Churches

As medieval London was almost entirely destroyed by the Great Fire of 1666, the churches that survived the flames are all the more precious. The Fire heralded the city's greatest era of church building, much of it under the supervision of Sir Christopher Wren, architect of St Paul's Cathedral. Later, the Victorians added yet more churches to London's burgeoning suburbs, one or two of which are especially worth seeking out.

▲ Westminster Abbey

This former medieval monastic church preserves both its cloisters and chapter house, and boasts some of the city's finest late Gothic architecture and funerary art from every age.

P.75 WESTMINSTER

▼ St Bartholomew-the-Great

Much altered, wonderfully ancient church which has the finest Norman chancel in London and some excellent pre-Fire monuments.

P.124 CLERKENWELL

▶ St Paul's Cathedral

The world's first Protestant cathedral is a Baroque masterpiece – test the acoustics in the whispering gallery and climb to the top of the dome.

P.130 THE CITY

▼ Westminster Cathedral

Bizarre, eye-catching neo-Byzantine Catholic cathedral with an ornate but eerily unfinished interior.

P.76 WESTMINSTER

▼ Temple Church

This early English Gothic church in the heart of the Inns of Court boasts a circular nave featuring battered medieval effigies of the Knights Templar.

P.120 HOLBORN

Royal London

Home to the most famous royal family in the world, London doesn't disappoint when it comes to pomp and circumstance. As well as the massing of "busbies" at the daily Changing of the Guard, there are much larger displays of royal pageantry to take in throughout the year. The crown jewels are always on public display, guarded by ludicrously overdressed Beefeaters at the Tower of London; and then, of course, there's the city's numerous royal palaces.

▲ Hampton Court Palace

Redesigned by Wren, this Tudor pile is without doubt the most magnificent of the country's royal palaces.

P.212 ▸ HAMPTON COURT

▼ Changing of the Guard

The colourful daily rituals of the Queen's Household Regiments, with the Horse Guards parading behind Whitehall and the Foot Guards looking after Buckingham Palace.

P.71 ▸ TRAFALGAR SQUARE AND WHITEHALL

▶ Trooping the Colour

Suitably spectacular summer show by the Household battalions in the presence of royalty.

P.236 ▶ ESSENTIALS

◀ Tower of London

A place of imprisonment for several monarchs, the Tower remains the safe-deposit box of the crown jewels, which feature some of the biggest diamonds in the world.

P.145 ▶ THE TOWER AND DOCKLANDS

▼ Royal Mews

Official garage for the royal family's fancy fleet of Daimlers, gilded coaches and immaculately groomed horses.

P.82 ▶ ST JAMES'S

▼ Buckingham Palace

The gaudy London home of Her Majesty is open to the public for just two months in the summer, while the royals holiday in Scotland.

P.80 ▶ ST JAMES'S

Tudor and Stuart London

Much of Tudor and Stuart London went up in smoke during the 1666 Great Fire of London, but some gems from the period do survive today from the grand residences of Hampton Court Palace and Ham House on the outskirts to the hammerbeamed Middle Temple Hall and wood-panelled Prince Henry's Room, on the edge of the City. The Golden Hinde and the Globe Theatre, meanwhile, are meticulous timber-framed reconstructions from London's glorious Elizabethan Renaissance.

▲ Ham House

Seventeenth-century stately home, just up the towpath from Richmond, with one of the finest Stuart interiors in the country.

P.209 ▶ KEW AND RICHMOND

▼ Golden Hinde

Seaworthy replica of the dinky timber ship in which Sir Francis Drake circumnavigated the globe.

P.162 ▶ BANKSIDE AND SOUTHWARK

▲ Middle Temple Hall

This sixteenth-century lawyers' dining hall boasts a fine hammerbeam roof, wood panelling and a richly carved Elizabethan screen.

P.119 ▸ HOLBORN

▼ Prince Henry's Room

Hidden gem at the top of Fleet Street, with Jacobean plasterwork and linenfold panelling that miraculously survived the Great Fire.

P.121 ▸ HOLBORN

▲ Globe Theatre

Relocated and reconstructed in the 1990s, the Globe gives a fascinating insight into the theatre of Shakespeare's day.

P.161 ▸ BANKSIDE AND
SOUTHWARK

▼ Hampton Court Palace

Magnificent Tudor palace on which both Cardinal Wolsey and Henry VIII spent a fortune.

P.212 ▸ HAMPTON COURT

Victorian London

During the reign of Queen Victoria (1837–1901), London trebled in size and became the largest city in the world, at the heart of an empire that stretched across the globe. Not surprisingly, the buildings of the era exude the wealth and confidence of that period. They also reflect the magpie-like tastes of the day, when architects tried to outdo each other in decorative detailing, borrowing from every previous architectural style and from all corners of the empire.

▲ Leadenhall Market

Cobblestones and graceful Victorian ironwork combine to create the City's most attractive market for luxury comestibles.

P.134 ▶ THE CITY

▼ Albert Memorial

This bombastic monument to Queen Victoria's consort is a riot of semi-precious stones, marbles, bronze and gilding.

P.170 ▶ HYDE PARK AND KENSINGTON GARDENS

▶ Palm House Kew Gardens

Decimus Burton's spectacular curvaceous hot-house is home to most of the world's known palm species.

P.208 ▶ KEW AND RICHMOND

◀ Brompton Oratory

Experience the smells and sights of an Italianate Roman Catholic church in this wonderfully atmospheric slice of neo-Baroque.

P.176 ▶ SOUTH KENSINGTON, KNIGHTSBRIDGE AND CHELSEA

▼ St Pancras Station

Victorian railway station fronted by a gloriously over-the-top red-brick Neo-Gothic hotel.

P.108 ▶ BLOOMSBURY

▼ Houses of Parliament

A gargantuan, confident neo-Elizabethan expression of nationhood, best known for its "Big Ben" clock-tower.

P.73 ▶ WESTMINSTER

Contemporary architecture

The economic boom of the 1980s witnessed London's first wave of contemporary architecture. Reflecting the nature of the times, the buildings were generally private office blocks, the most famous of which are the then-groundbreaking Lloyds Building and Canary Wharf. New offices continue to spring up city-wide, and since the turn of the millennium there's been a new wave of lottery-funded structures such as the Millennium Bridge, and public buildings like the new City Hall.

▲ Millennium Bridge

After a wobbly start, Norman Foster's flashy millennial footbridge, connecting St Paul's Cathedral with the Tate Modern, has proved a hit with locals and tourists alike.

P.159 ▸ BANKSIDE AND SOUTHWARK

▲ The Gherkin

The latest lofty addition to the City skyline is Norman Foster's unusual cone-shaped affair for Swiss Re insurance company.

P.134 ▸ THE CITY

▼ City Hall (GLA)

Bearing a close resemblance to a giant car headlight, Norman Foster's eco-friendly headquarters for the Greater London Authority occupies a prominent position on the Thames by Tower Bridge.

P.164 ▸ BANKSIDE AND SOUTH-WARK

▶ Canary Wharf

Loved and hated in equal measure, Cesar Pelli's stainless steel skyscraper is the centrepiece of the Canary Wharf Docklands development.

P.149 ▸ THE TOWER AND DOCKLANDS

▼ Serpentine Gallery and pavilions

The gallery and the annually commissioned summertime tea pavilions have added architectural merit to the green groves of the park.

P.170 ▸ HYDE PARK AND KENSINGTON GARDENS

▲ Lloyds Building

Lloyds' high-tech City offices, designed by Richard Rogers in the mid-1980s, are still strikingly contemporary and more successful than many younger upstarts.

P.133 ▸ THE CITY

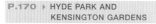

London from up high

It's only when you take a bird's-eye view that you realize just how vast London is. The most far-reaching vistas are from the London Eye, but even here you can barely make out the edge of the city. What you do notice, though, is that London has only a small number of very tall buildings, allowing church spires to rise above the rooftops, and that the city has a wonderfully idiosyncratic patchwork layout, woven over several centuries.

▲ Westminster Cathedral

A lift inside the stripy campanile takes you high above the rooftops of Westminster.

P.76 ▶ WESTMINSTER

▼ Parliament Hill

North London's favourite kite-flying spot, at the southern tip of Hampstead Heath, offers a fabulous skyline panorama.

P.195 ▶ HAMPSTEAD AND
HIGHGATE

▶ St Paul's Cathedral Dome

A head for heights and the ability to climb five hundred steps are needed to enjoy a rooftop view over the City here.

P.130 ▸ THE CITY

◀ Oxo Building

The free public viewing platform on the eighth floor of this former meat-processing factory gives a lovely view over the South Bank.

P.154 ▸ SOUTH BANK AND AROUND

▼ Tower Bridge

The elevated walkways of this landmark bridge provide the ultimate up- and down-river vistas.

P.148 ▸ THE TOWER AND DOCKLANDS

▼ London Eye

The city's giant Ferris wheel provides both the most expensive and the most superlative view over the capital.

P.154 ▸ SOUTH BANK AND AROUND

Indulgent London

If you've got the time and the money, London is a great place in which to indulge yourself – whether in the bar of a luxury hotel, the chair of one of the city's leading hair salons or at a table in a Michelin-starred restaurant.

Steam baths have been popular here since the Restoration in 1660, and there's an abundance of places around, with most offering treatments and massages as an optional extra.

▲ Dinner at Gordon Ramsay

Experience some of the capital's most sublime cooking at this Michelin-starred restaurant, run by the famously bad-tempered Glaswegian former footballer.

P.178 ▸ SOUTH KENSINGTON, KNIGHTSBRIDGE AND CHELSEA

▲ The Rookery

London features some first-class hotels, not-withstanding The Rookery, Farringdon's finest hidden gem. Spend a night in one of its sump-tuously decorated rooms, and imagine you've travelled back to the eighteenth century.

P.222 ▸ ESSENTIALS

▶ The Sanctuary

Full-on women-only pamper zone, where you can swim naked in the pool, jump in a jacuzzi or loll about in the sauna and steam room.

P.239 ▶ ESSENTIALS

▲ Ironmonger Row Baths

Old-fashioned steam bath, sauna and plunge-pool on the edge of the City, with optional massage and rest beds to collapse on afterwards.

P.239 ▶ ESSENTIALS

▼ Cocktails at St Martins Lane

Kick back at the hotel's Light Bar, one of the city's most stylish spots to enjoy a drink, with excellent DJs playing Thursday to Saturday.

P.221 ▶ COVENT GARDEN

Kids' London

There's plenty to delight kids in London. Top children's attractions such as London Zoo, the London Aquarium and the Natural History Museum are more or less guaranteed to go down well (and the latter has the added advantage of being free), as are the open spaces, glasshouses and subterranean aquariums of Kew Gardens and the state-of-the-art Diana Memorial Playground in Kensington Gardens. Finally, don't underestimate the value of London's public transport as a source of fun.

▼ Diana Memorial Playground

The city's most sophisticated, imaginative and popular outdoor playground, just a short walk from Diana's former home.

P.172 ▸ HYDE PARK AND KENSINGTON GARDENS

▲ London Aquarium

Large and popular South Bank aquarium, where kids can stroke the rays and gawp at the sharks.

P.155 ▸ SOUTH BANK AND AROUND

► Double-decker bus

Head upstairs on an old double-decker for a free tour of some of London's most famous sights, from Hyde Park to St Paul's Cathedral via Trafalgar Square.

P.235 ▶ ESSENTIALS

◄ London Zoo

Opened in 1828 as the world's first scientific zoo, and still a guaranteed hit with children of all ages.

P.188 ▶ REGENT'S PARK AND CAMDEN

▼ Natural History Museum

With animatronic dinosaurs and an earthquake simulator, the Natural History Museum is sure to prove a winner.

P.173 ▶ SOUTH KENSINGTON, KNIGHTSBRIDGE AND CHELSEA

▼ Kew Gardens

From the steaming Palm House to the giant waterlillies, there's enough wide open spaces to explore here to keep most kids happy.

P.208 ▶ KEW AND RICHMOND

Riverside London

Until the 1820s, the Thames was London's main thoroughfare, and some of the city's finest buildings were built along the riverfront. The steady decline in river traffic during the last century left the Thames quieter than ever before, a trend that has happily been reversed in the last decade. From the revitalized South Bank to the phoenix-like Docklands, the traffic-free portions of riverbank have again become a focal point, with pubs, cafés, restaurants, museums and other attractions jostling for space.

▲ Richmond

Elegant Thames-side suburb where you can have a drink overlooking the water, rent rowing boats or stroll along the bucolic towpath.

P.208 ▸ KEW AND RICHMOND

▲ Bankside

Thanks to the Tate Modern, Millennium Bridge and Shakespeare's Globe, the water-side entertainment district of Tudor and Stuart London is pulling in the crowds once again.

P.159 ▸ BANKSIDE AND SOUTHWARK

▲ South Bank

The traffic-free riverside path here connects numerous attractions, theatres and galleries, as well as affording by far the best views of the Thames's photogenic north bank.

P.152 ▸ SOUTH BANK AND AROUND

▼ Docklands

The transformation of London's moribund dock system into a world-class business district is a maritime miracle.

P.149 ▸ THE TOWER AND DOCKLANDS

▼ Old Royal Naval College

This symmetrical Baroque masterpiece enjoys the best riverside setting in the whole of London.

P.201 ▸ GREENWICH

Free London

London can be an expensive place for locals and tourists alike, but there are lots of things to enjoy in the city which are one hundred percent free. Aside from the numerous museums and galleries which don't charge entry, there are plenty of slightly more offbeat activities which don't cost a thing, from musical treats and upscale auctions to political sparring matches.

▲ Evensong at St Paul's Cathedral

The most moving way to experience this great Protestant cathedral is during choral evensong.

P.130 ▶ THE CITY

▼ Foyer gigs in the Royal Festival Hall

One of the joys of a stroll along the South Bank is the chance to catch one of the free lunchtime concerts in the RFH foyer.

P.152 ▶ SOUTH BANK AND AROUND

▲ Lunchtime concerts

Free lunchtime classical concerts take place in churches all over the City and parts of the West End.

P.70 ▶ TRAFALGAR SQUARE AND WHITEHALL

▲ Sotheby's auction

Buying might make a dent in your pocket, but viewing and attending an auction costs nothing.

P.88 ▶ PICCADILLY AND MAYFAIR

◀ Kenwood House

An exquisite eighteenth-century interior and top-drawer Old Masters can all be seen for free at English Heritage's flagship property overlooking Hampstead Heath.

P.196 ▶ HAMPSTEAD AND HIGHGATE

Dead London

In medieval times, only royalty and the nobility were commemorated after their death – and the iconoclasm of the Reformation and the Great Fire of 1666 mean that very little medieval funerary art has survived. However, in the nineteenth century, the emergence of an aspirational middle class prompted more Londoners to opt for permanent memorials and ostentatious funerals. Their legacy can be seen in London's vast suburban Victorian cemeteries, established to cope with the new fashion for funereal opulence.

WORKERS OF ALL LANDS

▲ Kensal Green

This canalside cemetery boasts the capital's most flamboyant funereal sculptures.

P.182 ▸ HIGH STREET KENSINGTON TO NOTTING HILL

▼ St Paul's Cathedral

The nave features some ludicrously pompous monuments to British imperialists, while the huge crypt specializes in artists.

P.130 ▸ THE CITY

▶ Westminster Abbey

When it comes to dead royalty, poets or politicians, the abbey wins hands down.

P.75 ▶ WESTMINSTER

▼ Highgate Cemetery

London's most convincingly Hammer Horror cemetery is most famous as the resting place of Karl Marx.

P.196 ▶ HAMPSTEAD AND HIGHGATE

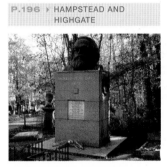

▲ Cenotaph

Edwin Lutyens' understated Whitehall memorial is a moving commemoration of the "glorious dead" from both world wars.

P.70 ▶ TRAFALGAR SQUARE AND WHITEHALL

▼ St Mary-at-Lambeth

The tiny graveyard here is home to the beautifully carved John Tradescant memorial and the grave of Captain Bligh of *Bounty* fame.

P.156 ▶ SOUTH BANK AND AROUND

Queasy London

London today is a fairly salubrious, modern metropolis, but many of its attractions prefer to glory in the city's murkier past. Medieval London was undoubtedly a muddy, unforgiving place but it was during the Victorian era when it really paid not to be too squeamish. The Gothic horror and hypocrisy of the period is perfectly illustrated by the cult surrounding Jack the Ripper, who still pulls in the punters even today, just as pre-anaesthetic operations did in the past.

▲ Madame Tussaud's

The ghoulish human fascination with murderers and serial killers is indulged in this infamous waxwork museum's Chamber of Horrors.

P.93 ▶ MARYLEBONE

▲ Smithfield Market

Each weekday morning around dawn, London's leading market for TK (town-killed) meat is a mass of bloody carcasses.

P.125 ▶ CLERKENWELL

▲ London Dungeon

Ham and Gothic it may be, but the grisly tableaux and ghost-train ride at the London Dungeon are as popular as ever.

P.163 ▶ BANKSIDE AND SOUTHWARK

▲ Hunterian Museum

Surgeon John Hunter's collection of jars of pickled body parts and skeletons is not one for the squeamish, but for those in search of oddities exhibited here, this a fascinating experience.

P.122 ▶ HOLBORN

▶ Old Operating Theatre and Herb Garret

Amputations were performed with great speed and skill at this pre-anaesthetic operating theatre – though often with fatal consequences.

P.163 ▶ BANKSIDE AND SOUTHWARK

London on stage

London has enjoyed a reputation for quality theatre since the time of Shakespeare, and despite the continuing dominance of blockbuster musicals and revenue-spinning star vehicles, the city still provides a platform for innovation. The largely pub-based fringe theatre scene is still going strong, and comedy is so big that London now boasts more dedicated venues than any other city in the world.

▼ Comedy Café

London's comedy scene is as varied as it is huge, but the acts at this purpose-built Hoxton venue are a cut above the rest.

P.144 ▶ HOXTON AND SPITALFIELDS

▲ West End musicals

Lavish blockbuster musicals dominate the West End theatre scene.

P.96 ▶ SOHO

▶ Shakespeare's Globe

This meticulous replica of an Elizabethan playhouse puts on rabble-rousing, open-air performances of plays by Shakespeare and his contemporaries.

P.161 ▶ BANKSIDE AND SOUTHWARK

57

◀ The Place

Established centre for contemporary dance featuring work from new as well as international choreographers.

P.110 ▶ BLOOMSBURY

▼ Donmar Warehouse

Covent Garden theatre with an outstanding reputation for classy revivals, new writing and star-studded casts.

P.118 ▶ COVENT GARDEN

▼ National Theatre

The South Bank's concrete carbuncle houses three excellent theatre spaces, and stages consistently good productions of everything from classics to new works.

P.154 ▶ SOUTH BANK AND AROUND

Musical London

For sheer range and variety, there's little to beat London's live music. As well as boasting two world-class opera houses and free lunchtime classical concerts held regularly at venues throughout the capital, the live music scene also encompasses all variations of classical, rock, blues, roots and world music. Most major artists include London in any European tour, and there's also a thriving underground scene, with lots of up-and-coming bands working the circuit.

▲ Astoria

Smack in the centre of London, this cavernous former theatre hosts regular gigs, often with a rock/indie slant.

P.103 ▸ SOHO

▲ Jazz Café

Camden's Jazz Café embraces all kinds of music, attracting top names from world music, roots, folk, R&B and hip-hop, as well as the jazz crowd.

P.191 ▸ REGENT'S PARK & CAMDEN

▲ Ronnie Scott's

London's most famous jazz club is an intimate venue in the heart of Soho, established way back in 1958.

P.103 ▸ SOHO

▲ Royal Opera House

Despite the money and effort involved in getting a ticket, it's definitely worth trying to catch a production at one of the world's finest opera houses.

P.113 ▸ COVENT GARDEN

◀ Wigmore Hall

Long-established chamber music venue with wonderful acoustics, just off Oxford Street.

P.95 ▸ MARYLEBONE

Literary and artistic London

London's streets are full of literary and artistic associations – from Shakespeare, Dickens and Marx to Orwell, Woolf and Freud. Everywhere you look there's a blue plaque, a statue or a memorial celebrating the city's writers, painters and thinkers. Some have left only memories, others first editions and works of art, and a few have been paid the ultimate homage via the transformation of their former homes into museums.

▲ Handel House Museum

Court composer Georg Frideric Handel spent the best part of his life in this Georgian terraced house, now refurbished as a period set-piece.

P.88 ▸ PICCADILLY AND MAYFAIR

▼ 2 Willow Road

The Hampstead abode of Hungarian modernist architect Ernö Goldfinger is filled with avant-garde artworks by such greats as Max Ernst, Marcel Duchamp, Man Ray and Henry Moore.

P.193 ▸ HAMPSTEAD AND HIGHGATE

▶ British Library

Home of artistic literary master-pieces such as the Lindisfarne Gospels, as well as original manuscripts by the likes of James Joyce.

P.104 ▶ BLOOMSBURY

◀ Freud Museum

Fleeing Nazi persecution, the father of psychoanalysis lived out his last months in this well-to-do Hampstead residence.

P.193 ▶ HAMPSTEAD AND HIGHGATE

▼ Keats House

Former home – now shrine – to the ultimate Romantic poet, who fell in love with the girl next door, became consumptive and died in Rome at the age of just 25.

P.193 ▶ HAMPSTEAD AND HIGHGATE

▼ Leighton House

Purpose-built studio and living space of the successful Victorian painter Lord Leighton, chum of the pre-Raphaelites and lover of the exotic.

P.180 ▶ HIGH STREET KENSINGTON TO NOTTING HILL

Festivals and events

London has an endless roster of festivals and events, with something happening somewhere almost every day of the year. The fortnight of grass-court tennis at Wimbledon is one of the great annual social events but, like the Proms classical music festival, it's open to all-comers provided you're prepared to queue. Carnival, London's mammoth street party, is equally democratic, but it's also worth catching more unusual events, such as the quaint narrowboat and Morris dancing celebration that is the IWA Cavalcade.

▲ Dance Umbrella

One of the world's leading contemporary dance festivals, with innovative productions staged all over the capital.

P.236 ▶ ESSENTIALS

▼ Proms

The world's most egalitarian classical music festival, featuring daily concerts in the Royal Albert Hall (and elsewhere), and culminating in the flag-waving nationalism of the "Last Night".

P.236 ▶ ESSENTIALS

▲ Notting Hill Carnival

Floats, costume bands, sound-systems, legions of food stalls and a fun-loving, heaving crowd make this huge street party unmissable.

P.236 ▸ ESSENTIALS

▼ IWA Canal Cavalcade

Colourful and old-fashioned narrowboat parade at the picturesque Little Venice junction of the Regent's and Grand Union canals.

P.236 ▸ ESSENTIALS

▲ Open House

Constantly expanding annual event which sees the city's most intriguing historic build- ings throw open their doors to the public for free in September.

P.236 ▸ ESSENTIALS

▼ Wimbledon Lawn Tennis Championships

Summertime grass-court venue of the most singular of tennis's four Grand Slam events – think strawberries and cream, and heroic British failures.

P.236 ▸ ESSENTIALS

Places

Trafalgar Square and Whitehall

Despite the scruffy urban pigeons and the traffic noise, Trafalgar Square is still one of London's grandest architectural set-pieces, and as such is prime tourist territory. Most folk head here for the National Gallery, at the top of the square, then linger by the fountains before wandering down the unusually broad avenue of Whitehall en route to the Houses of Parliament and Westminster Abbey. Whitehall itself is synonymous with the faceless, pinstriped bureaucracy who run the various governmental ministries located here, but it's also the venue for the most elaborate Changing of the Guard, which usually attracts a small crowd of onlookers.

Trafalgar Square

As one of the few large public squares in London, Trafalgar Square has been a focus for political demonstrations since it was laid out in the 1820s. Most days, however, it's scruffy urban pigeons that you're more likely to encounter, as they wheel around the square hoping some unsuspecting visitor will feed them (though, it is, in fact, illegal to do so). Along with its fountains, the square's central focal point is the deeply patriotic **Nelson's Column**, which stands 170ft high and is topped by a 17ft statue of the one-eyed, one-armed admiral who defeated the French at the 1805 Battle of Trafalgar. Nelson himself is actually quite hard to see – not so the giant bronze lions at the base of the column, which provide a popular photo opportunity.

National Gallery

Trafalgar Square ☎ 020/7747 2885, 🖥 www.nationalgallery.org.uk. Daily 10am–6pm, Wed till 9pm. Free.

Despite housing more than 2300 paintings, the main virtue of the National Gallery is not so much the collection's size, but its range, depth and sheer quality. A quick tally of the **Italian** masterpieces, for

▼ FOUNTAINS, TRAFALGAR SQUARE

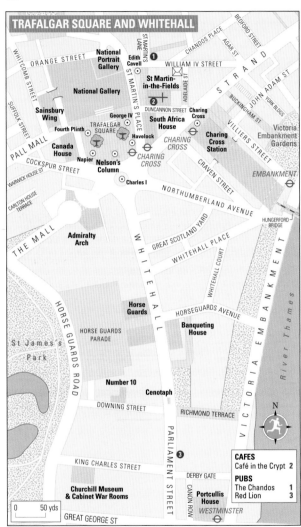

TRAFALGAR SQUARE AND WHITEHALL

BEDFORD STREET
CHANDOS PLACE
AGAR ST
ST MARTIN'S LANE
ORANGE STREET
National Portrait Gallery
Edith Cavell ①
WILLIAM IV STREET
STRAND
JOHN ADAM ST
WHITCOMB STREET
National Gallery
St Martin-in-the-Fields ②
BUCKINGHAM ST
YORK BLDGS
Sainsbury Wing
George IV
DUNCANNON STREET
Charing Cross
VILLIERS STREET
Victoria Embankment Gardens
SUFFOLK STREET
Fourth Plinth
TRAFALGAR SQUARE
South Africa House
Charing Cross
Canada House
Havelock
CHARING CROSS
Charing Cross Station
PALL MALL
Napier
Nelson's Column
CHARING CROSS
CRAVEN STREET
EMBANKMENT
COCKSPUR STREET
WARWICK HOUSE ST
Charles I
NORTHUMBERLAND AVENUE
HUNGERFORD BRIDGE
CARLTON HOUSE TERRACE
Admiralty Arch
GREAT SCOTLAND YARD
WHITEHALL PLACE
WHITEHALL COURT
THE MALL
WHITEHALL
River Thames
HORSE GUARDS ROAD
Horse Guards
HORSEGUARDS AVENUE
VICTORIA EMBANKMENT
St James's Park
HORSE GUARDS PARADE
Banqueting House
Number 10
Cenotaph
DOWNING STREET
RICHMOND TERRACE
N
PARLIAMENT STREET
KING CHARLES STREET
DERBY GATE
CANON ROW
Churchill Museum & Cabinet War Rooms
Portcullis House
WESTMINSTER
0   50 yds
GREAT GEORGE ST

CAFES
Café in the Crypt 2

PUBS
The Chandos 1
Red Lion 3

© Crown copyright

example, includes works by Uccello, Botticelli, Mantegna, Piero della Francesca, Veronese, Titian, Raphael, Michelangelo and Caravaggio. From **Spain** there are dazzling pieces by El Greco, Velázquez and Goya; from the **Low Countries**, van Eyck, Memlinc and Rubens, and an array of Rembrandt paintings that features some of his most searching portraits. Poussin, Claude, Watteau and the only Jacques-Louis David paintings in the country are the early highlights of a **French** contingent that has a particularly strong showing of Cézanne and the Impressionists. **British** art is also well represented, with important works by Hogarth, Gainsborough, Stubbs and Turner, though for twentieth-century British art – and many more Turners – you'll need to move on to Tate Britain on Millbank (see p.77).

To view the collection chronologically, begin with the **Sainsbury Wing**, the softly-softly, postmodern 1980s adjunct which is linked to – and playfully imitates – the original Neoclassical building. However, with more than a thousand paintings on permanent display, you'll need stamina to see everything in one day, so if time is tight your best bet is to home in on your areas of special interest, having picked up a gallery plan at one of the information desks. **Audioguides**, with a brief audio commentary on virtually all of the paintings on display, is available for a "voluntary contribution" of £4. Much better are the gallery's **free guided tours** (daily 11.30am & 2.30pm, plus Wed 6 & 6.30pm, Sat also 12.30 & 3.30pm), which set off from the Sainsbury Wing foyer, and focus on a representative sample of works.

National Portrait Gallery

St Martin's Place ☎020/7306 0055, ⓦwww.npg.org.uk. Daily 10am–6pm, Thurs & Fri till 9pm. Free. Founded in 1856 to house uplifting depictions of the good and the great, the National Portrait Gallery has some fine individual works. However, many of the studies are of less interest than their subjects, and the overall impression is of an overstuffed shrine to famous Brits rather than a museum offering any insight into the history of portraiture. Nevertheless, it is fascinating to trace who has been deemed worthy of admiration at any moment: aristocrats and artists in previous centuries, warmongers and imperialists in the early decades of the twentieth century, writers and poets in the 1930s and 1940s, and latterly, retired footballers, politicians and film and pop stars. The NPG's audioguide gives useful biographical background information and is available in return for a "voluntary

PLACES Trafalgar Square and Whitehall

▼ UCELLO'S *BATTLE OF SAN ROMANO*, NATIONAL GALLERY

PLACES

Trafalgar Square and Whitehall

▲ BRUNEL PORTRAIT, NPG

contribution". The gallery's **special exhibitions** (for which there's often an entrance charge) are well worth seeing – the photography shows, in particular, are usually excellent.

St Martin-in-the-Fields

Duncannon St ⓦ www.stmartin-in -the-fields.org. Mon–Sat 10am–8pm, Sun noon–8pm. Free. Something of a blueprint for eighteenth-century churches across the Empire, St Martin-in-the-Fields is fronted by a magnificent Corinthian portico and topped by an elaborate, and distinctly unclassical, tower and steeple. Completed in 1726, the interior is purposefully simple, though the Italian plasterwork on the barrel vaulting is exceptionally rich; it's best appreciated while listening to one of the church's free **lunchtime concerts** or ticketed, candle-lit evening performances (call ☎020/7839 8362 for timings and information). There's a licensed café in the roomy **crypt**, not to mention a shop, gallery and

brass-rubbing centre (Mon–Sat 10am–6pm, Sun noon–6pm).

Whitehall

During the sixteenth and seventeenth centuries Whitehall was synonymous with royalty, serving as the permanent residence of England's kings and queens. The original Whitehall Palace was the London seat of the Archbishop of York, confiscated and greatly extended by Henry VIII after a fire at Westminster forced him to find alternative accommodation; it was here that he celebrated his marriage to Anne Boleyn in 1533, and where he died fourteen years later. From the sixteenth century onwards, nearly all the key governmental ministries and offices migrated here, rehousing themselves on an ever-increasing scale. The royalty, meanwhile, moved out to St James's after a fire destroyed most of Whitehall Palace in 1698.

The statues dotted along Whitehall today recall the days when this street stood at the centre of an empire on which the sun never set, while just beyond the Downing Street gates, in the middle of the road, stands Edwin Lutyens' **Cenotaph**, commemorating the dead of both world wars. Eschewing any kind of Christian imagery, the plain monument is inscribed simply with the words "The Glorious Dead" and remains the focus of the country's Remembrance Sunday ceremony, held here in early November.

Banqueting House

Whitehall ⓦ www.hrp.org.uk. Mon–Sat 10am–5pm. £4.50. One of the few sections of Whitehall Palace to escape the 1698 fire was the

▲ ST-MARTIN-IN-THE-FIELDS

Banqueting House, one of the first Palladian buildings to be built in England. The one room open to the public has no original furnishings, but is well worth seeing for the superlative **Rubens ceiling paintings** commissioned by Charles I in the 1630s, depicting the union of England and Scotland, the peaceful reign of his father, James I, and finally his apotheosis. Charles himself walked through the room for the last time in 1649, when he stepped onto the executioner's scaffold from one of its windows.

Horse Guards

Whitehall ⓦ www.army.mod.uk /ceremonialandheritage. Outside this modest building (once the old palace guard house) two mounted sentries of the **Queen's Household Cavalry** and two horseless colleagues, all in ceremonial uniform, are posted daily from 10am to 4pm. With nothing in particular to guard nowadays, the sentries are basically here for the tourists, though they are under orders not to smile. Try to coincide your visit with the **Changing of the Guard** (see box below).

10 Downing Street

ⓦ www.number-10.gov.uk. Since the days of Margaret Thatcher, London's most famous address has been hidden behind wrought-iron security gates. A pretty plain, seventeenth-century terraced house, no. 10 has been home to every British prime minister since it was presented to Robert Walpole, Britain's first PM, by George II in 1732.

Changing of the Guard

The Changing of the Guard takes place at two separate London locations: the Foot Guards hold theirs outside Buckingham Palace (April–July daily 11.30am; Sept–March alternate days; no ceremony if it rains), but the more impressive one is held on Horse Guards Parade, where a squad of twelve mounted Household Cavalry in full livery arrives from Hyde Park to relieve the guards at Horse Guards on Whitehall (Mon–Sat 11am, Sun 10am) – alternatively, if you miss the whole thing, turn up at 4pm for the elaborate daily inspection by the Officer of the Guard, who checks the soldiers haven't knocked off early.

▲ SOUTH AFRICA HOUSE, TRAFALGAR SQUARE

Churchill Museum and Cabinet War Rooms

King Charles St ☎020/7930 6961, ⓦcwr.iwm.org.uk. Daily 9.30am–6pm. £11. In 1938, in anticipation of Nazi air raids, the basement of the civil service buildings on the south side of King Charles Street was converted into the **Cabinet War Rooms**. It was here that Winston Churchill directed operations and held Cabinet meetings for the duration of World War II and the rooms have been left pretty much as they were when they were finally abandoned on VJ Day 1945, making for an atmospheric underground trot through wartime London. Also in the basement is the excellent

Churchill Museum. You can hear snippets of Churchill's most famous speeches and check out his trademark bowler, spotted bow tie and half-chewed Havana, not to mention his wonderful burgundy zip-up "romper suit".

Cafés

Café in the Crypt

St Martin-in-the-Fields, Duncannon St. Mon–Wed 10am–8pm, Thurs–Sat 10am–11pm, Sun noon–8pm. The self-service buffet food is nothing special, but there are regular veggie dishes, and the atmospheric location below the church is very central.

Pubs

The Chandos

29 St Martin's Lane. Mon–Sat 11am–11pm, Sun noon–10.30pm. If you can get one of the booths downstairs, or the leather sofas upstairs in the Opera Room, then you'll find it difficult to leave.

Red Lion

48 Parliament St. Mon–Fri 11am–11pm, Sat 11am–9pm, Sun noon–8pm. Old-fashioned late-Victorian pub popular with politicians, who can be called to parliamentary votes by a division bell in the bar.

Westminster

Political, religious and regal power has emanated from Westminster for almost a millennium. It was King Edward the Confessor who first established this spot as London's royal and ecclesiastical power base in the eleventh century, building his palace and abbey some three miles upstream from the City of London, and the embryonic English parliament met in the abbey from the fourteenth century onwards.

Westminster remains home to the Houses of Parliament today, and as such it's a popular tourist spot, with visitors drawn here by Big Ben, one of the city's most familiar landmarks, and Westminster Abbey, London's most historic church. A short walk upriver, Tate Britain houses the finest permanent collection of British art in the country.

Houses of Parliament

Parliament Square ☎ 020/7219 3000, ⓦ www.parliament.uk. Also known as the Palace of Westminster, the Houses of Parliament are one of London's best-known monuments and the ultimate symbol of a nation once confident of its place at the centre of the world. The city's finest example of Victorian Gothic Revival, the complex is distinguished above all by the ornate, gilded clock tower popularly known as **Big Ben**, after the thirteen-ton main bell that strikes the hour (and is broadcast across the airwaves by the BBC).

The original medieval palace burnt to the ground in 1834, but Westminster Hall survived, and its huge oak hammerbeam roof, and sheer scale make it one of the most magnificent secular medieval halls in Europe – you get a glimpse of it en route to the public galleries.

To watch the proceedings in either the House of Commons or the Lords, simply join the queue for the **public galleries** (known as Strangers' Galleries) outside St Stephen's Gate. The public are let in slowly (from 4pm Mon, 1pm Tues–Thurs, 10am Fri); the security checks

▼ HOUSES OF PARLIAMENT

© Crown copyright

are very tight, and the whole procedure can take an hour or more. If you want to avoid the queues, turn up an hour or more later, when the crowds have usually thinned; phone ☎020/7219 4272 to check the place isn't closed for the holidays.

To see **Question Time** (Mon 2.30pm, Tues–Thurs 11.30am), when the House is at its most raucous and entertaining, you really need to book a ticket several weeks in advance from your local MP if you're a

resident UK citizen, or your home country's embassy (see p.237) in London if you're not. If you're here in late summer, you can also see Parliament by way of a **guided tour (**Mon, Fri & Sat 9.15am–4.30pm, Tues, Wed & Thurs 1.15–4.30pm; Aug also Tues 9.15am–1.15pm; £7; booking line ☎0870/906 3773), in which visitors get to walk through the two chambers, see some of the state rooms reserved for the Queen, and admire Westminster Hall. It's a good idea to book in advance, or you

▲ TAXI LIGHT, PARLIAMENT SQUARE

can simply head for the ticket office on Abingdon Green, opposite Victoria Tower and its adjacent gardens.

Jewel Tower

Abingdon St. Daily: April–Oct 10am–5pm; Nov–March 10am–4pm. £2.60. The Jewel Tower is another remnant of the medieval palace. It formed the southwestern corner of the original exterior fortifications (there's a bit of moat left, too), and was constructed in around 1365 by Edward III as a giant strongbox for the crown jewels. These days, it houses an excellent exhibition on the history of parliament – worth checking out before you visit the Houses of Parliament.

St Margaret's Church

Parliament Square ⓦwestminster -abbey.org. Mon–Fri 9.30am–3.45pm, Sat 9.30am–1.45pm, Sun 2–5pm. Free. Sitting in the shadow of Westminster Abbey, St Margaret's has been the unofficial parliamentary church since the entire Commons arrived here unannounced in 1614 to unmask religious Dissenters among the MPs.

The present building dates back to 1523, and its most noteworthy furnishing is the colourful Flemish stained-glass window above the altar, which commemorates the marriage of Henry VIII and Catherine of Aragon (depicted in the bottom left- and right-hand corners).

Westminster Abbey

Parliament Square ⓦwww .westminster-abbey.org. Mon–Fri 9.30am–4.45pm, Wed until 7pm, Sat 9.30am–1.45pm. £10. The venue for every coronation since William the Conqueror, and the site of just about all royal burials in the five hundred years from Henry III to George II, Westminster Abbey embodies much of England's history. There are scores of memorials to the nation's most famous citizens, too, and the interior is crammed with reliefs and statues.

Entry is via the north transept, cluttered with monuments to politicians – and traditionally known as **Statesmen's Aisle** – shortly after which you come to the abbey's most dazzling architectural set piece, the **Lady Chapel**, added by Henry VII in 1503 as his future resting place. With its intricately carved vaulting and fan-shaped gilded pendants, the chapel represents the final spectacular gasp of the English Perpendicular style. The public are no longer admitted to the **Shrine of Edward the Confessor**, the sacred heart of the building (except on a guided verger tour; £4), though you do get to inspect Edward I's **Coronation Chair**, a decrepit oak throne dating from around 1300 and still used for coronations. Nowadays, the abbey's royal tombs are upstaged by **Poets' Corner**, in the south transept. The first occupant, Geoffrey Chaucer, was buried here, in 1400, not because he was a poet but because he lived nearby. By the eighteenth century, however, this zone had become an artistic pantheon, and since then has been filled with tributes to all shades of talent from William Blake to John Betjeman. From the south transept, you can view the central sanctuary, site of the coronations, and the wonderful **Cosmati floor mosaic**, constructed in the thirteenth century by Italian craftsmen, and often covered by a carpet to protect it.

Doors in the south choir aisle lead to the **Great Cloisters** (daily 8am–6pm; free with Abbey ticket), rebuilt after a fire in 1298. At the eastern end of the cloisters lies the octagonal **Chapter House** (daily 10.30am–4pm; free), where the House of Commons met from 1257. The thirteenth-century decorative paving tiles and wall-paintings have survived intact. Close by is the **Abbey Museum** (daily 10.30am–4pm; free), filled with generations of bald royal death masks and wax effigies. From the cloisters you can make your way to the little-known **College Garden** (Tues–Thurs: April–Sept 10am–6pm; Oct–March 10am–4pm; free), a 900-year-old stretch of green which now provides a quiet retreat; brass band concerts take place in July and August between 12.30 and 2pm.

It's only after exploring the cloisters that you get to see the **nave** itself: narrow, light and, at over a hundred feet in height, by far the tallest in the country; you exit via the west door.

▼ LUTHER KING STATUE, WESTMINSTER ABBEY

Westminster Cathedral

Victoria St ⓦ www.rcdow.org.uk. Mon–Fri & Sun 7am–7pm, Sat 8am–7pm. Free. Begun in 1895, the stripy neo-Byzantine, Roman Catholic Westminster Cathedral is one of London's most surprising churches, as well as one of the last – and the wildest – monuments to the Victorian era. Constructed

▲ WILLIAM BLAKE'S *NEWTON*, TATE BRITAIN

from more than twelve million terracotta-coloured bricks and decorated with hoops of Portland stone, it culminates in a magnificent 274ft tapered **campanile**, served by a lift (April–Nov daily 9.30am–12.30pm & 1–5pm; Dec–March Thurs–Sun same hours; £2). The interior is still only half finished, so to get an idea of what the place should eventually look like, explore the series of side chapels whose rich, multicoloured decor makes use of over one hundred different types of marble from around the world. Be sure, too, to check out the low-relief Stations of the Cross, sculpted by Eric Gill during World War I.

Tate Britain

Millbank ☎020/7887 8008, ⊛www.tate.org.uk. Daily 10am–5.50pm. Free. A purpose-built gallery founded in 1897 with money from Henry Tate, inventor of the sugar cube, Tate Britain is now devoted almost exclusively to British art from 1500 to the present day. In addition, the gallery also showcases contemporary British artists and continues to sponsor the Turner Prize, the country's most prestigious modern-art award.

The pictures are rehung more or less annually, but always include a fair selection of works by British artists such as Hogarth, Constable, Gainsborough, Reynolds and Blake, plus foreign artists like van Dyck who spent much of their career over here. The ever-popular **Pre-Raphaelites** are well represented, as are established twentieth-century greats including Stanley Spencer and Francis Bacon alongside living artists such as David Hockney and Lucien Freud. Lastly, don't miss the Tate's outstanding **Turner collection**, displayed in the Clore Gallery.

Shops

Blewcoats School Gift Shop

23 Caxton St ☎020/7222 2877,

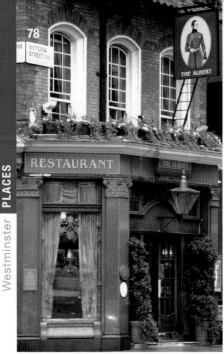

▲ THE *ALBERT* PUB

Mon–Thurs 9.30am–5.30pm, Fri 9am–4pm. Pick up copies of *Hansard* (the word-for-word account of parliament), plus the government's white and green papers.

Tate Britain Gift Shop

Millbank ☎ 020/7887 8876, ⓦ www .tate.org.uk. Daily 10am–5.50pm. Lots of art posters, from Constable to Turner Prize nonsense, plus loads of funky, arty accessories.

Pubs

Albert

52 Victoria St. Mon–Sat 11am–11pm, Sun noon–10.30pm. Roomy High Victorian pub, with big bay windows, glass partitions and a beautiful original ceiling and carved wooden bar.

Westminster Arms

9 Storey's Gate. Mon–Fri 11am–11pm, Sat 11am–6pm, Sun noon–5pm. A real parliamentary pub, packed wall-to-wall with MPs, and with a division bell in the bar.

ⓦ www.nationaltrust.org.uk. Mon–Fri 10am–5.30pm (Thurs until 7pm), Sat 10am–4pm. National Trust gift shop in a pretty little Georgian schoolhouse, selling toiletries, tapestries, waterproof hats, preserves and books ranging from gardening to architecture.

Parliamentary Bookshop

12 Bridge St ☎ 020/7219 3890, ⓦ www.bookshop.parliament.uk.

St James's

An exclusive little enclave sandwiched between St James's Park and Piccadilly, St James's was laid out in the 1670s close to the royal seat of St James's Palace. Regal and aristocratic residences overlook nearby Green Park and the stately avenue of The Mall, gentlemen's clubs cluster along Pall Mall and St James's Street, while jacket-and-tie restaurants and expense-account gentlemen's outfitters line Jermyn Street. Hardly surprising, then, that most Londoners rarely stray into this area. Plenty of folk, however, frequent St James's Park, with large numbers heading for the Queen's chief residence, Buckingham Palace, and the adjacent Queen's Gallery and Royal Mews.

The Mall

The tree-lined sweep of The Mall – London's nearest equivalent of a Parisian boulevard – was laid out in the first decade of the twentieth century as a memorial to Queen Victoria. These days, it's best to try and visit on a Sunday, when it's closed to traffic. The bombastic Admiralty Arch was erected to mark the eastern entrance to The Mall, just off Trafalgar Square, while at the other end, in front of Buckingham Palace, stands the ludicrously overblown Victoria Memorial, Edward VII's tribute to his mother.

St James's Park

ⓦ www.royalparks.gov.uk. The south side of The Mall gives on to St James's Park, the oldest of London's royal parks, having been drained and enclosed for hunting purposes by Henry VIII. It was landscaped by Nash in the 1820s, and today its tree-lined lake is a favourite picnic spot for Whitehall's civil servants. Pelicans chill out at the eastern end (feeding takes place daily at 3pm), and there are exotic ducks, swans and geese aplenty. From the bridge across the lake there's also a fine view over to Westminster and the jumble of domes and pinnacles

▼ ST JAMES'S PARK

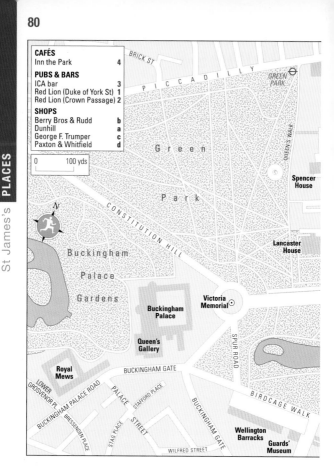

CAFÉS
Inn the Park   4

PUBS & BARS
ICA bar   3
Red Lion (Duke of York St)   1
Red Lion (Crown Passage)   2

SHOPS
Berry Bros & Rudd   b
Dunhill   a
George F. Trumper   c
Paxton & Whitfield   d

0   100 yds

BRICK ST

PICCADILLY

GREEN PARK

QUEEN'S WALK

Green

Park

Spencer House

CONSTITUTION HILL

Buckingham

Palace

Gardens

Lancaster House

Buckingham Palace

Victoria Memorial

Queen's Gallery

SPUR ROAD

Royal Mews

BUCKINGHAM GATE

LOWER GROSVENOR PL

BUCKINGHAM PALACE ROAD

PALACE STREET

STAFFORD PLACE

BRESSENDEN PLACE

STAG PLACE

BUCKINGHAM GATE

BIRDCAGE WALK

Wellington Barracks

Guards' Museum

WILFRED STREET

along Whitehall, with the London Eye peeking over it all.

Guards' Museum

Birdcage Walk. Daily 10am–4pm. £2.
The Neoclassical facade of the Wellington Barracks, built in 1833 and fronted by a parade ground, runs along the south side of St James's Park. In a bunker opposite the barracks' modern chapel, the Guards' Museum endeavours to explain the complicated evolution of the Queen's Household Regiments, and provide a potted military history since the Civil War. Among the exhibits are the guards' glorious scarlet and blue uniforms, a lock of Wellington's hair and a whole load of war booty, from Dervish prayer mats plundered from Sudan in 1898 to items taken from an Iraqi POW during the Gulf War. The museum also displays (and sells) an impressive array of toy soldiers.

Buckingham Palace

Buckingham Gate ⓦ www.royal.gov.
uk. Aug & Sept daily 9.45am–6pm.

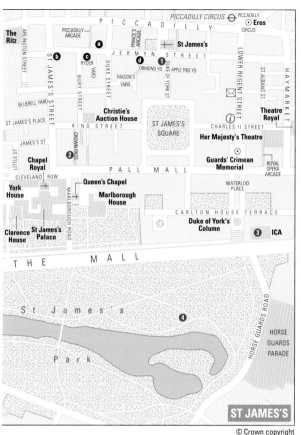

© Crown copyright

Advance booking on ☏ 020/7766 7300.
£14. The graceless colossus of
Buckingham Palace, popularly
known as "Buck House",
has served as the monarch's
permanent London residence
only since the accession of
Victoria in 1837 (if the Queen
is at home, the Royal Standard
flies from the roof of the palace).
Bought by George III in 1762,
the building was overhauled
by Nash in the late 1820s, and
again by Aston Webb in time
for George V's coronation in
1913, producing a Neoclassical
monolith that's about as bland as
it's possible to be.

For two months of the
year, the hallowed portals are
grudgingly nudged open to
the public; timed tickets are
sold from the marquee-like
box office in Green Park at
the western end of The Mall.
The interior, however, is a bit
of an anticlimax: of the palace's
660 rooms, you're permitted
to see around twenty, and
there's little sign of life as the
Queen decamps to Scotland
every summer. For the other

▲ CHANGING OF THE GUARD

ten months of the year there's little to do here, as the palace is closed to visitors – not that this deters the crowds who mill around the railings and gather in some force to watch the **Changing of the Guard** (see box, p.71).

Queen's Gallery

Buckingham Gate ⓦ www.royal. gov.uk. Daily 10am–5.30pm. £7.50. The changing exhibitions at the Queen's Gallery are drawn from the Royal Collection; the vast array of artworks snapped up by the royal family which is three times larger than that at the National Gallery. Among the thousands of works the curators have to choose from are some incredible masterpieces by Michelangelo, Reynolds, Gainsborough, Vermeer, van Dyck, Rubens, Rembrandt and Canaletto, as well as numerous Fabergé eggs and heaps of Sèvres china.

Royal Mews

Buckingham Palace Rd ⓦ www.royal. gov.uk. Aug & Sept daily 10am–5pm; Oct–July daily except Fri 11am–4pm. £6.50. There's more pageantry on show at the Nash-built Royal Mews. The horses can be viewed in their luxury stables, along with an exhibition of equine accoutrements, but it's the royal carriages that are the main attraction. The most ornate is the Gold State Coach made for George III in 1762, smothered in 22-carat gilding and weighing four tons, its axles supporting four life-size figures. The Mews also houses the Royal Family's gleaming fleet of five Rolls Royce Phantoms and three Daimlers.

St James's Palace

Marlborough Rd ⓦ www.royal.gov.uk. Originally built by Henry VIII for Anne Boleyn, it was here that Charles I chose to sleep the night before his execution, so as not to have to listen to his scaffold being erected in Whitehall. When Whitehall Palace burnt to the ground in 1698, St James's became the principal royal residence until the court moved down the road to Buckingham Palace under Queen Victoria. The imposing red-brick gate-tower that forms the main entrance, and the Chapel Royal, are all that remain of the original Tudor palace. The rambling complex is off-limits to the public,

with traffic careering down it nose to tail day and night. Infinitely more pleasant places to window-shop are the various nineteenth-century arcades here, originally built to protect shoppers from the mud and horse-dung on the streets, but now equally useful for escaping exhaust fumes.

Burlington Arcade

ⓦ www.burlington-arcade.co.uk. Mon–Sat 9am–6pm. Awash with mahogany-fronted jewellers and gentlemen's outfitters, the Burlington Arcade is Piccadilly's longest and most expensive nineteenth-century arcade. It was built in 1819 for Lord Cavendish, then owner of neighbouring Burlington House, to prevent commoners throwing rubbish into his garden. Upholding Regency decorum, it is still illegal to whistle, sing, hum, hurry, carry large packages or open umbrellas on this small stretch – the arcade's beadles (known as Burlington Berties), in their Edwardian frock-coats and gold-braided top hats, take the prevention of such criminality very seriously.

Royal Academy

ⓦ www.royalacademy.org.uk. Daily 10am–6pm, Fri till 10pm. £4–10 depending on the exhibition. The Royal Academy of Arts (RA) occupies the enormous Burlington House, one of the few survivors of the aristocratic mansions that once lined Piccadilly. The country's first-ever formal art school, the Academy was founded in 1768 by a group of English painters including Thomas Gainsborough and Joshua Reynolds, the first president, whose statue now stands in the main courtyard, palette in hand. The college

has always had a conservative reputation for its teaching, and its exhibitions tend to be crowd-pleasers, interspersed with the occasional controversial show guaranteed to grab the headlines. However, the Academy is best known for the **Summer Exhibition**, which opens in June and runs until mid-August and remains an essential stop on the social calendar of upper middle-class England. Anyone can enter paintings in any style, and the lucky winners get hung, in rather close proximity, and sold. Supposed gravitas is added by the RA "Academicians", who are allowed to display six of their own works – no matter how awful. The result is a bewildering display, which gets annually panned by the critics. As well as hosting exhibitions, the RA has a small selection of works from its own collection on **permanent display** in the

▼ BURLINGTON ARCADE

newly restored white and gold John Madejski Fine Rooms (Tues–Fri 1–4.30pm, Sat & Sun 10am–6pm; guided tours Tues–Fri 1pm; free). Highlights include a Rembrandtesque self-portrait by Reynolds, plus works by the likes of John Constable, Stanley Spencer and David Hockney.

Bond Street and around

While Oxford Street, Regent Street and Piccadilly have all gone downmarket, Bond Street has carefully maintained its exclusivity. It is, in fact, two streets rolled into one: the southern half, laid out in the 1680s, is known as Old Bond Street; its northern extension, which followed less than fifty years later, is New Bond Street. Both are pretty unassuming architecturally, but the shops that line them – and those of neighbouring Conduit Street and South Molton Street – are among the flashiest in London, dominated by perfumeries, jewellers and designer clothing emporia such as Versace, Gucci and Yves Saint-Laurent.

In addition to fashion, Bond Street is also renowned for its auction houses, the oldest of which is **Sotheby's, at no. 34–35** (Ⓦ www.sothebys .com). Despite a price-fixing

scandal in 2002 that resulted in the imprisonment of its former chairman and a £12 million fine, business is still booming. The viewing galleries (free) are open to the public, as are the auctions themselves. Bond Street's **art galleries** are another favourite place for the wealthy to offload their heirlooms; for contemporary art, head for neighbouring Cork Street. Both locations' galleries have impeccably presented and somewhat intimidating staff, but if you're interested, walk in and look around. They're only shops, after all.

Handel House Museum

25 Brook St Ⓦ www.handelhouse.org. Tues–Sat 10am–6pm, Thurs till 8pm, Sun noon–6pm. £5. The German-born composer **Georg Frideric Handel** (1685–1759) spent the best part of his life in London, producing all his best-known works at what's now the Handel House Museum. The composer used the ground floor as a sort of shop where subscribers could buy scores, while the first floor was employed as a rehearsal room. Although containing few original artefacts, the house has been painstakingly restored, and further atmosphere is provided by music students who come to practise on the house's harpsichords. More formal performances take place on Thursday evenings from 6.30pm (£8.50). Access to the house is via the chic cobbled yard at the back.

Oxford Street

Ⓦ www.oxfordstreet .co.uk. The old Roman road to Oxford has been London's main shopping mecca for

▼ ART DECO CLOCK, SELFRIDGES

Afternoon tea

The classic English afternoon tea – assorted sandwiches, scones and cream, cakes and tarts and, of course, lashings of tea – is available all over London, but is best sampled at one of the capital's top hotels; a selection of the best venues are picked out below. Book ahead, and leave your jeans and trainers at home – most hotels will expect men to wear a jacket of some sort, though only The Ritz insists on jacket and tie. Expect to pay up to £30 per person.

Claridge's Brook St ☎020/7409 6307, ⊛www.savoy-group.co.uk. Daily 3–5.30pm.

The Dorchester 54 Park Lane ☎020/7629 8888, ⊛www.dorchesterhotel.com. Daily 3–6pm.

The Lanesborough Hyde Park Corner ☎020/7259 5599, ⊛www.lanesborough .com. Mon–Sat 3.30–6pm, Sun 4–6pm.

The Ritz Piccadilly ☎020/7493 8181, ⊛www.theritzhotel.co.uk. Daily 11.30am, 1.30, 3.30 & 5.30pm.

The Savoy Strand ☎020/7420 2356, ⊛www.savoy-group.co.uk. See map p.112. Mon–Fri 2–3.30pm & 4–6pm, Sat & Sun noon–1.30pm, 2–3.30pm & 4–6pm.

the last hundred years. Today, despite successive recessions and sky-high rents, this aesthetically unremarkable two-mile hotchpotch of shops is still one of the world's busiest streets. East of Oxford Circus, it forms the northern border of Soho; to the west, the one great landmark is Selfridges, a huge Edwardian pile fronted by giant Ionic columns, with the Queen of Time riding the ship of commerce and supporting an Art Deco clock above the main entrance. The store was opened in 1909 by Chicago millionaire Gordon Selfridge, who flaunted its 130 departments under the slogan, "Why not spend a day at Selfridges?"; he was later pensioned off after running into trouble with the Inland Revenue.

Shops

Browns
23–27 & 50 South Molton St ☎020/7514 0052, ⊛www. brownsfashion.com. Mon–Sat 10am–6.30pm, Thurs 10am–7pm. London's largest range of designer wear, with big international names under the same roof as the more cutting-edge, up-and-coming designers, and catering equally well for women as for men.

Charbonnel et Walker
1 Royal Arcade, 28 Old Bond St ☎020/7491 0939, ⊛www.charbonnel .co.uk. Mon–Sat 10am–6pm. Established in 1875, this is where Her Majesty binges on chocolate, which comes presented in the most exquisite wrapping.

Fortnum & Mason
181 Piccadilly ☎020/7734 8040, ⊛www.fortnumandmason.com. Mon–Sat 10am–6.30pm, Sun noon–6pm. Beautiful and eccentric store offering gorgeously presented and pricey food; also specializes in designer clothes, furniture and stationery.

Hamleys
188–196 Regent St ☎0870/333 2455, ⊛www.hamleys.com. Mon–Fri 10am–8pm, Sat 9.30am–8pm, Sun noon–6pm. Possibly the world's largest toy shop, and certainly

a feast for the eyes of most small children, with lots of gadget demonstrations going on throughout its six floors of mayhem.

Hatchards

187 Piccadilly ☎020/7439 9921, ⓦwww.hatchards.co.uk. Mon–Sat 9.30am–7pm, Sun noon–6pm. The Queen's official bookseller, Hatchards holds its own when it comes to quality fiction, royal biography and history.

Liberty

210–220 Regent St ☎020/7734 1234, ⓦwww.liberty.co.uk. Mon–Sat 10am–7pm, Thurs till 8pm, Sun noon–6pm. A fabulous, partly mock-Tudor emporium of luxury. Best known for its fabrics, though it is, in fact, a full-blown department store.

Marks & Spencer

458 Oxford St ☎020/7935 7954, ⓦwww.marksandspencer.co.uk. Mon–Fri 8am–9pm, Sat 9am–8pm, Sun noon–6pm. The largest London branch of this British institution offers a huge range of own-brand clothes, food, homeware and furnishings.

Selfridges

400 Oxford St ☎0870/837 7377, ⓦwww.selfridges.com. Mon 10am–8pm, Tues–Sat 9.30am–8pm, Thurs till 9pm, Sun noon–6pm. London's first great department store, and still one of its best: a huge, airy mecca of clothes, food and furnishings.

Waterstone's

203–206 Piccadilly ☎020/7851 2400, ⓦwww.waterstones.co.uk. Mon–Sat 10am–10pm, Sun noon–6pm. This flagship bookstore – Europe's largest – boasts a café, bar, gallery and events rooms as well as five floors of books.

Cafés

Mômo Tearoom

25 Heddon St. Mon–Sat noon–1am, Sun noon–10.30pm. Serving reasonably priced and delicious snacks, this is London's ultimate Arabic pastiche café, with tables and hookahs spilling out onto the pavement of a quiet little Mayfair alleyway.

Sotheby's

34–35 New Bond St ⓦwww.sothebys.com. Mon–Fri 9.30am–4.45pm. Sotheby's café is by no means cheap, but the lunches are exquisitely prepared, and the excellent afternoon teas are a fraction of the price of the nearby hotels.

The Wolseley

160 Piccadilly ⓦwww.thewolseley.com. Mon–Fri 7am–midnight, Sat & Sun 11.30–midnight (Sun 11pm). A lofty and stylish 1920s interior, attentive, non-snooty service and Viennese-inspired food. Given the glamour levels it's surprisingly affordable too – a great place for breakfast or a cream tea.

Restaurants

Kiku

17 Half Moon St ☎020/7499 4208, ⓦwww.kikurestaurant.co.uk. Mon–Sat noon–2.30pm & 6.30–10.15pm, Sun 5.30–9.45pm. "Kiku" translates as pricey, but for top-quality sushi and sashimi, this place doesn't charge the earth. Take a seat at the traditional sushi bar and wonder at the dexterity of the knife man. Set lunch £13.50.

Truc Vert

42 North Audley St ☎020/7491 9988 ⓦwww.trucvert.co.uk. Mon–Sat 7.30am–10pm, Sun 9.30am–4pm. An

upmarket but friendly restaurant, offering quiche, salads, pâtés, cakes and pastries. The menu changes daily and begins early with breakfast; also has a small deli section. Mains £13–16.

Pubs and bars

Audley
41 Mount St. Mon–Sat 11am–11pm, Sun noon–10.30pm. A grand Mayfair pub, with its original Victorian burgundy lincrusta ceiling, chandeliers and clocks.

Claridge's
49 Brook St ⓦ www.savoy-group. com. Mon–Sat noon–1am, Sun 4pm–midnight. The bar here has a tasteful Art Deco feel, with terribly English waiters and splendid cocktails from £8 each.

Dorchester
63 Park Lane ⓦ www.dorchesterhotel .com. Mon–Sat noon–11pm, Sun noon–10.30pm. Wildly over-the-top gilded, mirrored Hollywood decor, big booths to ease into,

and jolly good cocktails at just under £10 a hit.

Guinea
30 Bruton Place. Mon–Fri 11am–11pm, Sat 6.30–11pm. Tiny, old-fashioned, flower-strewn mews pub, serving good Young's bitter and excellent steak-and-kidney pies.

Ye Grapes
16 Shepherd Market. Mon–Sat 11am–11pm, Sun noon–10.30pm. Busy Victorian free house, with a good selection of real ales from a number of breweries and an open fire – a great local in the heart of Mayfair.

Clubs and venues

Dover Street
8–9 Dover St ☎ 020/7491 7509 ⓦ www.doverst.co.uk. Mon–Sat. Cover charge (£6–15) from 10pm. Enjoyable central restaurant and jazz, bar hosting blues, R&B, jazz Latin and soul bands every night followed by a DJ until 3am.

▼ CAFÉ CULTURE BEHIND OXFORD STREET

Marylebone

Marylebone may not have quite the pedigree and snob value of Mayfair, but it's still a wealthy and aspirational area. Built in the eighteenth century, its mesh of smart Georgian streets and squares survives more or less intact today, and compared to the brashness of nearby Oxford Street, the backstreets of Marylebone are a pleasure to wander, especially the chi-chi, village-like quarter around the High Street. In fact, the area only really gets busy and touristy around the north end of Baker Street, home of the fictional detective Sherlock Holmes, and one of London's biggest visitor attractions, Madame Tussaud's waxworks' extravaganza.

Wallace Collection

Hertford House, Manchester Square
ⓦ www.wallacecollection.org. Daily
10am–5pm. Free. Housed in a miniature eighteenth-century French chateau, the Wallace Collection is an old-fashioned place, with exhibits piled high in glass cabinets, paintings covering every inch of wall space and a bloody great armoury. The collection is best known for its eighteenth-century **French paintings** (especially Watteau); look out, too, for Franz Hals' *Laughing Cavalier*, Titian's *Perseus and Andromeda*, Velázquez's *Lady with a Fan* and Rembrandt's affectionate portrait of his teenage son, Titus. Labelling can be pretty terse and paintings occasionally move about, so you might want to consider renting an audioguide (£3).

RIBA

66 Portland Place ☎ 020/7580
5533, ⓦ www.riba.org. Mon–Fri
8am–6pm, Tues until 9pm, Sat
8am–5pm. Free. With its sleek 1930s Portland-stone facade, the Royal Institute of British Architects headquarters is easily the finest building on Portland Place. Inside, the main staircase remains a wonderful period piece, with etched glass balustrades, walnut veneer and two large columns of black marble rising up on either side. You can view the interior en route to the institute's often

▼ MAIN STAIRCASE, RIBA

© Crown copyright

RESTAURANTS		CAFÉS		PUBS		CLUBS & LIVE VENUES	
Fairuz	7	Eat & Two Veg	2	Barley Mow	3	Wigmore Hall	10
Phoenix Palace	1	Golden Hind	9	Dover Castle	6		
The Providores	4	Patisserie Valerie		O'Conor Don	8	SHOPS	
		at Sagne	5			Daunt Books	a

thought-provoking first-floor architectural exhibitions (free) and to its café, or if you visit for one of the Tuesday-evening talks (6.30pm; £8) held here. The excellent ground-floor bookshop is also worth a browse.

Madame Tussaud's

Marylebone Rd ☎0870/400 3000, ⓦwww.madame-tussauds.com. Mon–Fri 9.30am–5.30pm, Sat & Sun 9am–6pm; school holidays daily 9am–5.30pm. £24. Madame Tussaud's waxworks have been pulling in the crowds ever since the good lady arrived in London from France in 1802 bearing the sculpted heads of guillotined aristocrats. The entrance fee

is extortionate, the likenesses occasionally dubious and the automated dummies inept, but you can still rely on finding London's biggest queues here – to avoid joining them, book your ticket over the phone or online in advance. After star-spotting and trawling through the irredeemably tasteless Chamber of Horrors (including Chamber Live where costumed actors jump out at you in the dark) the Tussaud's finale is a manic five-minute "ride" through the history of London in a miniaturized taxi cab. Tickets for Madame Tussaud's also allow you to watch a thirty-minute high-tech presentation, usually on a celebrity/

Hollywood-inspired theme, projected onto the domed auditorium that once housed the London Planetarium.

Sherlock Holmes Museum

239 Baker St ⦿ www.sherlock
-holmes.co.uk. Daily 9.30am–6pm.
£6. Sherlock Holmes's fictional address was 221b Baker Street, hence the number on the door of the Sherlock Holmes Museum. Stuffed full of Victoriana and life-size models of characters from the books, it's an atmospheric and very competent exercise in period reconstruction. You can stroll in and out of the rooms, and don a deerstalker to have your picture taken by the fireside, looking like the great detective himself.

Shops

Daunt Books

83 Marylebone High St ⦿020/7224 2295, ⦿www.dauntbooks.co.uk. Mon–Sat 9am–7.30pm, Sun 11am–6pm.

▼ PATISSERIE VALERIE CAKES

Wide and inspirational range of travel literature as well as the usual guidebooks, presented by expert staff in the beautiful, galleried interior of this famous shop.

Cafés

Eat & Two Veg

50 Marylebone High St. Mon–Sat 9am–11pm, Sun 10am–10pm. A lively and modern veggie restaurant, with an eclectic menu featuring Thai, Greek and Italian dishes; some vegan and soya protein choices.

Golden Hind

73 Marylebone Lane. Mon–Fri noon–3pm & 6–10pm, Sat 6–10pm. Marylebone's heritage fish-and-chip restaurant, founded in 1914, serves classic cod and chips from around a fiver, as well as slightly fancier fare.

Patisserie Valerie at Sagne

105 Marylebone High St ⦿www.
patisserie-valerie.co.uk. Mon–Fri 7.30am–7pm, Sat 8am–7pm, Sun 9am–6pm. Founded as Swiss-run *Maison Sagne* in the 1920s, and preserving its wonderful decor from those days, the café is now run by Soho's fab patisserie makers, and is without doubt Marylebone's finest.

Restaurants

Fairuz

3 Blandford St ⦿020/7486 8108.
Mon–Sat noon–11.30pm, Sun noon–10.30pm. One of London's more accessible Middle Eastern restaurants, with an epic list of mezze, delicate and fragrant charcoal grills and one or two oven-baked dishes. Get here early to secure one of the

nook-and-crannyish, tent-like tables. Mains £9–16.

Phoenix Palace
3–5 Glentworth St ☎020/7486 3515. Mon–Sat noon–11.30pm, Sun 11am–10.30pm. The menu here stretches off into the farthest corners of Chinese chefly imagination, and it's worth a careful read. Better still, the cooking is good and the portions large. Mains £7–25.

The Providores
109 Marylebone High St ☎020/7935 6175, ⓦwww.theprovidores .co.uk. Mon–Fri 9am–11pm, Sat 10am–11pm, Sun 10am–10pm. Outstanding fusion restaurant split into two distinct areas: snacky Tapa Room downstairs and full-on restaurant upstairs. On either level the food, which may sound like an untidy assemblage on paper, is original and wholly satisfying. Mains £18–25.

Pubs and bars

Barley Mow
8 Dorset St. Mon–Sat 11am–11pm. This local pub tucked away in the backstreets of Marylebone has pawnbrokers' snugs and serves a range of real ales.

Dover Castle
43 Weymouth Mews. Mon–Fri 11.30am–11pm, Sat 12.30–11pm. A traditional, quiet boozer hidden away down a labyrinthine and picturesque Marylebone mews. Green upholstery, dark wood and a nicotine-stained lincrusta ceiling add to the atmosphere.

O'Conor Don
88 Marylebone Lane ⓦwww .oconordon.com. Mon–Fri noon–11pm. Stripped of the usual trappings this stout-loving pub is a cut above the average, with excellent Guinness, a pleasantly easy-going pace and Irish food on offer.

Clubs and venues

Wigmore Hall
36 Wigmore St ☎020/7935 2141, ⓦwww.wigmore-hall.org.uk. With near-perfect acoustics, this classical and chamber music/ song recital venue is a favourite with artists and audiences alike – book well in advance.

PLACES

Marylebone

▼ O'CONOR DON PUB

Soho

Soho is one of London's most diverse, busy and characterful areas, and is very much the heart of the West
End. It's been the city's premier red-light district for
centuries, and retains an unorthodox and slightly raff-
ish air that's unique for central London. Conventional
sights are few and far between, yet it's a great area to
wander through, even if you just take in the lively fruit
and vegetable market on Berwick Street; whatever the
hour, however, there's always something going on. Most
folk head here to visit one of the many cinemas or theatres, or to grab a bite to eat or a drink at the incredible
variety of cafés, bars and restaurants, including a whole
array of inexpensive Chinese places that pepper the tiny
enclave of Chinatown to the south. Soho is also a very
upfront gay mecca, with bars and cafés concentrated
around the Old Compton Street area.

Leicester Square

By night, when the big cinemas
and nightclubs are doing brisk
business and the buskers are
entertaining passers-by, Leicester
Square is one of the most
crowded places in London; on a
Friday or Saturday night, it can
seem as if half the youth of the
city's suburbs have congregated
here, supplemented by a vast
number of tourists. By day,
queues form for theatre and
concert deals at the square's
half-price ticket booth, while
clubbers hand out flyers to
likely looking punters.

It wasn't until the mid-
nineteenth century that the
square began to emerge as
an entertainment zone, with
accommodation houses (for
prostitutes and their clients)
and music halls such as the
grandiose Empire and the
Hippodrome (just off the
square), both of which still
stand today. **Cinema** moved in
during the 1930s – a golden age
evoked by the sleek black lines
of the Odeon on the east side
– and maintains its grip on the
area. The Empire is the favourite
for big red-carpet premieres
and, in a rather
half-hearted
imitation of
the Hollywood
tradition,
there are even
handprints-
of-the-stars
indented into
the pavement
of the square's
southwestern
corner.

▼ CHARLIE CHAPLIN STATUE, LEICESTER SQUARE

Half-price theatre tickets

The Society of London Theatre (www.officiallondontheatre.co.uk) runs the Half
Price Ticket Booth in Leicester Square, now known as tkts (Mon–Sat 10am–7pm,
Sun noon–3.30pm; www.tkts.co.uk), which sells on-the-day tickets for all the
West End shows at discounts of up to fifty percent, though they tend to be in the
top end of the price range, are limited to four per person, and carry a service
charge of £2.50 per ticket.

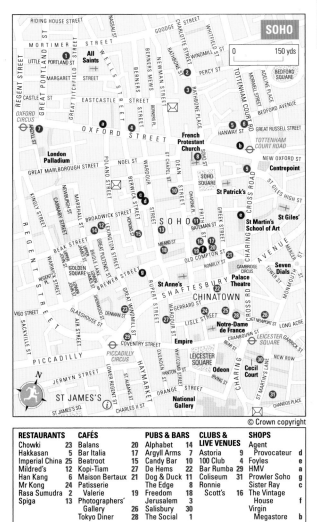

© Crown copyright

RESTAURANTS		CAFÉS		PUBS & BARS		CLUBS & LIVE VENUES		SHOPS	
Chowki	23	Balans	20	Alphabet	14	Astoria	9	Agent	
Hakkasan	5	Bar Italia	17	Argyll Arms	7	100 Club	4	Provocateur	d
Imperial China	25	Beatroot	15	Candy Bar	10	Bar Rumba	29	Foyles	e
Mildred's	12	Kopi-Tiam	27	De Hems	22	Coliseum	31	HMV	a
Han Kang	6	Maison Bertaux	21	Dog & Duck	11	Ronnie		Prowler Soho	g
Mr Kong	24	Patisserie		The Edge	8	Scott's	16	Sister Ray	c
Rasa Sumudra	2	Valerie	19	Freedom	18			The Vintage	
Spiga	13	Photographers'		Jerusalem	3			House	f
		Gallery	26	Salisbury	30			Virgin	
		Tokyo Diner	28	The Social	1			Megastore	b

Chinatown

A self-contained jumble of shops, cafés and restaurants, Chinatown is one of London's most distinct and popular ethnic enclaves. Centred around **Gerrard Street**, it's a tiny area of no more than three or four blocks, thick with the aromas of Chinese cooking and peppered with ersatz touches. Few of London's 60,000 Chinese actually live in Chinatown, but it nonetheless remains a focus for the community: a place to do business or the weekly shopping, celebrate a wedding, or just meet up for meals – particularly on Sundays, when the restaurants overflow with Chinese families tucking into dim sum. Most Londoners come to Chinatown simply to eat – easy and inexpensive enough to do. Cantonese cuisine predominates, and you're unlikely to be disappointed wherever you go.

Charing Cross Road

Charing Cross Road, which marks Soho's eastern border, boasts the highest concentration of **bookshops** anywhere in London. One of the first to

▼ EATING OUT IN CHINATOWN

open here, in 1906, was Foyles at no. 119 – De Valera, George Bernard Shaw, Walt Disney and Conan Doyle were all once regular customers. You'll find more of Charing Cross Road's original character at the string of specialist and secondhand bookshops south of Cambridge Circus. One of the nicest places for specialist and antiquarian book-browsing is Cecil Court, the southernmost pedestrianized alleyway between Charing Cross Road and St Martin's Lane.

Photographers' Gallery

5 & 8 Great Newport St ⓦ www .photonet.org.uk. Mon–Sat 11am–6pm, Sun noon–6pm. Free. Established in 1971 as the first of its kind in London, the Photographers' Gallery hosts excellent temporary photographic exhibitions, often featuring leading contemporary photographers, that are invariably worth a browse. Note that the gallery has exhibition spaces at two separate addresses, with a café at no. 5 and a good bookshop at no. 8.

Old Compton Street

If Soho has a main drag, it has to be Old Compton Street, which runs parallel with Shaftesbury Avenue. The corner shops, peep shows, boutiques and trendy cafés here are typical of the area and a good barometer of the latest Soho fads. Soho has been a permanent fixture on

▲ SOHO THEATRE

the **gay scene** since the last century, though nowadays, it's not just gay bars, clubs and cafés jostling for position on Old Compton Street: there's a gay-run houseshare agency, a financial advice outfit and, even more convenient, a gay taxi service.

Shops

Agent Provocateur

6 Broadwick St ☎020/7439 0229, ⓦwww.agentprovocateur.com. Mon–Sat 11am–7pm (Thurs till 8pm), Sun noon–5pm. Upmarket lingerie store for those with an interest in the kitsch, sexy and glamorous.

Foyles

113–119 Charing Cross Rd ☎020/7437 5660, ⓦwww.foyles .co.uk. Mon–Sat 9.30am–9pm, Sun noon–6pm. Long-established bookstore with a big Silver

Moon feminist section, and Ray's Jazz Shop and café on the first floor.

HMV

150 Oxford St ☎020/7631 3423, ⓦwww.hmv.co.uk. Mon–Sat 9am–8.30pm (Thurs till 9pm), Sun noon–6pm. All the latest releases, as you'd expect, but also an impressive backlist, a reassuring amount of vinyl and a good classical section.

Prowler Soho

5–7 Brewer St ☎020/7734 4031, ⓦwww.prowlerstores.co.uk. Mon–Sat 11am–10pm, Sun 1–9pm. A gay and lesbian household name, stocking lots of fetish gear and erotica, plus a great range of literature, art, postcards and gifts.

Sister Ray

34–35 Berwick St ☎020/7734 3297, ⓦwww.sisterray.co.uk. Mon–Sat 9.30am–8pm, Sun noon–6pm. Up-to-the minute indie sounds, plus

▲ THE VINTAGE HOUSE, SOHO

lots of electronica and some forays into the current dance scene. Most releases available on vinyl as well as CD.

The Vintage House

42 Old Compton St ☎020/7437 2592, ⓦwww.vintagehouse.co.uk. Mon–Fri 9am–11pm, Sat 9.30am–11pm, Sun noon–10pm. Wines, brandies and more than 1400 whiskies line the shelves of this family-run drinker's paradise.

Virgin Megastore

14–16 Oxford St ☎020/7631 1234, ⓦwww.virginmega.co.uk. Mon–Sat 9am–10pm, Sun noon–6pm. The rock-heavy mainstream floor is better stocked than the specialist sections, but there's a little of everything else, and plenty of books, magazines, T-shirts and assorted music ephemera.

Cafés

Balans

34 Old Compton St ☎020/7439 3309, ⓦwww.balans.co.uk. Mon–Thurs 8am–5am, Fri & Sat 8am–6am, Sun 8am–2am. Enduringly busy Soho institution with a full restaurant menu including a lengthy brunch section makes it the obvious solution to mid- or post-party wooziness.

Bar Italia

22 Frith St. Nearly 24hr; closed Mon–Fri 4–6am. This tiny café is a Soho institution, serving coffee, croissants and sandwiches more or less around the clock – as it has been doing since 1949.

Beatroot

92 Berwick St. Mon–Sat 9am–9pm, Sun noon–7.30pm. Great little veggie café by the market, doling out hot savoury bakes, stews and salads (plus delicious cakes) in boxes of varying sizes – all under £5.

Kopi-Tiam

9 Wardour St. Daily 11am–11pm. Bright, cheap Malaysian café serving up curries, coconut rice, juices and "herbal soups" to local Malays, all for around a fiver.

Maison Bertaux
28 Greek St. Daily 8.30am–8pm.
Long-standing, old-fashioned
and terribly French Soho
patisserie, with seating on two
floors. The wonderful offerings
here are made on the premises
and are among the best in the
West End.

Patisserie Valerie
44 Old Compton St ⓦwww.patisserie
-valerie.co.uk. Mon–Fri 7.30am–8.30pm,
Sat 8am–8.30pm, Sun 9am–6.30pm.
Popular coffee, croissant and cake
emporium dating from the 1950s
and attracting a loud-talking, arty
crowd.

Photographers' Gallery
5 Great Newport St. Mon–Sat
11am–5.30pm (Thurs till 7.30pm), Sun
noon–5.30pm. Bench seats within
one of the gallery buildings let
you check out the photographs
on display whilst tucking into
generously filled rolls and tasty
cakes.

Tokyo Diner
2 Newport Place. Daily noon–midnight.
Friendly eatery serving fast
food, Tokyo style. Minimalist
decor lets the sushi do the
talking, which – if the number
of Japanese who frequent the
place is anything to go by – it
does fluently.

Restaurants

Chowki
2–3 Denman St ⓣ020/7439 1330. Daily
noon–11.30pm. Large, cheap Indian
restaurant serving authentic
homestyle food in stylish
surroundings. The regional feast is
great value at £11.

Hakkasan
8 Hanway Place ⓣ020/7927 7000.
Mon–Wed noon–3pm & 6pm–midnight,
Thurs–Fri noon–3pm & 6–12.30am,
Sat noon–4.30pm & 6–12.30am.
Impressively designed Chinese
restaurant serving novel, well-
presented, fresh, delicious and
expensive food.

Imperial China
White Bear Yard, 25a Lisle St
ⓣ020/7734 3388. Mon–Sat noon–
11.30, Sun 11.30am–10.30pm. Large
restaurant tucked into a little
courtyard off Lisle Street; fresh
and bright, with dim sum that's
up there with the best, service
that is "Chinatown brusque",
and a menu with eminently
reasonable prices.

Mildred's
45 Lexington St ⓣ020/7494 1634
ⓦwww.mildreds.co.uk. Mon–Sat
noon–11pm. Fresher and more
stylish than many veggie
restaurants, the stir-fries,
pasta dishes and burgers are
wholesome, delicious and
inexpensive.

Han Kang
16 Hanway St ⓣ020/7637 1985. Mon–
Sat noon–3pm & 6–10.30pm. Small
non-descript Korean restaurant
that serves some of the best
Korean food in the capital; the
three-course lunch, in particular,
is excellent value at £6.50.

Mr Kong
21 Lisle St ⓣ020/7437 7923. Mon–Sat
noon–2.45am, Sun noon–1.45am.
One of Chinatown's finest, with
a chef-owner who pioneered
modern Cantonese cuisine:
order from the "Today's" and
"Chef's Specials" menu, and
don't miss the mussels in black-
bean sauce.

Rasa Samudra
5 Charlotte St ⓣ020/7637 0222
ⓦwww.rasarestaurants.com. Mon–Sat
noon–3pm & 6–11pm. Smart, pricey,

fishy south Indian restaurant which produces classy dishes that would be more at home in Mumbai than London.

Spiga

84–86 Wardour St ☎020/7734 3444. Wed–Sat noon–3am, Sun noon–10.30pm. A pleasantly casual but upmarket Italian affair, with a lively atmosphere, a serious wood-fired oven and cool designer looks.

Pubs and bars

Alphabet

61–63 Beak St ⓦwww.alphabetbar. com. Mon–Fri noon–11pm, Sat 4–11pm. Upstairs is light and spacious with decadent leather sofas, a great choice of European beers, and mouthwatering food; downstairs, there are dimmed coloured lights and car seats strewn around.

Argyll Arms

18 Argyll St. Mon–Sat 11am–11pm, Sun noon–10.30pm. A stone's throw from Oxford Circus, this is a serious find: a great Victorian pub that has preserved many of its original features and serves good real ales.

Candy Bar

4 Carlisle St ⓦwww.thecandybar. co.uk. Mon–Thurs 5–11.30pm, Fri & Sat 5pm–2am, Sun 5–11pm. The crucial, cruisey vibe makes this the hottest girl-bar in central London.

De Hems

11 Macclesfield St. Mon–Sat noon–midnight, Sun noon–10.30pm. Probably your best bet in Chinatown, this is London's official Dutch pub, and has been since the 1890s; a simple wood-panelled affair with

Oranjeboom on tap and Belgian beers in bottles.

Dog & Duck

18 Bateman St. Mon–Sat 11am–11pm, Sun 11am–10.30pm. Tiny Soho pub that retains much of its old character, beautiful Victorian tiling and mosaics, and a good range of real ales.

The Edge

11 Soho Square ⓦedgesoho.co.uk. Mon–Thurs 11am–midnight, Fri & Sat noon–1am, Sun noon–10.30pm. Busy, style-conscious and pricey Soho café/bar spread over several floors, although this doesn't seem to stop everyone ending up on the pavement, especially in summer. Food daily, DJs most nights.

Freedom

60–66 Wardour St. Mon–Sat 11am–3am, Sun 11am–midnight. Hip, busy, late-opening place, popular with a straight/gay Soho crowd. Great juices and healthy food in the daytime, cocktails and overpriced beer in the evening.

Jerusalem

33–34 Rathbone Place. Mon noon–11pm, Tues & Wed noon–midnight, Thurs & Fri noon–1am, Sun 7pm–1am. All chandeliers and velvet drapes, this place attracts a more dressed-up crowd enjoying the house DJs who play Thurs, Fri and Sat evenings.

Salisbury

90 St Martin's Lane. Mon–Fri 11am–midnight, Sat noon–11pm, Sun noon–10.30pm. One of the most superbly preserved Victorian pubs in London – and certainly the most central – with cut, etched and engraved windows, bronze statues, red-velvet seating and a fine lincrusta ceiling.

The Social

5 Little Portland St ⓦwww.thesocial.com. Mon–Fri noon–midnight, Sat 1pm–midnight. Industrial club-bar with great DJs playing everything from rock to rap, a truly hedonistic-cum-alcoholic crowd and great snacks – beans on toast and fish-finger sarnies – for when you get an attack of the munchies.

Clubs and venues

Astoria

157 Charing Cross Rd ⓦwww.meanfiddler.com. One of London's best and most central medium-sized venues, this large, balconied one-time theatre tends to host popular bands from a real variety of genres, as well as the popular G-A-Y club.

100 Club

100 Oxford St ⓦwww.the100club.co.uk. Doors open 7.30pm. An unpretentious, inexpensive and fun jazz venue with an incredible vintage – it's been going strong for more than sixty years.

Bar Rumba

36 Shaftesbury Ave ⓦwww.barrumba.co.uk. Open until 3/4am. Fun, smallish West End club venue with a mix of regular nights ranging from salsa, R&B and dance to drum'n'bass. Pop in early evening (when it's free) to sample some cocktails during happy hour.

Coliseum

St Martin's Lane ☎0870/145 0200, ⓦwww.eno.org. English National Opera differs from its Royal Opera House counterpart in that all its operas are sung in English, productions tend to be more experimental, and the cost is far less.

Ronnie Scott's

47 Frith St ⓦwww.ronniescotts.co.uk. The most famous jazz club in London: small and smoky and still going strong. The place for top-line names, who play two sets – one at around 10pm, the other after midnight. Book a table, or you'll have to stand.

▼ FREEDOM BAR, SOHO

Bloomsbury

Bloomsbury was built over in grid-plan style from the 1660s onwards, and the formal, bourgeois Georgian squares laid out then remain the area's main distinguishing feature. In the twentieth century, Bloomsbury acquired a reputation as the city's most learned quarter, dominated by the dual institutions of the British Museum and London University, and home to many of London's chief book publishers, but perhaps best known for its literary inhabitants, among them T.S. Eliot and Virginia Woolf. Only in its northern fringes does the character of the area change dramatically, as you near the two busy main-line train stations of Euston and King's Cross.

PLACES

Bloomsbury

British Museum

Great Russell St ⓦ www.british -museum.ac.uk. Mon–Wed, Sat & Sun 10am–5.30pm, Thurs & Fri 10am–8.30pm. Free. One of the great museums of the world, the British Museum contains an incredible collection of antiquities, prints, drawings and books, all housed under one roof. Begun in 1823, the building itself is the grandest of London's Greek Revival edifices, with its central **Great Court** (Mon–Wed & Sun 9am– 6pm, Thurs–Sat 9am–11pm) featuring a remarkable curving glass-and-steel roof designed by Norman Foster. At the Court's centre stands the copper-domed former **Round Reading Room** (daily 10am–5.30pm) of the British Library, where Karl Marx penned *Das Kapital*.

The BM's collection of **Roman and Greek antiquities** is unparalleled, and is most famous for the Parthenon sculptures, better known as the Elgin Marbles after the British aristocrat who walked off with the reliefs in 1801. Elsewhere, the **Egyptian collection** is easily the most significant outside Egypt, ranging from monumental sculptures to the ever-popular mummies and their ornate outer caskets. Also on display is the Rosetta Stone, which enabled French professor, Champollion, to finally unlock the secret of Egyptian hieroglyphs. Other highlights include a splendid series of **Assyrian reliefs** from Nineveh, and several extraordinary artefacts from **Mesopotamia** such as the enigmatic Ram in the Thicket (a goat

▼ BLOOMSBURY GROUP PLAQUE, GORDON SQUARE

BLOOMSBURY

CAFÉS		PUBS & BARS		CLUBS & LIVE		SHOPS		
Coffee Gallery	8	King's Bar	3	VENUES		Atlantis Bookshop	f	Persephone
Fryer's Delight	9	The Lamb	4	The Cross	1	Gay's the Word	b	Books c
Wagamama	6	Museum		The Place	2	Gosh!	d	Playin' Games e
		Tavern	7			James Smith		Stern's Music a
RESTAURANT						& Sons	g	
Cigala	5							

statuette in lapis lazuli and shell) and the remarkable hoard of goldwork known as the Oxus Treasure.

The leathery half-corpse of the 2000-year-old Lindow Man, discovered in a Cheshire bog, and the Anglo-Saxon treasure from the Sutton Hoo ship burial, by far the richest single archeological find made in Britain, are among the highlights of the **Prehistoric** and **Roman Britain** collection. The **medieval** and **modern**

collections, meanwhile, range from the twelfth-century Lewis chessmen carved from walrus ivory, to twentieth-century exhibits such as a copper vase by Frank Lloyd Wright.

The **King's Library**, in the east wing, displays some of the museum's earliest acquisitions, brought back from the far reaches of the British Empire, everything from Javanese puppets to a model gamelan orchestra, collected by Stamford Raffles. The sheer range and volume of items on display, with their terse (and in some cases non-existent) labels, is a deliberate attempt to illustrate the acquisitive magpie tastes of the eighteenth-century collector, epitomized by Hans Sloane himself, the BM's founder.

Don't miss the museum's expanding **ethnographic collection**, too, including the atmospheric Mexican and North American galleries, plus the African galleries in the basement. In the north wing of the museum, closest to the back entrance on Montague Place, there are also fabulous Asian treasures including ancient Chinese porcelain, ornate snuffboxes, miniature landscapes and a bewildering array of Buddhist and Hindu gods.

Foundling Museum

40 Brunswick Square ⓦ www. foundlingmuseum.org.uk. Tues–Sat 10am–6pm, Sun noon–6pm. £5.

The Foundling Museum tells the fascinating story of the Foundling Hospital, London's first home for abandoned children founded in 1756 by retired sea captain Thomas Coram. As soon as it was opened, it was besieged, and soon forced to reduce its admissions drastically and introduce a ballot system. Among the most tragic exhibits are the tokens left by the mothers in order to identify the children should they ever be in a position to reclaim them: these range from a heart-rending poem to a simple enamel pot label reading "ale". The museum also boasts an impressive **art collection** including works by artists such as Hogarth, Gainsborough and Reynolds, now hung in the eighteenth-century interiors carefully preserved in their entirety from the original hospital.

Dickens' House

48 Doughty St ⓦ www. dickensmuseum.com. Mon–Sat 10am–5pm, Sun 11am–5pm. £5.
Despite the plethora of blue plaques marking the residences of local luminaries, Dickens' House is Bloomsbury's only literary museum. Dickens moved here in 1837 shortly after his marriage to Catherine Hogarth, and they lived here for two years, during which time he wrote *Nicholas Nickleby* and *Oliver Twist*. Although the author painted a gloomy Victorian world in his books, the drawing room here, in which he entertained his literary friends, was decorated in a rather upbeat Regency style. Letters, manuscripts and first editions, the earliest known portrait (a miniature painted by his aunt in 1830) and the reading copies

he used during extensive lecture tours in Britain and the States are the rewards for those with more than a passing interest in the novelist. You can also watch a film about his life (30min).

London University

Ⓦ www.lon.ac.uk. London has more students than any other city in the world (over half a million at the last count), which isn't bad going for a city that only organized its own University in 1826, more than six hundred years after the likes of Oxford and Cambridge. The university started life in Bloomsbury, but it wasn't until after World War I that the institution really began to take over the area.

This piecemeal development means that departments are spread over a wide area, though the main focus is between the 1930s Senate House skyscraper on Malet Street, behind the British Museum, and the Neoclassical University College (UCL; Ⓦ www.ucl.ac.uk), near the top of Gower Street. UCL is home to London's most famous art school, the Slade, which puts on temporary exhibitions from its collection at the **Strang Print Room** (term-time Wed–Fri 1–5pm; other times call ☎020/7679 2540 to check hours; free), in the south cloister of the main quadrangle. Also on display in the south cloisters is the fully-clothed skeleton of philosopher Jeremy Bentham (1748–1832), one of the university's founders, topped by a wax head and wide-brimmed hat.

London University Museums and the Brunei Gallery

On the first floor of London University's D.M.S. Watson building on Malet Place, the **Petrie Museum of Egyptian Archeology** (Ⓦ www.petrie .ucl.ac.uk; Tues–Fri 1–5pm, Sat 10am–1pm; free) has a couple of rooms jam-packed with antiquities, the bulk of them from excavations carried out in the 1880s by the then UCL Professor of Egyptology, including the world's oldest dress, an understandably ragged pleated garment worn by an Ancient Egyptian teenager around 3000 BC. Tucked away in the southeast corner of Gordon Square, at no. 53, there's more specialist interest at the **Percival David Foundation of Chinese Art** (Ⓦ www .pdfmuseum.org.uk; Mon–Fri 10.30am–5pm; free), which boasts two floors of top-notch Chinese ceramics, bequeathed to the University, while the temporary exhibitions of photography and art at the **Brunei Gallery** (Ⓦ www .soas.ac.uk/gallery; Mon–Fri 10.30am–5pm; free), which is part of the School of Oriental and African Studies, are usually well worth visiting; call ☎020/7898 4915 to see what's on. There's also a café on the ground floor, and a secluded Zen-like rooftop garden.

British Library

96 Euston Rd ☎020/7412 7332, Ⓦ www.bl.uk. Mon & Wed–Fri 9.30am–6pm, Tues 9.30am–8pm, Sat 9.30am–5pm, Sun 11am–5pm. Free. Opened in 1998 as the country's most expensive public building (over £250 million), it was hardly surprising that the British Library drew fierce criticism from all sides. Certainly, the exterior's red-brick brutalism is horribly out of fashion, but the interior of the library has met with general approval and the

high-tech exhibition galleries are superb.

The library's reading rooms are accessible to its members only, but its exhibition galleries are open to all. These are situated to the left as you enter; straight ahead is the spiritual heart of the BL, a multistorey glass-walled tower housing the vast **King's Library**, collected by George III and donated to the museum by George IV in 1823; to the side of the King's Library are the pull-out drawers of the philatelic collection.

The first of the three exhibition galleries to head for is the dimly lit **John Ritblat Gallery**, where a superlative selection of ancient manuscripts, maps, documents and precious books, including the Magna Carta and the richly illustrated Lindisfarne Gospels, are displayed. One of the most appealing innovations is "Turning the Pages", a small room off the main gallery where you can "turn" the pages of selected texts on a computer terminal. The Workshop of Words, Sounds and Images is a hands-on exhibition of more universal appeal, where you can design your own literary publication, while the Pearson Gallery of Living Words puts on excellent temporary exhibitions, for which there is sometimes an admission charge.

St Pancras & King's Cross stations

Euston Rd. Completed in 1876, the former Midland Grand Hotel's majestic sweep of Neo-Gothic lancets, dormers and chimneypots forms the facade of St Pancras Station, where Eurostar trains will arrive as of 2007. The adjacent King's Cross Station, opened in 1850, is a mere shed in comparison. King's Cross is more famous, however, as this is the station from which **Harry Potter** and his wizarding chums leave for school on the *Hogwarts Express* from platform 9 ¾. The scenes from the film are, in fact, shot between platforms 4 and 5, as 9 and 10 are unphotogenic side-platforms.

▼ *RUSSELL HOTEL*, RUSSELL SQUARE

Shops

Atlantis Bookshop

49a Museum St ☎020/7405 2120,
ⓦwww.theatlantisbookshop.com.
Mon–Sat 10.30am–6pm. Splendid
occult-oriented place, with the
perfect ambience for browsing
through books and magazines
covering spirituality, psychic
phenomena, witchcraft and the
like.

Gay's the Word

66 Marchmont St ☎020/7278 7654,
ⓦwww.gaystheword.co.uk. Mon–Sat
10am–6.30pm, Sun 2–6.30pm.
An extensive collection of
lesbian and gay classics, pulps,
contemporary fiction and non-
fiction, plus cards, calendars and
weekly lesbian discussion groups
and readings.

Gosh!

39 Great Russell St ☎020/7636
1011, ⓦwww.goshlondon.com. Daily
10am–6pm (Thurs & Fri till 7pm). All
kinds of comics for all kinds of
readers, whether you're casually
curious or a serious collector.

James Smith & Sons

53 New Oxford St ☎020/7836 4731,
ⓦwww.james-smith.co.uk. Mon–Fri
9.30am–5.25pm, Sat 10am–5.25pm.
A survivor from an earlier time
(it was established in 1830), this
beautiful and venerable shop
purveys hip-flasks, portable seats
and canes, but its main trade is
in umbrellas.

Persephone Books

59 Lamb's Conduit St ☎020/7242
9292, ⓦwww.persephonebooks.co.uk.
Mon–Fri 10am–6pm. The attractive
bookshop of a publishing house
which specializes in neglected
early twentieth-century fiction,
poetry, biography and cook
books, mostly by women.

Playin' Games

33 Museum St ☎020/7323 3080.
Mon–Sat 10am–6pm, Sun noon–6pm.
Two floors of traditional board
games (Scrabble, Cluedo, etc),
plus backgammon, war games,
fantasy games and more.

Stern's Music

293 Euston Rd ☎020/7387 5550
ⓦwww.sternsmusic.com. Mon–Sat
10.30am–6.30pm. World famous
for its global specialisms, this
expert store has an unrivalled
stock of African music, and
excellent selections from pretty
much everywhere else in the
world, too.

Cafés

Coffee Gallery

23 Museum St. Mon–Fri 8.30am–
5.30pm, Sat 10am–7pm, Sun
noon–7pm. Excellent small café
serving mouthwatering Italian
sandwiches, and a few more
substantial dishes at lunchtime.
Get there early to grab a seat.

Fryer's Delight

19 Theobald's Road. Mon–Sat noon–
10pm. Fish and chips done to
perfection at a very reasonable
price in a no-nonsense, formica-
tabled chippie.

Wagamama

4 Streatham St ⓦwww.wagamama
.com. Mon–Sat noon–11pm, Sun
12.30–10pm. Much copied since,
this was the pioneer of austere,
minimalist, canteen-style noodle
bars, which serves filling main
meals for under £10.

Restaurants

Cigala

54 Lamb's Conduit St ☎020/7405
1717, ⓦwww.cigala.co.uk. Daily

12.30–10.45pm. Simple dishes, strong flavours, fresh ingredients and real passion are evident at this smart, Iberian restaurant, where a two-course set menu will set you back around £15.

Pubs and bars

King's Bar

Great Russell Hotel, Russell Square. Mon–Sat 7–1am, Sun 7am–midnight. The magnificent high ceilings and wood panelling of this Victorian hotel bar provide a great place in which to luxuriate. It's also a lot less posh – and more fun – than most hotel bars, and you get free bowls of nibbles.

The Lamb

94 Lamb's Conduit St. Mon–Sat 11am–11pm, Sun 11am–4pm & 7–10.30pm. Pleasant Young's pub with a marvellously well-preserved Victorian interior of mirrors, old wood and "snob" screens.

Museum Tavern

49 Great Russell St. Mon–Sat 11am–11pm, Sun noon–10.30pm. Large and characterful old pub, right opposite the main entrance to the British Museum, and the erstwhile drinking hole of Karl Marx.

Clubs and venues

The Cross

Arches 27–31, York Way ⓦwww .the-cross.co.uk. Fri 11pm–5am, Sat 10pm–6am. Hidden underneath the arches, the favourite flavours of this renowned club are hard house, house and garage. It's bigger than you imagine, but always rammed with chic clubby types, and there's a cool garden – perfect for those chill-out moments.

The Place

17 Duke's Road ⓦwww.theplace .org.uk. Small dance theatre presenting the work of new choreographers and student performers, and hosts some of the finest small-scale contemporary dance from across the globe.

Covent Garden

Covent Garden's transformation from a fruit, vegetable and flower market into a fashion-conscious shopping quarter was one of the most miraculous developments of the 1980s. Some three centuries ago the piazza served as the great playground (and red-light district) of eighteenth-century London. The Royal Opera House, alongside the area's buskers and numerous theatres, are survivors in this tradition, but in addition, there are now year-round stalls selling everything from antiques to Union Jack T-shirts, as well as numerous unusual shops, the occasional funfair and an annual Christmas market. Nearby, the old warehouses around Neal Street boast some of the most fashionable shops in the West End, selling everything from shoes to skateboards.

Covent Garden Piazza

ⓦwww.coventgardenmarket.co.uk. London's oldest planned square, laid out in the 1630s by Inigo Jones, Covent Garden Piazza was initially a great success – its novelty value alone ensured a rich and aristocratic clientele for the surrounding properties. Over the next century, though, the tone of the place fell as the fruit and vegetable **market** expanded, and theatres and coffee houses began to take over the peripheral buildings. Eventually, a large covered market was constructed in the middle of the square, but when the flower market closed in 1974, it was very nearly demolished to make way for an office development. Instead, the elegant Victorian market hall and its largely pedestrianized, cobbled piazza were restored to house shops, restaurants and arts-and-crafts stalls. Boosted by high-quality buskers and street entertainers, the piazza is now one of London's major tourist attractions, its success prompting a wholesale gentrification of the streets all around.

▼ COVENT GARDEN BICYCLE TAXIS

St Paul's Church

Covent Garden Piazza ⓦwww.actorschurch.org. The only remaining parts of the original piazza are the two rebuilt sections of arcading on the north side, and St Paul's Church on the west side. The proximity of so many theatres has earned

PLACES

Covent Garden

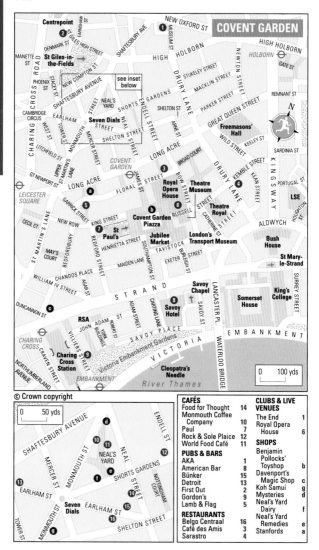

© Crown copyright

CAFÉS		CLUBS & LIVE VENUES	
Food for Thought	14	The End	1
Monmouth Coffee Company	10	Royal Opera House	6
Paul	7	SHOPS	
Rock & Sole Plaice	12	Benjamin	
World Food Café	11	Pollocks' Toyshop	b
PUBS & BARS		Davenport's Magic Shop	c
AKA	1	Koh Samui	d
American Bar	8	Mysteries	g
Bünker	15	Neal's Yard	
Detroit	13	Dairy	f
First Out	2	Neal's Yard	
Gordon's	9	Remedies	e
Lamb & Flag	5	Stanfords	a
RESTAURANTS			
Belgo Centraal	16		
Café des Amis	3		
Sarastro	4		

it the nickname of the "**Actors' Church**", and it's filled with memorials to international thespians from Boris Karloff to Gracie Fields. The space in front of the church's Tuscan portico – where Eliza Doolittle was discovered selling violets by Henry Higgins in George Bernard Shaw's *Pygmalion* – is now a legalized venue for buskers and street performers, who must audition for a slot months in advance. Round the back, the churchyard provides a tranquil respite from the activity outside – access is from King Street, Henrietta Street or Bedford Street.

London's Transport Museum

Covent Garden Piazza ☎020/7565 7299, ⓦwww.ltmuseum.co.uk. Daily 10am–6pm, Fri opens 11am. £5.95. Covent Garden's former flower market hall now serves as a retirement home for the old buses, trains and trams of London's Transport Museum, which is undergoing a thorough refurbishment but will open again in summer 2007. The ever-popular collection also has enough interactive fun – touch-screen computers, vehicles to climb on and the odd costumed conductor – to keep most children amused. There's usually a good smattering of stylish maps and posters on display, too, and you can buy reproductions, plus countless other tube, bus and tram paraphernalia, at the shop on the way out.

Theatre Museum

Russell St ☎020/7943 4700, ⓦtheatremuseum.org. Tues–Sun 10am–6pm. Free. Also housed in the old flower market hall, the Theatre Museum displays three centuries of memorabilia from the Western performing arts. The corridors of glass cases cluttered with props, programmes and costumes are not especially exciting, but the temporary exhibitions tend to be a lot more fun, as are the workshops, make-up demonstrations and occasional live performances. The museum also runs a booking service for West End shows and has an unusually good selection of cards and posters.

Royal Opera House

Bow St ☎020/7304 4000, ⓦwww. royaloperahouse.org. The arcading in the northeast corner of the piazza was rebuilt as part of the new millennium multi-million pound refurbishment of the Royal Opera House, whose main Neoclassical facade, dating from 1811, opens onto Bow Street (which you can reach via a passageway in the corner of the arcading). As part of the redevelopment, the market's spectacular wrought-iron Floral Hall (daily 10am–3pm) was transformed into the opera house's new first-floor foyer; both this and the glorious terrace overlooking the piazza, beyond the *Amphitheatre* bar/restaurant, are open to the public. **Backstage tours** (Mon–Fri 10.30am, 12.30 & 2.30pm, Sat also 11.30am; £9) of the opera house are also available.

PLACES Covent Garden

▼ ROYAL OPERA HOUSE

▲ SOMERSET HOUSE COURTYARD FOUNTAINS

Strand

Once famous for its riverside mansions, and later its music halls, the Strand is a shadow of its former self today, characterized more by the young homeless who shelter in the shop doorways at night. On the south side of the Strand, a blind side street – where the traffic drives on the right – leads to the Savoy, built in 1889 and still London's grandest hotel. César Ritz was the original manager, Guccio Gucci started out as a dishwasher here, and the list of illustrious guests is endless.

Bush House

Strand ⊛ www.bbc.co.uk/worldservice. Home of the BBC's World Service since 1940, Bush House was actually built by the American speculator Irving T. Bush, whose planned trade centre flopped in the 1930s. The giant figures on the north facade and the inscription, "To the Eternal Friendship of English-speaking Nations", thus refer to the friendship between the US and Britain, and are not, as many people assume, the

declaratory manifesto of the current occupants.

Victoria Embankment

Built between 1868 and 1874, the Victoria Embankment was the inspiration of French engineer Joseph Bazalgette, whose project simultaneously relieved congestion along the Strand, provided an extension to the underground railway and sewage systems, and created a new stretch of parkland with a riverside walk – no longer much fun due to the volume of traffic that barrels along it, though it does afford some good views over the water. London's oldest monument, **Cleopatra's Needle**, languishes little-noticed on the Thames side of the embankment. The 60-foot-high, 180-ton stick of granite in fact has nothing to do with Cleopatra – it's one of a pair originally erected in Heliopolis in 1475 BC (the other one is in New York's Central Park).

Somerset House

Victoria Embankment ☏020/7845 4600, ⊛www.somerset-house.org.uk. Courtyard and terrace daily 10am–11pm,

interior daily 10am–6pm. Free. Sole
survivor of the grand edifices
which once lined this stretch of
the riverfront, Somerset House's
four wings enclose an elegant and
surprisingly large courtyard. From
March to October, a wonderful
55-jet fountain spouts straight
from the courtyard's cobbles; in
winter, an ice rink is set up in its
place. The monumental Palladian
building itself was begun in
1776 by William Chambers as
a purpose-built governmental
office development, but now also
houses a series of museums and
galleries.

The south wing, overlooking
the Thames, is home to the
**Hermitage Rooms (Ⓦwww
.hermitagerooms.com; £5)**,
featuring changing displays
of anything from paintings
to Fabergé eggs drawn from
St Petersburg's Hermitage
Museum, and the **Gilbert
Collection (Ⓦwww.gilbert
-collection.org.uk; £5)**,
displaying decorative artworks
from European silver and gold
to micromosaics, clocks, portrait
miniatures and snuffboxes.

In the north wing are the
**Courtauld Institute galleries
(Ⓦwww.courtauld.ac.uk; £5**,

free Mon 10am–2pm), chiefly
known for their dazzling
collection of Impressionist and
Post-Impressionist paintings.
Among the most celebrated
works are a small-scale version
of Manet's nostalgic *Bar at the
Folies-Bergère,* Renoir's *La Loge,*
and Degas's *Two Dancers,* plus
a whole heap of Cézanne's
canvases, including one of
his series of *Card Players.* The
Courtauld also boasts a fine
selection of works by the likes
of Rubens, van Dyck, Tiepolo
and Cranach the Elder, as well
as twentieth-century paintings
and sculptures by, among
others, Kandinksy, Matisse,
Dufy, Derain, Rodin and
Henry Moore.

Shops

Benjamin Pollock's Toyshop

44 The Market ☎020/7379 7866,
Ⓦwww.pollocks-coventgarden.
co.uk. Mon–Sat 10.30am–6pm,
Sun 11am–4pm. Beautiful, old-
fashioned toys, for grown-ups
as well as children: toy theatres,
glove puppets, jack-in-the-boxes
and so on.

▼ BENJAMIN POLLOCK'S TOYSHOP

Davenport's Magic Shop

5–7 Charing Cross Tube Arcade, Strand ☏020/7836 0408, ⓦwww.davenportsmagic.co.uk. Mon–Fri 9.30am–5.30pm, Sat 10.30am–4.30pm. The world's oldest family-run magic business, stocking a huge array of marvellous tricks for amateurs and professionals.

Koh Samui

65 Monmouth St ☏020/7240 4280. Mon–Sat 10am–6.30pm. The leading promoter of young British designers such as Matthew Williamson, this one-stop boutique offers a highly selective range of womenswear with an elegant, eclectic and feminine feel.

Mysteries

9–11 Monmouth St ☏020/7240 3688. Mon–Fri 10am–7pm, Sat 10am–6pm, Sun noon–6pm. Strangely compulsive shop that stocks just about every occult-related book, magazine, accessory, crystal and piece of ephemera you can imagine. Psychic readings are on offer too.

Neal's Yard Dairy

17 Shorts Gardens ☏020/7240 5700. ⓦwww.nealsyarddairy.co.uk. Mon–Thurs 11am–6.30pm, Fri & Sat 10am–6.30pm. London's finest cheese shop, with a huge selection of quality cheeses from around the British Isles, as well as a few exceptionally good ones from further afield. You can taste before you buy.

Neal's Yard Remedies

15 Neal's Yard ☏020/7379 7222, ⓦwww.nealsyardremedies.com. Mon–Wed 10.30am–7pm, Thurs 10.30am–7.30pm, Fri 10am–7pm, Sat 9am–7.30pm, Sun 11am–6pm. Fabulously scented, beautifully presented, entirely efficacious herbal cosmetics, toiletries and other remedies.

Stanfords Map and Travel Bookshop

12–14 Long Acre ☏020/7836 1321, ⓦwww.stanfords.co.uk. Mon–Fri 9am–7.30pm, Tues from 9.30am, Thurs until 8pm, Sat 10am–7pm, Sun noon–6pm. The world's largest specialist travel bookshop, stocking pretty much any map of anywhere, plus a huge range of guides and travel literature.

Cafés

Food for Thought

31 Neal St. Mon–Sat noon–8.30pm, Sun noon–5pm. Long-established but minuscule bargain veggie café – the tasty and filling menu changes twice daily, and includes vegan and wheat-free options. Expect to queue, and don't expect to linger at peak times.

Monmouth Coffee Company

27 Monmouth St. Mon–Sat 8am–6.30pm. The marvellous aroma hits you when you walk in. Pick and mix your coffee from a fine selection, then settle into one of the cramped wooden booths and flick through the daily newspapers on hand.

Paul

29 Bedford St. Mon–Fri 7.30am–9pm, Sat & Sun 9am–9pm. Seriously French, classy boulangerie with a wood-panelled café at the back. Try one of the chewy *fougasses*, quiches or tarts, before launching into the exquisite patisserie.

Rock & Sole Plaice

47 Endell St. Daily 11.30am–10.30pm. A no-nonsense traditional fish-and-chip shop in central London. Takeaway, eat in or out at one of the pavement tables.

World Food Café

14 Neal's Yard. Mon–Fri 11.30am–5pm,
Sat 11.30am–4.30pm. First-floor
veggie café that comes into
its own in summer, when the
windows are flung open and
you can gaze down upon trendy
humanity as you tuck into
pricey but tasty dishes from all
corners of the globe.

Restaurants

Belgo Centraal

50 Earlham St ☎020/7813 2233,
ⓦwww.belgo-restaurants.com.
Mon–Thurs noon–11.30pm, Fri & Sat
noon–midnight, Sun noon–10.30pm.
Massive metal-minimalist cavern
serving excellent kilo buckets of
moules marinière, with frites and
mayonnaise, washed down with
Belgian beers and waffles for
dessert. The lunchtime and early
evening specials, for around £6,
are a bargain for central London.
Mains £9–13.

Café des Amis

11–14 Hanover Place, off Long Acre
☎020/7379 3444, ⓦwww
.cafedesamis.co.uk. Mon–Sat
11.30am–11pm. Modern, clean
and bright French wine bar and
restaurant whose menu darts
from influence to influence:
salmon terrine with guacamole
meets confit of halibut and
pumpkin gnocchi. The
set menus are good
value. Mains £15–19.

Sarastro

126 Drury Lane
☎020/7836 0101,
ⓦwww.sarastro-
restaurant.com. Daily
noon–11.30pm. Busy,
over-the-top opera-
themed restaurant,
where you can
hear young starlets

perform live (Mon & Sun),
whilst enjoying food from the
eastern Med. Mains £9–13.

Pubs and bars

AKA

18 West Central St ⓦwww.the-end
.co.uk. Mon–Fri 6pm–3am, Sat 7pm–
7am, Sun 9pm–4am. Minimalist
club-bar, with a chrome balcony
overlooking the main floor,
a well-stocked bar and food
courtesy of the local *Pizza
Express*.

American Bar

The Savoy, Strand. Mon–Sat 2pm–1am.
Utterly gorgeous Art Deco bar
that's famous for its cocktails
(a snip at £10 a throw). Dress
code is jacket and tie, or at least
very smart. A jazz pianist plays
from 7pm.

Bünker

41 Earlham St ⓦwww.bunkerbar.
com. Mon–Sat noon–11pm, Sun
noon–10pm. Busy, brick-vaulted
basement bar with wrought-iron
pillars, lots of brushed steel and
pricey, strong brews, most made
on the premises.

Detroit

35 Earlham St ⓦwww.detroit-bar.com.
Mon–Sat 5pm–midnight. Cavernous

PLACES

Covent Garden

▼ BELGO CENTRAAL

▲ AMERICAN BAR, THE SAVOY

Lamb & Flag

33 Rose St. Mon–Thurs 11am–11pm, Fri & Sat 11am–10.45pm, Sun noon–10.30pm. Busy, tiny and highly atmospheric pub, hidden away down an alley between Garrick Street and Floral Street. John Dryden was attacked here in 1679 after scurrilous verses had been written about one of Charles II's mistresses (by someone else as it turned out).

underground venue with an open-plan bar area, secluded Gaudíesque booths, a huge range of spirits and excellent cocktails. DJs playing funk and retro take over Thurs–Sat.

First Out

52 St Giles High St ⓦwww .firstoutcafebar.com. Mon–Sat 10am–11pm, Sun 11am–10.30pm. The West End's original gay café/bar: upstairs is airy and non-smoking, downstairs dark and foggy. On Fridays there's a busy pre-club warm-up session for women; gay men are welcome as guests.

Gordon's

47 Villiers St. Mon–Sat 11am–11pm, Sun noon–10pm. Cavernous, shabby, atmospheric wine bar specializing in ports. The excellent and varied wine list, decent buffet food and genial atmosphere make this a favourite with local office workers, who spill outdoors in the summer.

Clubs and venues

Donmar Warehouse

41 Earlham St ☎020/7240 4882, ⓦwww.donmar-warehouse.com. Theatre noted for its new plays and top-quality reappraisals of the classics.

The End

18 West Central St ⓦwww.endclub .com. Open until 3am or later. Designed for clubbers by clubbers, The End is well known for its focus on tech-house and drum'n'bass at weekends, and has one of the best sound systems in the world.

Royal Opera House

Bow St ☎020/7304 4000, ⓦwww. royaloperahouse.org. The ROH still has a deserved reputation for snobbery, and is ludicrously overpriced. Tickets are very hard to come by so try the day seats which are put on sale from 10am on the day of a performance.

Holborn

Holborn (pronounced "Hoe-bun") is a fascinating area to explore. Strategically placed between the royal and political centre of Westminster and the financial might of the City, this wedge of land became the hub of the English legal system in the early thirteenth century. Hostels, known as Inns of Court, were established where lawyers could eat, sleep and study English Common Law; even today, in order to qualify, every aspiring barrister must study at one of the Inns, whose archaic, cobbled precincts dominate the area and exude the rarefied atmosphere of an Oxbridge college.

Temple

Temple is the largest and most complex of the Inns of Court, and is made up of two Inns: Middle Temple (ⓦwww .middletemple.org.uk) and **Inner Temple (ⓦ**www.innertemple .org.uk). A few very old buildings survive here, but the overall scene is dominated by neo-Georgian reconstructions that followed the devastation of the Blitz. Still, the maze of courtyards and passageways is fun to explore – especially after dark, when Temple is gas-lit.

Medieval students ate, attended lectures and slept in the **Middle Temple Hall** (Mon–Fri 10am–noon & 3–4pm; free), still the Inn's main dining room. Constructed in the 1560s, the hall provided the setting for many great Elizabethan masques and plays – probably including Shakespeare's *Twelfth Night*, which is believed to have been premiered here in 1602. The hall is worth a visit for its fine hammerbeam roof, wooden panelling and decorative Elizabethan screen.

▲ ROYAL COURTS OF JUSTICE

© Crown copyright

The two Temple Inns share use of the complex's oldest building, **Temple Church** (ⓦwww.templechurch.com; Wed–Sun 11am–4pm), built in 1185 by the Knights Templar. An oblong chancel was added in the thirteenth century, and the whole building was damaged in the Blitz, but the original round church – modelled on the Holy Sepulchre in Jerusalem – still stands, with its striking Purbeck-marble piers, recumbent marble effigies of knights, and tortured grotesques grimacing in the spandrels of the blind arcading.

Royal Courts of Justice

Strand ☎020/7947 6000, ⓦwww .hmcourts-service.gov.uk. Mon–Fri 9am–4.30pm. Free. Home to the Court of Appeal and the High Court, the Royal Courts of Justice are where England's most important civil cases are tried.

Appeals and libel suits are heard here – countless pop and soap stars have battled it out with the tabloid press, while appeals have led to freedom for those wrongfully imprisoned, such as the high-profile Birmingham Six and Guildford Four. The fifty-odd courtrooms are open to the public, though you have to go through stringent security checks first (strictly no cameras allowed).

Fleet Street

In 1500, one Wynkyn de Worde, a pupil of William Caxton, moved the Caxton presses from Westminster to Fleet Street, in order to be close to the Inns of Court (lawyers were among his best customers) and to the clergy of St Paul's, who comprised the largest literate group in the city. Britain's first daily newspapers were published here, and by the nineteenth century, all the major national and provincial dailies had their offices and printing presses in the Fleet Street district. Since the 1980s, all but a handful of the press headquarters that once dominated this part of town have relocated to the Docklands and elsewhere. Nonetheless, Fleet Street still offers one of the grandest approaches to the City, thanks to the view across to Ludgate Hill and beyond to St Paul's Cathedral.

Prince Henry's Room

17 Fleet St ⓦ www .cityoflondon.gov.uk/phr. Mon–Sat 11am–2pm. Free. The first floor of this fine Jacobean house, with its distinctive timber-framed bay windows, now contains material relating to the diarist Samuel Pepys (1633–1703), who was born in nearby Salisbury Court and baptized at St Bride's. Even if you've no interest in Pepys, the wooden-panelled room itself is worth a look – it contains one of the finest Jacobean plasterwork ceilings in London, and a lot of original stained glass.

St Bride's

Fleet St ⓦ www.stbrides.com. Mon–Fri 9am–5pm, Sat 11am–3pm. Free. To get a sense of old-style Fleet Street, head for the so-called "journalists' and printers' cathedral", the church of St Bride's, which boasts Christopher Wren's tallest and most exquisite spire (said to be the inspiration for the tiered wedding cake). The crypt contains a little museum (same hours as church) of Fleet Street history, with information on the *Daily Courant* and the *Universal Daily Register*, which later became *The Times*, claiming to be "the faithful recorder of every species of intelligence . . . circulated for a particular set of readers only".

▲ ST BRIDE'S SPIRE

Dr Johnson's House

17 Gough Square ⓦwww
.drjohnsonshouse.org. May–Sept
Mon–Sat 11am–5.30pm; Oct–April
Mon–Sat 11am–5pm. £4.50. Despite
appearances, Dr Johnson's House
is the only authentic eighteenth-
century building on Gough
Square. It was here the great
savant, writer and lexicographer
lived from 1747 to 1759 whilst
compiling the 41,000 entries
for the first dictionary of the
English language. The grey-
panelled rooms of the house are
peppered with period furniture
and lined with portraits and
etchings, including one of
Johnson's servant Francis Barber.
Two first-edition copies of the
great *Dictionary* are on display,
while the open-plan attic, in
which Johnson and his six
helpers put the tome together,
is now lined with explanatory
panels on lexicography.

Lincoln's Inn

Lincoln's Inn Fields/Chancery Lane,
☎020/7405 1393, ⓦwww.lincolnsinn
.org.uk. Mon–Fri 9am–6pm. Free.
Lincoln's Inn was the first
– and in many ways is the
prettiest – of the Inns of Court,
having miraculously escaped
the ravages of the Blitz; famous
alumni include Thomas More,
Oliver Cromwell and Margaret
Thatcher. The main entrance
is the diamond-patterned,
red-brick Tudor gateway on
Chancery Lane, adjacent to
which is the early seventeenth-
century **chapel** (Mon–Fri
noon–2pm), with its unusual
fan-vaulted open undercroft and,
on the first floor, a late Gothic
nave, hit by a zeppelin in World
War I and much restored since.
The Inn's fifteenth-century **Old
Hall** (open by appointment),
where the lawyers used to live
and where Dickens set the

case Jarndyce versus Jarndyce
in *Bleak House*, features a fine
timber roof, linenfold panelling
and an elaborate, early Jacobean
screen.

Hunterian Museum at the Royal College of Surgeons

Royal College of Surgeons, Lincoln's
Inn Fields ⓦwww.rcseng.ac.uk. Tues–
Sat 10am–5pm. Free. Containing
the unique specimen collection
of the surgeon-scientist
John Hunter (1728–93), the
Hunterian Museum first opened
in 1813, and was beautifully
refurbished in 2005. Since most
of the exhibits are jars of pickled
skeletons and body pieces, it's
certainly not a museum for the
squeamish. Among the prize
exhibits are the skeletons of
the Irish giant, Charles Byrne
(1761–83), who was seven feet
seven inches tall, and the Sicilian
midget Caroline Crachami
(d.1824), who was just one foot
ten and a half inches when she
died at the age of 3.

Sir John Soane's Museum

13 Lincoln's Inn Fields ⓦwww.soane.
org. Tues–Sat 10am–5pm, candle-
lit first Tues of the month 6–9pm.
Free. The chief architect of
the Bank of England, Sir John
Soane (1753–1837) was an
avid collector who designed
this house not only as a home
and office, but also as a place
to stash his large assortment
of art and antiquities; opened
up as a museum, it's now one
of London's best-kept secrets.
Arranged much as it was in
his lifetime, the ingeniously
planned house has an informal,
treasure-hunt atmosphere,
with surprises in every alcove.
The star exhibits are Hogarth's
satirical *Election* series and his
merciless morality tale *The
Rake's Progress,* as well as the

alabaster sarcophagus of Seti I. At 2.30pm every Saturday, a fascinating, hour-long **guided tour** (£3) takes you round the museum and the enormous research library next door, which contains architectural drawings, books and exquisitely detailed architectural models of Pompeiian and Paestum temples in cork and wood.

Pubs and bars

Black Friar

174 Queen Victoria St. Mon–Sat 11am–11pm, Sun noon–10.30pm. Gorgeous, utterly original pub, with Art Nouveau marble friezes of boozy monks and a wonderful highly decorated alcove, all dating from 1905.

Cittie of Yorke

22 High Holborn. Mon–Fri 11.30am–11pm, Sat noon–11pm. One of London's most venerable pubs, with a vaulted cellar bar, wood panelling, cheap Sam Smith's beer and a grand quasi-medieval wine hall, whose cosy cubicles were once the preserve of lawyers and their clients.

Na Zdrowie

11 Little Turnstile. Mon–Fri 12.30–11pm, Sat 6–11pm. Great Polish bar hidden in an alleyway behind Holborn tube, with a wicked selection of flavoured vodkas and beers, and good, cheap Polish food.

Old Bank of England

194 Fleet St. Mon–Fri 11am–11pm. Not the actual Bank of England, but the former Law Courts' branch, this imposing High Victorian banking hall is now a magnificently opulent ale and pie pub.

Ye Olde Cheshire Cheese

Wine Office Court, 145 Fleet St. Mon–Sat 11am–11pm, Sun noon–3.30pm. A famous seventeenth-century watering hole, with real fires and several snug, dark-panelled bars. Popular with tourists, but by no means exclusively so.

Ye Olde Mitre

1 Ely Court, off Hatton Garden. Mon–Fri 11am–11pm. Wonderfully atmospheric pub dating back to 1546 whose low-ceilinged, wood-panelled rooms are packed with history and which offers some unusual ales.

▼ MARBLE FRIEZES, *BLACK FRIAR*

Clerkenwell

A typical London mix of Georgian and Victorian town-houses, housing estates, loft conversions and art studios, Clerkenwell has been transformed over the last decade or so. On the edge of London's financial sector, this formerly workaday district – a centre for lockmaking, clockmaking, printing and jewellery – is now a fashionable enclave for media companies and outlets for designer furniture catering for the area's new loft-dwelling residents. Well off the conventional tourist trail, there's only a smattering of minor sights here, but the area's main highlight is its abundance of trendy restaurants, bars and clubs.

Old Bailey

Newgate St ⓦ www.cjsonline.org.
Mon–Fri 10.30am–1pm & 2–4pm.
Free. The Central Criminal Court, more popularly known as the Old Bailey, was built on the site of the notoriously harsh Newgate Prison, where folk used to come to watch public hangings. The current, rather pompous Edwardian building is distinguished by its green dome, surmounted by a gilded statue of Justice, unusually depicted

without blindfold, holding her sword and scales. The Old Bailey is now the venue for all the country's most serious criminal court cases; you can watch the proceedings from the visitors' gallery, but note that bags, cameras, mobiles, personal stereos and food and drink are not allowed in, and there is no cloakroom.

St Bartholomew-the-Great

Cloth Fair ⓦ www.greatstbarts
.com. Tues–Fri 8.30am–5pm, Sat 10.30am–1.30pm, Sun 8.30am–1pm & 2.30–8pm; mid-Nov to mid-Feb closes 4pm Tues–Fri. Free. Begun in 1123, St Bartholomew-the-Great is London's oldest and most exquisite parish church. Its half-timbered Tudor gatehouse on Little Britain Street incorporates a thirteenth-century arch that once formed the entrance to the nave; above, a wooden statue of St Bartholomew stands

▼ JUSTICE ATOP THE OLD BAILEY

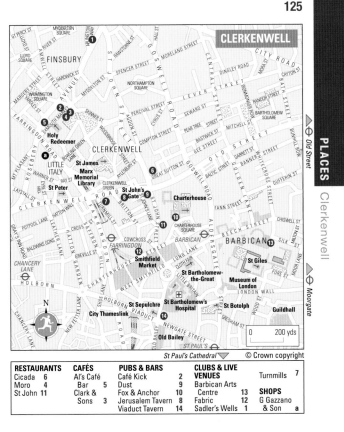

St Paul's Cathedral   © Crown copyright

RESTAURANTS		CAFÉS		PUBS & BARS		CLUBS & LIVE			
Cicada	6	Al's Café		Café Kick	2	VENUES		Turnmills	7
Moro	4	Bar	5	Dust	9	Barbican Arts			
St John	11	Clark &		Fox & Anchor	10	Centre	13	SHOPS	
		Sons	3	Jerusalem Tavern	8	Fabric	12	G Gazzano	
				Viaduct Tavern	14	Sadler's Wells	1	& Son	a

holding the knife with which
he was flayed. One side of the
medieval cloisters survives to
the south, immediately to the
right as you enter the church.
The rest is a confusion of
elements, including portions
of the transepts and, most
impressively, the chancel, where
stout Norman pillars separate
the main body of the church
from the ambulatory. There are
various pre-Fire monuments
to admire, the most prominent
being the tomb of Rahere,
court jester to Henry I, which
shelters under a fifteenth-
century canopy north of the
main altar.

Smithfield

Blood and guts were regularly
spilled at Smithfield long
before today's meat market
was legally sanctioned here in
the seventeenth century. For
more than three centuries it
was a popular venue for **public
executions**: the Scottish hero,
William Wallace, was hanged,
disembowelled and beheaded
here in 1305, and the Bishop
of Rochester's cook was boiled
alive in 1531, but the local
speciality was burnings, which
reached a peak in the mid-
sixteenth century during the
reign of "Bloody" Mary, when
hundreds of Protestants were

burned at the stake for their beliefs. These days, Smithfield is dominated by its **meat market**, housed in a colourful and ornate Victorian market hall on Charterhouse Street; if you want to see it in action, get here early – the activity starts around 4am and is all over by 9am or 10am. The compensation for getting up at this ungodly hour are the early licensing laws which apply to certain local pubs, which mean you can get a hearty breakfast and an early morning pint from the local pubs.

Museum of London

London Wall, Barbican ☎020/7600 3699, ⓦwww.museumoflondon .org.uk. Mon–Sat 10am–5.50pm, Sun noon–5.50pm. Free. Despite London's long pedigree, very few of its ancient structures are still standing. However, numerous Roman, Saxon and Elizabethan remains have been discovered during the City's various rebuildings, and many of these finds are now displayed at the Museum of London. The permanent exhibition provides an imaginative and educational trot through London's past from prehistory to the present day. Specific exhibits to look out for include the Bucklersbury Roman mosaic; the sarcophagus, coffin and skeleton of a wealthy Roman woman found in Spitalfields; and the Lord Mayor's heavily gilded coach (still used for state occasions). The real strength of the museum, though, lies in the excellent temporary exhibitions, lectures, walks and videos it organizes throughout the year.

Barbican

A monumental concrete ghetto built over the heavily bombed Cripplegate area, the Barbican is both a residential complex and home to the infamously user-repellent **Barbican Arts Centre (ⓦ**www.barbican.org .uk) on Silk Street, London's supposed answer to Paris's Pompidou Centre which was formally opened in 1982. The complex, containing a huge concert hall, two theatres, a cinema and a library, serves as home to the London Symphony Orchestra and the capital's chapter of the Royal Shakespeare Company, and stages regular free gigs in the foyer area. The zone's solitary prewar building is the heavily restored sixteenth-century church of **St Giles Cripplegate** (Mon–Fri 11am–4pm).

Marx Memorial Library

37a Clerkenwell Green ☎020/7253 1485, ⓦwww.marxlibrary.net. Mon–Thurs 1–2pm or by appointment; closed Aug. Free. Housed in a former Welsh Charity School, the Marx Memorial Library was where Lenin edited seventeen editions of the Bolshevik paper *Iskra* in 1902–03. The library was founded in 1933 in response to the book burnings taking place in Nazi Germany, and the poky little back room where Lenin worked is maintained as it was then, as a kind of shrine – even the original lino survives. You're free to view the Lenin Room, where there's an original copy of *Iskra*, and the workerist *Hastings Mural* from 1935, but to consult the unrivalled collection of books and pamphlets on the labour movement you need to become a library member.

Exmouth Market

ⓦwww.exmouth-market.com. Exmouth Market is at the

▲ LENIN, MARX MEMORIAL LIBRARY

epicentre of newly fashionable Clerkenwell. The old market proper has been reduced to a raggle-taggle of tatty stalls and a pie-and-mash shop, but the rest of the street has been colonized by modish new shops, bars and restaurants. The only striking building is the church of the **Holy Redeemer**, which upholds the Catholic traditions of the Church of England. In keeping with its Roman tendencies, it boasts an unusual Italianate campanile, and, inside, Stations of the Cross and a large baldachin.

Shops

G Gazzano & Son

167–169 Farringdon Rd ☎020/7837 1586. Mon–Fri 8am–5.15pm, Sat 8am–5pm, Sun 10am–2pm. This fabulous establishment has been keeping the area in Italian fare for a century, and the old wooden cabinets are still holding up under the weight of all that good-quality food.

Cafés

Al's Café Bar

11–13 Exmouth Market. Mon, Tues & Sun 8am–11pm, Wed–Sat 8am–2am. A designer greasy spoon with a local media-luvvie clientele, which serves up Italian breads, Mediterranean dishes, nachos, decent coffee and good soups alongside the chips and grills. In the evening, it's more bar than café.

Clark & Sons

46 Exmouth Market. Mon–Thurs 10.30am–4pm, Fri 10.30am–5.30pm, Sat 10.30am–5pm. Exmouth Market has undergone something of a trendy transformation, so it's all the more surprising to find this genuine pie-and-mash shop still going strong.

Restaurants

Cicada

132 St John St ☎020/7608 1550, ⓦwww.cicada.nu. Mon–Fri noon–

11pm, Sat 6–11pm. This modern barrestaurant, with its retro chocolate leatherette seating, offers an unusual pan-Asian menu that ranges from fishy *tom yum* to ginger noodles or sushi.

Moro

34–36 Exmouth Market ☎020/7833 8336. Mon–Fri 12.30–2.30pm & 7–10.30pm, Sat 7–10.30pm. Modern, spartan restaurant that typifies the new face of the area and attracts a clientele to match. *Moro* is a place of pilgrimage for disciples of the wood-fired oven and Moorish food.

St John

26 St John St ☎020/7251 0848, ⊛www.stjohnrestaurant.co.uk. Mon–Fri noon–3pm & 6–11pm, Sat 6–11pm. Minimalist former smokehouse that's now a decidedly old-fashioned English restaurant specializing in offal. The cooking is of a very high standard. Booking essential.

Pubs and bars

Café Kick

43 Exmouth Market ⊛www.cafekick. co.uk. Mon–Sat noon–11pm, Sun noon–10.30pm. Stylish take on a local French-style café/bar, with three busy table-football games to enliven the atmosphere.

Dust

27a Clerkenwell Rd. Tues & Wed 5pm–midnight, Thurs 5pm–2am, Fri & Sat 5pm–4am. £3–5 Fri & Sat. High-ceilinged bar in a former watchmaker's factory. Great cocktails, a small dancefloor and quality DJs at the weekend playing house, soul, funk and hip-hop.

Fox & Anchor

115 Charterhouse St. Mon–Fri 7am–9pm. Handsome Smithfield Market pub that's famous for its early opening hours and huge breakfasts (served 7–10am).

Jerusalem Tavern

55 Britton St. Mon–Fri 11am–11pm. Small, atmospheric converted Georgian coffee house, serving tasty food at lunchtimes, along with an excellent range of draught beers.

Viaduct Tavern

126 Newgate St. Mon–Fri noon–11pm. Glorious Victorian gin palace, built in 1869 opposite what was then Newgate Prison and is now the Old Bailey. The walls are beautifully decorated with oils of faded ladies representing Commerce, Agriculture and the Arts.

Clubs and venues

Barbican

Silk St ☎020/7638 8891, ⊛www .barbican.org.uk. With the resident London Symphony Orchestra, the Barbican is one of the outstanding arenas for classical music, as well as folk and world music. The theatrical spectacles range from puppetry and musicals to new drama works, and of course Shakespeare. Programming is much more adventurous than it was, and free music in the foyer is often very good.

Fabric

77a Charterhouse St ⊛www .fabriclondon.com. Open until 5am Fri & 7am Sat. Cavernous, underground, brewery-like space with a devastating sound system. Friday is Fabric Live, a mix of drum'n'bass, hip-hop and

▲ *VIADUCT TAVERN'S* DECORATED INTERIOR

live acts. Saturday concentrates on house, techno and electro played by underground DJs from around the globe.

Sadler's Wells

Rosebery Ave ⓦ www.sadlers-wells
.com. Home to Britain's best contemporary dance companies, and host to the finest international companies, Sadler's Wells also puts on theatre pieces and children's shows.

Turnmills

63b Clerkenwell Rd ⓦ www.turnmills
.co.uk. Fri 10.30pm–7.30am, Sat 10pm–7am, Sun 6am–noon. The place to come if you want to sweat from dusk till dawn. Trance, house and techno with top-name guest DJs rule Friday's weekly Gallery night, while Saturday plays host to bi-monthly parties.

The City

The City is where London began, and its boundaries today are only slightly larger than those marked by the Roman walls and their medieval successors. However, you'll find few visible leftovers of London's early days, since four-fifths of it burned down in the Great Fire of 1666. With the notable exception of St Paul's Cathedral and Wren's numerous smaller churches, what you see now is mostly the product of the Victorian construction boom, postwar reconstruction and the latest office-building frenzy that began in the 1980s. The majority of Londoners lived and worked in or around the City up until the eighteenth century – nowadays, however, over a million commuters spend the best part of Monday to Friday here, but only a few thousand actually live here. It's best to try and visit during the week, since many pubs, restaurants and even some tube stations and tourist sights close down at the weekend.

St Paul's Cathedral

Ludgate Hill ⊕ www.stpauls
.co.uk. Mon–Sat 8.30am–4pm.
£9. Designed by Christopher
Wren and completed in 1710,
St Paul's remains a dominating
presence in the City despite
the encroaching tower blocks.
Topped by an enormous lead-
covered dome that's second in
size only to St Peter's in Rome,
its showpiece west facade is
particularly magnificent, and is
most impressive at night when
bathed in sea-green arc lights.
However compared to its great
rival, Westminster Abbey, St
Paul's is a soulless but perfectly
calculated architectural set piece,
a burial place for captains rather
than kings.

The best place to appreciate
the building's glory is from
beneath the **dome**, adorned
(against Wren's wishes) by
trompe l'oeil frescoes. The most
richly decorated section of the
cathedral is the **chancel**, where
the late Victorian mosaics of

birds, fish, animals and greenery
are particularly spectacular.
The intricately carved oak and
lime-wood choir stalls, and the
imposing organ case, are the
work of Wren's master carver,
Grinling Gibbons.

Beginning in the south aisle, a
series of stairs lead to the dome's
three galleries, the first of which
is the internal **Whispering
Gallery**, so called because of
its acoustic properties – words
whispered to the wall on one
side are distinctly audible over
one hundred feet away on the
other, though you often can't
hear much above the hubbub.
Of the two exterior galleries,
the best views are from the tiny
Golden Gallery, below the
golden ball and cross which top
the cathedral.

Although the nave is crammed
full of overblown monuments
to military types, burials in
St Paul's are confined to the
crypt, reputedly the largest in
Europe. The whitewashed walls

and bright lighting, however, make this one of London's least atmospheric mausoleums, but **Artists' Corner** here does boast as many painters and architects as Westminster Abbey has poets, including Christopher Wren himself. The star tombs, though, are those of Nelson and Wellington, both occupying centre stage and both with more fanciful monuments upstairs.

It's well worth attending one of the cathedral's **services**, if only to hear the ethereal choir, who perform during most evensongs (Mon–Sat 5pm), and on Sundays at 10am, 11.30am and 3.15pm.

Paternoster Square

The Blitz destroyed the area immediately to the north of St Paul's, incinerating all the booksellers' shops and around six million books. In their place a brazenly modernist pedestrianized piazza was built, only to be torn down quite recently and replaced with post-classical office blocks in Portland stone and a Corinthian column topped by a gilded urn. One happy consequence of the square's redevelopment is that **Temple Bar**, the last surviving City gate, which used to stand at the top of Fleet Street, has found its way back to London after over a hundred years of exile, languishing in a park in Hertfordshire. Designed by Wren himself, the triumphal arch, looking weathered but clean, now forms the entrance to Paternoster Square from St Paul's, with the Stuart monarchs, James I and Charles II, and their consorts occupying the niches.

Guildhall

Aldermanbury Street ⓦwww .cityoflondon.gov.uk. May–Sept daily 10am–5pm; Oct–April Mon–Sat 10am–5pm. Free. Situated at the geographical centre of the City, Guildhall has been the area's administrative seat for over eight hundred years. It remains the headquarters of the Corporation of London, the City's governing body, which still uses it for many formal civic occasions. Architecturally, however, it's not quite the beauty it once was, having been badly damaged in both the Great Fire and the Blitz, and scarred by the addition of a grotesque 1970s concrete cloister and wing. Nonetheless, the Great Hall, basically a postwar reconstruction of the fifteenth-century original, is worth a brief look, as is the **Clockmakers' Museum** (Mon–Fri 9.30am–4.30pm; free), a collection of over six hundred timepieces, including one of the clocks that won John Harrison the Longitude prize. Also worth a visit is the purpose-built **Guildhall Art Gallery** (Mon–Sat 10am–5pm, Sun noon–4pm;

▼ MAGOG STATUE, GUILDHALL

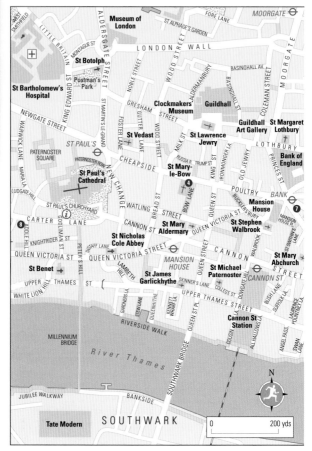

£2.50, free Fri and daily after 3.30pm), which contains one or two exceptional works, such as Rossetti's *La Ghirlandata* and Holman Hunt's *The Eve of St Agnes*, plus a massive painting depicting the 1782 Siege of Gibraltar, commissioned by the Corporation. In the basement, you can view the remains of a **Roman amphitheatre**, dating from around 120 AD, which was discovered during the gallery's construction.

Bank of England

Threadneedle St ⓦwww .bankofengland.co.uk. Mon–Fri 10am–5pm. Free. Established in 1694 by William III to raise funds for the war against France, the Bank of England stores the gold reserves of seventy or so central banks around the world, but not, ironically, of Britain itself. British gold reserves are kept in the Federal Reserve Bank of New York, where they were moved during World

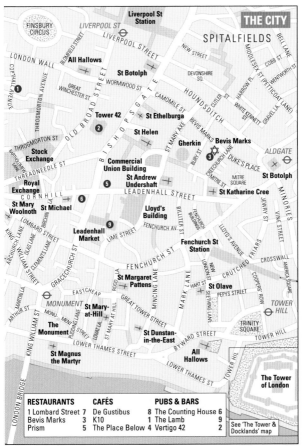

THE CITY

SPITALFIELDS

ALDGATE

RESTAURANTS		CAFÉS		PUBS & BARS	
1 Lombard Street	7	De Gustibus	8	The Counting House	6
Bevis Marks	3	K10	1	The Lamb	9
Prism	5	The Place Below	4	Vertigo 42	2

See 'The Tower & Docklands' map

© Crown copyright

War II. All that remains of the original building, on which John Soane spent the best part of his career (from 1788 onwards), is the windowless, outer curtain wall, which wraps itself round the 3.5-acre island site. However, you can view a reconstruction of Soane's Bank Stock Office, with its characteristic domed skylight, in the **museum** (Mon–Fri 10am–5pm; free), which has its entrance on Bartholomew Lane. The permanent exhibition here includes a scaled-down model of Soane's bank and a Victorian-style diorama of the night in 1780 when the bank was attacked by rioters. Sadly most of the gold bars are fakes, but there are specimens of every note issued by the Royal Mint over the centuries.

Lloyd's and the Gherkin

East of Bank, and beyond Bishopsgate, on Lime Street,

-134**134**

City churches

The City is crowded with churches (ⓦ www.cityoflondonchurches.com) – well over forty at the last count, the majority of them built or rebuilt by Wren after the Great Fire. Those particularly worth seeking out include **St Stephen Walbrook** (Mon–Thurs 10am–4pm, Fri 10am–3pm), on Walbrook, Wren's most spectacular church interior after St Paul's, with sixteen Corinthian columns arranged in clusters around a central coffered dome, and exquisite dark-wood furnishings by Grinling Gibbons. On Lombard Street, **St Mary Woolnoth** (Mon–Fri 7.45am–5pm) is a typically idiosyncratic creation of Nicholas Hawksmoor, one of Wren's pupils, featuring an ingenious lantern lit by semicircular clerestory windows, and a striking altar canopy held up by barley-sugar columns. The interior of Wren's **St Mary Abchurch** (Mon–Thurs 10am–2pm), on Abchurch Lane, is dominated by an unusual and vast dome fresco, painted by a local parishioner and lit by oval lunettes, while the superlative lime-wood reredos is again by Gibbons.

 stands Richard Rogers' glitzy **Lloyd's Building** – a vertical version of Rogers' own Pompidou Centre – a startling array of glass and blue steel pipes. The most popular of the City buildings of the 1980s, it's now been eclipsed by its near neighbour, Norman Foster's glass diamond-clad **Gherkin**,

▼ THE GHERKIN, THE CITY

officially known as 30 St Mary Axe. It's obscenely large – at 590ft in height – but most Londoners seem to quite like it for its cheeky shape.

Note that neither building is open to the public.

Leadenhall Market

Leadenhall St. Mon–Fri 11am–2pm. The picturesque cobbles and richly painted, graceful Victorian cast-ironwork of Leadenhall Market date from 1881. Inside, the traders cater mostly for the lunchtime City crowd, their barrows laden with exotic seafood and game, fine wines, champagne and caviar.

Bevis Marks Synagogue

Bevis Marks ⓦ www.sandp.org. Guided tours Wed & Fri noon, Sun 11.15am. £2. Hidden away in a little courtyard behind a modern red-brick office block, the Bevis Marks Synagogue was built in 1701 by Sephardic Jews who had fled the Inquisition in Spain and Portugal. It's the country's oldest surviving synagogue, and the roomy, rich interior gives an idea of just how wealthy the worshippers were at the time. The Sephardic community has now dispersed across London and the congregation has dwindled, but the magnificent array of chandeliers ensure that it's a popular venue for candle-lit Jewish weddings.

Monument

Monument St. Daily 9am–5.30pm. £2. The Monument was designed by Wren to commemorate the Great Fire of 1666. A plain Doric column crowned with spiky gilded flames, it stands 202ft high, making it the tallest isolated stone column in the world; if it were laid out flat it would touch the site of the bakery where the Fire started, east of the Monument. The bas-relief on the base, now in very bad shape, depicts Charles II and the Duke of York in Roman garb conducting the emergency relief operation. The 311 steps to the viewing gallery once guaranteed an incredible view; nowadays it is somewhat dwarfed by the buildings surrounding it.

▲ THE MONUMENT

Cafés

De Gustibus

53–55 Carter Lane. Mon–Fri 7am–5pm. Award-winning bakery that constructs a wide variety of sandwiches, bruschetta, croque monsieur and quiche to eat in or take away.

K10

20 Copthall Ave. Mon–Fri 11.30am–3pm & takeaway till 6pm. Remarkably good, inexpensive sushi outlet, with a busy takeaway section upstairs, and a *kaiten* (conveyor-belt) dining area downstairs.

The Place Below

St Mary-le-Bow, Cheapside Ⓦ www .theplacebelow.co.uk. Mon–Fri 7.30am–3pm. This café serving imaginative vegetarian dishes is something of a find in the midst of the City. Added to that, the wonderful Norman crypt makes for a very pleasant place in which to dine.

Restaurants

1 Lombard Street

1 Lombard St ☏020/7929 6611, Ⓦwww.1lombardstreet.com. Closed Sat & Sun. Set in a former banking hall, this place comprises a buzzy circular bar under a suitably imposing glass dome, a classy, pricey City brasserie and a restaurant serving straightforward Michelin-starred French fare. Brasserie

mains £10–28; restaurant mains £24–33.

Bevis Marks

Bevis Marks ☎020/7283 2220, ⓦwww.bevismarkstherestaurant .com. Mon–Thurs noon–3pm & 5.30–7.15pm, Fri noon–3pm. Stylish restaurant in the glassed-over courtyard outside Bevis Marks Synagogue, serving expensive, modern British kosher dishes (steak and Guinness pie, roast salmon) as well as traditional Jewish fare (*krupnik, matzo balls*). Mains £12–18.

Prism

147 Leadenhall St ☎020/7256 3888, ⓦwww.harveynichols.com. Mon–Fri 11.30am–3pm & 6–11pm. A very slick expense-account restaurant in another old banking hall, with a fashionably long bar, suave service and a menu comprised of well-judged English favourites with modernist influences. Mains £16–26.

Pubs and bars

The Counting House

50 Cornhill. Mon–Fri 11am–11pm. Another wonderful City bank conversion, with fantastic high ceilings, a glass dome, chandeliers and a central oval bar.

The Lamb

Leadenhall Market. Mon–Fri 11am–9pm. A great pub right in the middle of Leadenhall Market, serving pricey but excellent roast beef sandwiches at lunchtime.

Vertigo 42

Tower 42, Old Broad St. Mon–Fri noon–3pm & 5–11pm. Rarefied drinking in this champagne bar, 42 floors above the City. Each seat has an astounding view of London; drinks' prices are correspondingly high, and light meals are on offer. Smart jeans and trainers acceptable; booking essential.

Hoxton and Spitalfields

Until recently, Hoxton was an unpleasant amalgam of wholesale clothing and shoe shops, striptease pubs and roaring traffic. But over the last ten years, the area has been colonized by artists, designers and architects and transformed itself into the city's most vibrant artistic enclave, peppered with contemporary art galleries and a whole host of very cool bars and clubs. Spitalfields, to the south, lies at the heart of the old East End, once the first port of call for thousands of immigrants over the centuries, and now best known for its Sunday markets and its cheap Bangladeshi curry houses.

Hoxton Square

The geographical focus of Hoxton's metamorphosis is Hoxton Square, a strange and not altogether happy assortment of light industrial units, many of them now converted into artists' studios arranged around a leafy, formal square. Despite the lack of aesthetic charm, the square is now an undisputedly fashionable place to live and work; several leading West End **art galleries** have opened up premises hereabouts, most prominently White Cube (Tues–Sat 10am–6pm; Ⓦwww .whitecube.com) at no. 48, which has been likened to a miniature Tate Modern, partly due to the glass roof that tops the building, and partly because it touts the likes of Damien Hirst, Tracey Emin and various other Turner Prize artists.

Geffrye Museum

Kingsland Rd ☎020/7739 9893, Ⓦwww.geffrye-museum.org .uk. Tues–Sat 10am–5pm, Sun noon–5pm. Free. Set back from the main road in a peaceful little enclave of eighteenth-century ironmongers' almshouses, Hoxton's one conventional tourist sight is the Geffrye Museum, dedicated to furniture design since

▲ WHITE CUBE GALLERY, HOXTON SQUARE

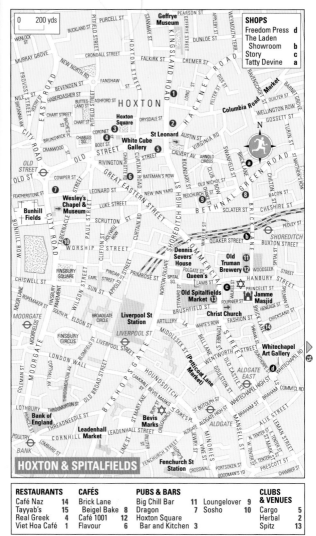

RESTAURANTS		CAFÉS		PUBS & BARS				CLUBS & VENUES	
Café Naz	14	Brick Lane		Big Chill Bar	11	Loungelover	9	Cargo	5
Tayyab's	15	Beigel Bake	8	Dragon	7	Sosho	10	Herbal	2
Real Greek	4	Café 1001	12	Hoxton Square				Spitz	13
Viet Hoa Café	1	Flavour	6	Bar and Kitchen	3				

1911. A series of period living rooms, ranging from the oak-panelled seventeenth century through refined Georgian and cluttered Victorian, leads to the excellent twentieth-century section and the museum's

pleasant café/restaurant.

One of the **almshouses** has been restored to its original condition and can be visited (first Sat of the month & first and third Wed; 11am, noon, 2pm & 3pm; £2).

Columbia Road Flower Market

Columbia Rd. Sun 8am–1pm. Columbia Road is the city's most popular market for flowers and plants; it's also the liveliest, with the loud and upfront stallholders catering to an increasingly moneyed clientele. As well as seeds, bulbs, potted plants and cut flowers from the stalls, you'll also find every kind of gardening accessory from the chi-chi shops that line the street, and you can keep yourself sustained with bagels, cakes and coffee from the local cafés.

Wesley's Chapel & House

49 City Rd www.wesleyschapel.org.uk. Mon–Sat 10am–4pm, Sun noon–1.45pm. Free. A place of pilgrimage for Methodists all over the world, Wesley's Chapel was built in 1777, and heralded the coming of age of the faith founded by **John Wesley** (1703–91). The interior is uncharacteristically ornate, with powder-pink columns of French jasper and a superb, Adam-style gilded plasterwork ceiling. Predictably enough, the **Museum of Methodism** in the basement has only a passing reference to the insanely jealous 40-year-old widow Wesley married, and who eventually left him. Wesley himself spent his last two years in Wesley's House, a delightful Georgian place to the right of the main gates. On display inside are his deathbed and an early shock-therapy machine he was particularly keen on.

Bunhill Fields

City Rd www.cityoflondon.gov.uk. April–Sept Mon–Fri 7.30am–7pm, Sat & Sun 9.30am–4pm; Oct–March closes 4pm. Originally used as a plague pit, Bunhill Fields was the main burial ground for Dissenters or Nonconformists (practising Christians who were not members of the Church of England) until 1852. It's no longer used for burials, but the flagstone paths and tall trees make it a popular lunchtime spot for local workers. The cemetery's three most famous incumbents are commemorated in the central paved area: William Blake's simple monument stands northeast of the obelisk to Daniel Defoe, while opposite lies John Bunyan's recumbent statue.

▼ COLUMBIA ROAD FLOWER MARKET

Petticoat Lane

Middlesex St. Daily except Sat 9am–2pm. Petticoat Lane (officially named Middlesex Street) may not be one of London's prettiest streets, but it does play host to one of the capital's longest-running Sunday markets, specializing in cheap (and often pretty tacky) clothing. As such, it's resolutely unfashionable, with old-style Cockney traders yelling out prices, others flogging pretty African and Indian fabrics, and lots of stalls selling pungent, partially tanned leather jackets with shoulder pads.

Whitechapel Art Gallery

80–82 Whitechapel High St ☎020/7522 7888, ⊛www .whitechapel.org. Tues–Sun 11am–6pm (Thurs until 9pm). Free. The East End institution that draws in more outsiders than any other is the Whitechapel Art Gallery, housed in a beautiful crenellated 1899 Arts and Crafts building. The gallery puts on some of London's most innovative exhibitions of contemporary art, as well as hosting the biennial Whitechapel Open, a chance for local artists to get their work shown to a wider audience. The complex also has a pleasant café overlooking Angel Alley, where there's a stainless steel anarchist portrait gallery courtesy of the Freedom Press bookshop (see p.142).

Brick Lane

Brick Lane lies at the heart of London's Bengali community, whose inexpensive curry houses dominate the "Banglatown" (southern) end of the street. The red-brick chimney half way up Brick Lane heralds the **Old Truman Brewery** (⊛www.trumanbrewery.com), founded in 1666 and the largest in the world at the end of the nineteenth century. It ceased operations in 1989 and is now a multimedia centre for music, fashion, art and IT. North of the brewery and railway arch are the streets that serve as the venue for **Brick Lane's Sunday market** of bric-a-brac (Sun 8am–2pm). There are in fact virtually no stalls on Brick Lane itself any more; instead the market extends west along Sclater Street, and east down Cheshire Street. The stalls are a real mixed bag nowadays, selling cheap hardware, fruit and veg, and CDs, and services to unlock mobiles phones; the shops, though, tend to be more designer accessories and interior

▼ BRICK LANE MARKET

▲ GEFFRYE MUSEUM

furnishings than old-fashioned junk.

Christ Church, Spitalfields

Commercial St ⓦ www.christ-churchspitalfields.org. Tues 11am–4pm, Sun 1–4pm. Free. Built between 1714 and 1729 to a characteristically bold design by Nicholas Hawksmoor, Christ Church features a huge 225-foot-high broach spire and giant Tuscan portico, raised on steps and shaped like a Venetian window (a central arched opening flanked by two smaller rectangles), a motif repeated in the tower and doors. Inside, there's a forest of giant columned bays, with a lion and a unicorn playing peekaboo on the top of the chancel beam and, opposite, London's largest Georgian **organ**. The recent, multi-million pound restoration programme has saved the church from falling down; sadly, it's also removed all the atmosphere the old decaying interior once had.

Old Spitalfields Market

Commercial St. Mon–Fri 10am–4pm, Sun 9am–5pm. The capital's premier wholesale fruit and vegetable market until 1991, Old Spitalfields Market now hosts a large, eclectic and fairly sophisticated selection of shops and stalls selling crafts, clothes, food and organic fruit and vegetables. Half the market was recently knocked down to make way for yet more boxy, glassy offices, courtesy of Norman Foster, but the red-brick and green-gabled eastern half of the original building, built in 1893, survives.

Dennis Severs' House

18 Folgate St ☎ 020/7247 4013, ⓦ www.dennissevershouse.co.uk. "Silent Night" Mon: April–Sept 8–11pm; Oct–March 6–9pm; £12. "The Experience" first and third Sun of each month 2–5pm; £8, plus following Mon noon–2pm. £5. Visiting the former home of the late American eccentric Dennis Severs is a bizarre and uncanny theatrical experience, which Severs once described as "passing through a frame into a painting". Visitors are free to explore the candle-lit

and log-fired Georgian house unhindered, and are left with the distinct impression that someone has literally just popped out: the house cat prowls, aromas of dinner waft up from the kitchen and the sound of horses' hooves can be heard from the cobbled street outside.

Shops

Freedom Press
Angel Alley, 84b Whitechapel High St ☎020/7247 9249, ⓦwww .freedompress.org.uk. Mon–Fri 10.30am–6pm, Sat 11am–5pm. Upholding a long East End tradition of radical politics, this small anarchist bookshop is packed with everything from Bakhunin to Chomsky.

The Laden Showroom
103 Brick Lane ☎020/7247 2431, ⓦwww.laden.co.uk. Mon noon–6pm, Tues–Sat 11am–6pm, Sun 10.30am–6pm. Emporium showcasing over forty independent designers, and is great for exuberant dressers on a budget. You can pick up Indian tunics, handmade customized T-shirts, batik bags and stripey bias-cut frocks. For similar secondhand gear, check out Rokit next door.

Story
4 Wilkes St ☎020/7377 0313. Tues–Sun 2–7pm. There's a whiff of Miss Haversham about the fading lace and Venetian mirrors in this exquisitely tasteful and eclectic shop, with everything – art, textiles, furniture, clothing – in shades of white or cream.

Tatty Devine
236 Brick Lane ☎020/7739 9009, ⓦwww.tattydevine.com. Mon–Fri 10am–6pm, Sat & Sun 11am–7pm. Funky shop which stocks (and

exhibits) wacky, tacky T-shirts and accessories by young designers: tape measure belts, safety-pin brooches and perspex earrings.

Cafés

Brick Lane Beigel Bake
159 Brick Lane. Daily 24hr. Classic takeaway bagel shop in the heart of the East End – unbelievably cheap, even for fillings such as smoked salmon with cream cheese.

Café 1001
1 Dray's Lane. Mon–Wed & Sun 8am–10.30pm, Thurs 8am–11pm, Fri & Sat 8am–midnight. Tucked in by the side of the Truman Brewery, off Brick Lane, this smoky café has a beaten-up studenty look, with lots of sofas to crash on. Mainstays are simple, filling sandwiches and delicious cakes. DJ sets every night.

Flavour
35 Charlotte Rd. Mon–Fri 8.30am–4pm, Sat 9am–4pm. Tiny Shoreditch café with just four stools, serving delicious Mediterranean lunch options: big soups, grilled tuna, salads and great pastries all freshly prepared.

Restaurants

Café Naz
46–48 Brick Lane ☎020/7247 0234, ⓦwww.cafenaz.co.uk. Daily noon–midnight. Self-proclaimed contemporary Bangladeshi restaurant that cuts an imposing modern figure on Brick Lane. The menu has all the standards plus a variety of baltis, the kitchen is open-plan, and the prices keen. Mains £5–10.

Tayyab's

83–89 Fieldgate St ☎020/7247 9543, ⓦwww.tayyabs.co.uk. Daily 5–11.30pm. Smart place serving straightforward Pakistani fare for over thirty years: good, freshly cooked and served without pretension. Prices remain low, booking is essential and service is speedy and slick. Mains £4–8.

Real Greek

15 Hoxton Market ☎020/7739 8212, ⓦwww.therealgreek.co.uk. Mon–Sat noon–3pm & 5.30–10.30pm. A world away from your average London Greek-Cypriot joint, with a lofty, busy *mezedopolio* and bar, where you can order a few *mezedes* (for under £5 each), and a more formal but modern restaurant serving authentic Greek main courses for £13–17.

Viet Hoa Café

72 Kingsland Rd ☎020/7729 8293. Mon–Fri noon–3.30pm & 5.30–11.30pm, Sat & Sun 12.30–11.30pm. Large, light and airy Vietnamese café in a street now heaving with similar places. Try one of the splendid "meals in a bowl", or the noodle dishes with everything from spring rolls to tofu. Mains around £5.

Pubs and bars

Big Chill Bar

94 Dray Walk ⓦwww.bigchill.net. Mon–Thurs & Sun noon–midnight, Fri & Sat noon–1am. Spin-off bar of the Big Chill multimedia company offering quality nightly DJs, cocktails and a general sense of fun. A mix of concrete and kitsch, the spacious bar manages to be style-conscious yet relaxed,

PLACES

Hoxton and Spitalfields

▼ LOUNGELOVER

with punters spilling out onto the tables on funky Dray Walk in warmer weather.

Dragon

5 Leonard St. Mon noon–midnight, Tues, Wed & Thurs noon–1am, Fri & Sat noon–2am, Sun noon–midnight. This discreetly signed, clubby pub with bare-brick walls and crumbling leather sofas attracts a bohemian mix of office workers and trendy Hoxtonites. Nightly DJs playing an eclectic mix from hip-hop to Sixties.

Hoxton Square Bar and Kitchen

2–4 Hoxton Square. Mon–Thurs & Sun 11am–midnight, Fri & Sat 11am–2am. Blade Runner-esque concrete bar that attracts artists, writers and wannabes with its mix of modern European food, kitsch-to-club soundtracks and worn leather sofas. Best in the summer, when the drinking spills into the square in a carnival spirit.

Loungelover

1 Whitby St ⓦ www.loungelover .co.uk. Tues–Thurs 6pm–midnight, Fri 6pm–1am, Sat 7pm–1am, Sun 4–10.30pm. Factory conversion with a bizarre array of opulently camp bric-a-brac, expertly slung together to create a trendy and unique cocktail bar. Drinks are very well executed and deservedly expensive. Reservations recommended.

Sosho

2a Tabernacle St ⓦ www.sosho3am .com. Mon 11.30am–10pm, Tues & Wed 11.30am–midnight, Thurs 11.30am–1am, Fri 11.30am–3am, Sat 7pm–3am. Cover charge at weekends. Very trendy club-bar, with good

cocktails and decent food; the ambience is chilled until the popular DJs kick in at 8.30pm (Wed–Sat).

Clubs and venues

Cargo

83 Rivington St ⓦ www.cargo-london .com. Mon–Thurs until 1am, Fri & Sat until 3am, Sun until midnight. *Cargo* plays host to a variety of excellent and often innovative club nights, from deep house to jazz, and often features live bands alongside the DJs.

Comedy Café

66 Rivington St ⓣ 020/7739 5706, ⓦ www.comedycafe.co.uk. Wed–Sat £5–15. Long-established, purpose-built club, often with impressive lineups. Free admission for the new-acts slot on Wednesday.

Herbal

10–14 Kingsland Rd ⓦ www.herbaluk .com Open usually Tues–Sun until 2 or 3am. An intimate two-floored venue comprising a cool New York-style loft and sweaty ground-floor club. A great place to check out drum'n'bass and breaks.

Spitz

Old Spitalfields Market, 109 Commercial St ⓦ www.spitz.co.uk. Mon–Wed until midnight, Thurs–Sat until 1am, Sun until 10.30pm. Friendly, small venue, where you can catch a diverse range of music including jazz, world, indie, folk, blues and electronica. The downstairs bistro hosts free live music up to four nights a week.

The Tower and Docklands

One of the city's main tourist attractions, the Tower of London was the site of some of the goriest events in the nation's history, and is somewhere all visitors should try and get to see. Immediately to the east are the remains of what was the largest enclosed cargo-dock system in the world, built in the nineteenth century to cope with the huge volume of goods shipped in along the Thames from all over the Empire. No one thought the area could be rejuvenated when the docks closed in the 1960s, but over the last 25 years, warehouses have been converted into luxury flats, waterside penthouse apartments have been built and a huge high-rise office development has sprung up around Canary Wharf.

Tower of London

Ⓦwww.hrp.org.uk. March–Oct Mon & Sun 10am–6pm, Tues–Sat 9am–6pm; Nov–Feb Mon & Sun 10am–5pm, Tues–Sat 9am–5pm. £15. One of the most perfectly preserved medieval fortresses in the country, the Tower of London sits beside the Thames surrounded by a wide, dry moat. Begun as a simple watchtower built by William the Conqueror

▲ DOCKLANDS LIGHT RAILWAY

Docklands Light Railway

The best way to visit Docklands is to take the Docklands Light Railway or DLR (☎020/7363 9700, Ⓦwww.tfl.gov.uk/dlr), whose driverless trains run on overhead tracks, and give out great views over the cityscape. DLR trains set off from Bank tube, or from Tower Gateway, close to Tower Hill tube and the Tower of London.

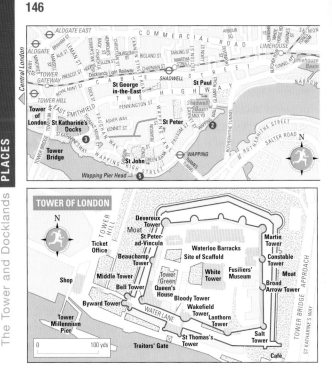

TOWER OF LONDON

the Tower is chiefly famous as a place of imprisonment and death, though it has been used variously as a royal residence, armoury, mint, menagerie, observatory and – a function it still serves – a safe-deposit box for the Crown Jewels. Before

▼ TOWER OF LONDON RAVEN

you set off to explore the complex, you should take one of the free guided tours, given every thirty minutes or so by one of the Tower's **Beefeaters** (officially known as Yeoman Warders). As well as giving a good introduction to the history, these ex-servicemen relish hamming up the gory stories.

Visitors today enter the Tower along Water Lane, but in times gone by most prisoners were delivered through Traitors' Gate, on the waterfront. The nearby **Bloody Tower** saw the murders of 12-year-old Edward V and his 10-year-old brother, and was used to imprison Walter Ralegh on three separate occasions, including an

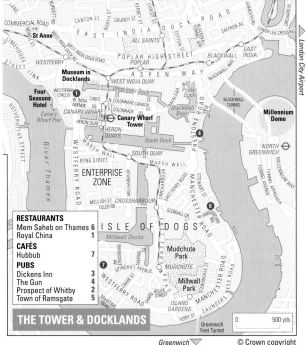

PLACES The Tower and Docklands

RESTAURANTS
Mem Saheb on Thames 6
Royal China 1
CAFÉS
Hubbub 7
PUBS
Dickens Inn 3
The Gun 4
Prospect of Whitby 2
Town of Ramsgate 5

THE TOWER & DOCKLANDS

Greenwich ▽

© Crown copyright

uninterrupted thirteen-year stretch.

The **White Tower**, at the centre of the complex, is the original "Tower", begun in 1076 and now home to displays from the Royal Armouries. Even if you've no interest in military paraphernalia, you should at least pay a visit to the Chapel of St John on the second floor; a beautiful Norman structure completed in 1080, it's the oldest intact church building in London. To the west of the White Tower is the execution spot on Tower Green where seven highly-placed but unlucky individuals were beheaded, among them Anne Boleyn and her cousin Catherine Howard (Henry VIII's second and fifth wives).

The **Crown Jewels**, of course, housed in the Waterloo Barracks are the major reason so many people flock to the Tower, but the moving walkways which take you past the loot are disappointingly swift, allowing you just 28 seconds' viewing during peak periods. The oldest piece of regalia is the twelfth-century Anointing Spoon, but the vast majority of exhibits, including the Imperial State Crown, postdate the Commonwealth (1649–60), when many of the royal riches were melted down for coinage or sold off. Among the jewels are the three largest cut diamonds in the world, including the legendary Koh-i-Noor, set into the Queen Mother's Crown in 1937.

▲ TOWER BRIDGE

Tower Bridge

ⓦwww.towerbridge.org.uk. Tower Bridge ranks with Big Ben as the most famous of all London landmarks. Completed in 1894, its Neo-Gothic towers are clad in Cornish granite and Portland stone, but conceal a steel frame which, at the time, represented a considerable engineering achievement, allowing a road crossing that could be raised to give tall ships access to the upper reaches of the Thames. The raising of the bascules (from the French for "see-saw") remains an impressive sight – phone ahead to find out when the bridge is opening (☎020/7940 3984). It's free to walk across the bridge, but you must pay to gain access to the elevated walkways (daily 9.30am–6pm; £5.50) linking the summits of the towers – closed from 1909 to 1982 due to their popularity with prostitutes and the suicidal. The views are pretty good and you get to visit the Engine Room on the south side of the bridge, where you can see the giant, and now defunct, coal-fired boilers and play some interactive engineering games.

St Katharine's Docks

ⓦwww.skdocks.co.uk. Built in the late 1820s to relieve the congestion on the River Thames, St Katharine's Docks were originally surrounded by high walls to protect the warehouses used to store luxury goods – ivory, spices, carpets and cigars – shipped in from all over the Empire. Nowadays, the docks are used as an upmarket marina, and the old warehouses house shops, pubs and restaurants that get a lot of passing trade thanks to the close proximity of the Tower. More appealing, however, are the old **swing bridges** over the basins (including a Telford footbridge from 1828), the boats themselves – you'll often see beautiful old sailing ships and Dutch barges – and the attractive Ivory House warehouse, with its clock tower, at the centre of the three basins. At its peak this warehouse received over 200 tons of ivory annually, and even mammoth tusks from Siberia.

Wapping High Street

Once famous for its boatyards and its three dozen riverside pubs, Wapping's Victorian atmosphere has been preserved, and as it lies just a short walk east of the Tower, this is easily the most satisfying part of Docklands to explore. Halfway along Wapping High Street is

Wapping Pier Head, the former entrance to the London Docks, flanked by grand, curvaceous Regency terraces. Here, you'll find one of the few surviving stairs down to the river beside the *Town of Ramsgate* pub; beneath the pub are the dungeons where convicts were chained before being deported to Australia. It was at the *Town of Ramsgate* that "Hanging" Judge Jeffreys was captured trying to escape disguised as a collier following the victory of William of Orange in 1688.

Canary Wharf

The geographical and ideological heart of the new Docklands is Canary Wharf, previously a destination for rum and mahogany, later tomatoes and bananas (from the Canary Islands – hence the name). Now a pedestrian-friendly business district, this is the one new Docklands area that you can happily stroll around, taking in the modern architecture and landscaping, looking out for some of the tongue-in-cheek sculptures, and perhaps having a drink overlooking one of the old wharves. Canary Wharf's name is, of course, synonymous with Cesar Pelli's landmark **tower**, officially known as One Canada Square. Britain's tallest building and the first skyscraper anywhere to be clad in stainless steel, it's an undeniably impressive sight, both close up and from a distance – its flashing pyramid-shaped pinnacle is a feature of the horizon at numerous points in London.

Museum in Docklands

West India Quay. ⓦ www. museumindocklands.org.uk. Daily 10am–6pm. £5. The last surviving Georgian warehouses of the West India Docks lie on the far side of a floodlit floating bridge at West India Quay. Amidst the dockside bars and restaurants, you'll find Warehouse No. 1, built in 1803 for storing rum, sugar, molasses, coffee and cotton, and now home to the Museum in Docklands which makes a visit to the area well worth the effort. Spread over several floors, the exhibits chart the history of London's docks, on both sides of the river from Roman times to the development of Canary Wharf. Highlights include a great model of old London Bridge, one side depicting it in 1440, the other around 1600, an eight-foot long watercolour showing the "legal quays" in the 1790s, just before the enclosed

▼ CANARY WHARF TOWER

The Dome

Clearly visible from Greenwich's riverside and park, the Dome is the archetypal millennial cock-up. Architecturally, it's eye-catching enough: over half a mile in circumference and 160ft in height, it's the world's largest dome, held up by a dozen, 300ft-tall yellow steel masts. But it's best known for the £800 million that was poured into it, and for the millennium exhibition and show, which was panned by the critics and dismantled after one year. Apart from a few one-off events, the Dome has remained (expensively) empty since then, though it's due to host the 2009 World Gymnastics Championships and be the 2012 Olympic venue for artistic gymnastics, trampolining and basketball.

docks eased congestion, and a reconstructed warren of late nineteenth-century shops and cobbled dockland streets. Those with kids should head for Mudlarks, on the ground floor, where children can learn a bit about pulleys and ballast, drive a DLR train or simply romp around the soft play area.

Island Gardens

Manchester Rd. At Island Gardens, the southernmost tip of the Isle of Dogs, the DLR heads under the Thames to Greenwich (see p.199), as does the 1902 Greenwich Foot Tunnel (open 24hr). The gardens themselves are nothing special, but the **view** is spectacular – this was

Christopher Wren's favourite Thames-side spot, from which he could contemplate his masterpieces across the river, the Royal Naval College and the Royal Observatory (see pp.201 & 203).

Cafés

Hubbub

269 Westferry Rd. Mon–Fri noon–2.30pm & 5.30–10.30pm, Sat & Sun 10am–5pm & 6–10.30pm. Within an arts centre in a converted former church, this is a real oasis in the desert of Westferry Road, offering decent fry-ups, sandwiches and a few fancier dishes.

▼ THE DOME

Restaurants

Mem Saheb on Thames

65–67 Amsterdam Rd ☏020/7538 3008. Mon–Fri noon–2.30pm & 6–11.30pm, Sat & Sun 6–11.30pm. Decent Indian restaurant with a superb view over the river to the Dome. Standard tandoori kebabs, plus the odd unusual dish like Rajasthani *khargosh* (rabbit and spinach), all for under £10.

Royal China

30 Westferry Circus ☏020/7221 2535. Mon–Thurs noon–11pm, Fri & Sat noon–11.30pm, Sun 11am–10pm. You can eat well from the full menu, but it's the dim sum that is most enticing here: the roast pork puff is famous and this may well be the place to finally take the plunge and try chicken's feet.

Pubs

Dickens Inn

St Katharine's Way. Mon–Sat 11am–11pm, Sun noon–10.30pm. Eighteenth-century timber-framed warehouse transported on wheels from its original site, and then much altered. Still, it's a remarkable building, with a great view, but very firmly on the tourist trail.

The Gun

27 Coldharbour. Mon–Sat 11am–11pm, Sun noon–10.30pm; open Sat & Sun from 10.30am for brunch but no alcohol. Old dockers' pub with a fresh lick of paint and lots of maritime memorabilia, an unrivalled view of the Dome from its outside deck, and a classy dining area serving very good Modern European food.

Prospect of Whitby

57 Wapping Wall. Mon–Fri 11am–11pm, Sat noon–11pm, Sun noon–10.30pm. London's most famous riverside pub, with a flagstone floor, a cobbled courtyard and great views.

Town of Ramsgate

62 Wapping High St. Mon–Sat noon–11pm, Sun noon–10.30pm. Dark, narrow, medieval pub located by Wapping Old Stairs, which once led down to Execution Dock. Admiral Bligh and Fletcher Christian were regular drinking partners here in pre-mutiny days.

South Bank and around

The South Bank has a lot going for it. As well as the massive waterside arts centre, it's home to a host of tourist attractions including the enormously popular London Eye observation wheel. With most of London sitting on the north bank of the Thames, the views from here are the best on the river, and thanks to the wide, traffic-free riverside boulevard, the whole area can be happily explored on foot. And a short walk from the South Bank lie one or two lesser-known but nonetheless absorbing sights such as the Imperial War Museum, which contains the country's only permanent exhibition devoted to the Holocaust.

South Bank Centre

The South Bank Centre is home to a whole variety of artistic institutions, the most attractive of which is the **Royal Festival Hall**, built in 1951 for the Festival of Britain and one of London's chief concert venues. With its open-plan, multi-level foyer, replete with café and bookshop and often hosting a free gig or exhibition, it's a great place to wander through during the day. Architecturally, the most depressing parts of the South Bank Centre are the grim-grey, concrete exteriors of the Queen Elizabeth Hall (QEH) and the more intimate Purcell Room, built in the 1960s to the north of the RFH in an uncompromisingly

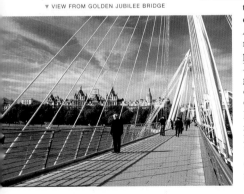

▼ VIEW FROM GOLDEN JUBILEE BRIDGE

Golden Jubilee Bridges

The best way to approach the South Bank is to walk from Embankment tube across the Hungerford Bridge, or the Golden Jubilee Bridges, as they are new known, a majestic, symmetrical double suspension footbridge that runs either side of Hungerford railway bridge, dishing out great river views on both sides, but particularly to the south towards Big Ben.

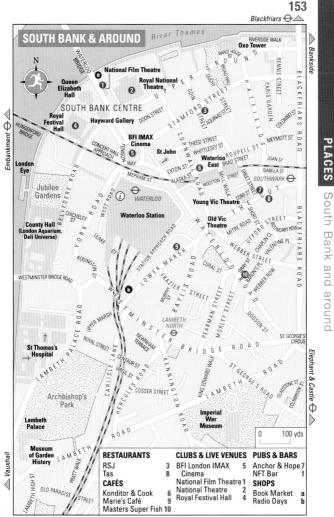

© Crown copyright

RESTAURANTS		CLUBS & LIVE VENUES		PUBS & BARS	
RSJ	3	BFI London IMAX	5	Anchor & Hope	7
Tas	8	Cinema		NFT Bar	1
CAFÉS		National Film Theatre	1	**SHOPS**	
Konditor & Cook	6	National Theatre	2	Book Market	a
Marie's Café	9	Royal Festival Hall	4	Radio Days	b
Masters Super Fish	10				

brutalist 1960s style. Above these two, with its strange rooftop neon sculpture, sits the **Hayward Gallery** (ⓦwww .hayward.org.uk; daily 10am–6pm, Tues & Wed until 8pm, Fri until 9pm; £7.50), one of the city's best venues for large-scale contemporary art exhibitions and retrospectives.

Tucked underneath Waterloo Bridge is the **National Film Theatre**, which screens London's most esoteric movies and has a decent café/bar. Behind the NFT, at the southern end of Waterloo Bridge, is the eye-catching glass-drum of the high-tech **BFI London IMAX**

▲ ROYAL FESTIVAL HALL, SOUTH BANK

Cinema. Lastly, on the east side of Waterloo Bridge, its series of horizontal concrete layers looking suspiciously like a multistorey car park, is the **National Theatre**, popularly known as "the National" or NT. It boasts three separate theatres – a Greek-style arena, a proscenium arch and a flexible studio – and puts on everything from Shakespeare to the latest David Hare.

Oxo Tower

ⓦwww.oxotower.co.uk. Daily until 10pm. The Oxo Tower started life as a power station before being converted into a meat-packing factory for the company that makes Oxo stock cubes – the lettering is spelt out in the windows of the main tower. The building now contains flats, browsable studio-shops for contemporary designers (Tues–Sun 11am–6pm) and an art gallery (daily 11am–6pm; free), whose exhibitions of contemporary photographs, paintings or sculptures are usually intriguing; on the top floor, there's a very swanky

restaurant and brasserie. You don't need to eat or drink here to enjoy the view from the top: just take the lift to the eighth-floor public viewing gallery.

London Eye

☎0870/5000 600, ⓦwww
.ba-londoneye.com. Daily: June–Sept 10am–9pm; Oct–May 10am–8pm. £13. London's most prominent recent landmark is the London Eye, the magnificently graceful observation wheel which spins slowly and silently over the Thames. Standing 443ft high, the wheel is the largest ever built, and it's constantly in slow motion – a full-circle "flight" in one of its 32 pods takes around thirty minutes, and lifts you high above the city. Unless you know your London landmarks well, you'll probably need to buy one of the Eye guides. At the top, you're at one of the few places (apart from a plane window) from which London looks a manageable size, as you can see right out to where the suburbs slip into the countryside. Ticket prices are high, though the engineering and the views are

awesome; queues can also be very bad at the weekend, so book in advance over the phone or online.

County Hall

The colonnaded crescent of County Hall is the only truly monumental building on the South Bank. Designed to house the now defunct London County Council, it was completed in 1933 and enjoyed its greatest moment of fame as headquarters of the GLC (Greater London Council), which was abolished by Margaret Thatcher in 1986 leaving London as the only European city without an elected authority. In 2000, the former GLC leader Ken Livingstone was elected as Mayor of London, and moved into the new GLA (Greater London Authority) building further downstream (see p.164). County Hall, meanwhile, is now in the hands of a Japanese property company, and currently houses several hotels, restaurants, an amusement arcade and a bizarre clutch of tourist attractions.

London Aquarium

Ⓦ www.londonaquarium .co.uk. Daily 10am–6pm or later. £11.75.

The most popular attraction in County Hall is the London Aquarium, laid out on two subterranean levels. With some super-large tanks, and everything from dog-face puffers to piranhas, this is an attraction that's pretty much guaranteed to please younger kids. The Touching Pool, where children can actually stroke the (non-sting) rays, is particularly popular. Impressive in scale, the aquarium is fairly conservative in design, though, with no walk-through tanks. Ask at the main desk for the times of the daily presentations.

Dalí Universe

Riverside Walk, County Hall Ⓦ www .daliuniverse.com. Daily 10am–6.30pm. £12. Three giant surrealist sculptures on the river-facing side of County Hall herald the Dalí Universe. Yet while Dalí was undoubtedly an accomplished and prolific artist, you'll be disappointed if you're expecting to see his "greatest hits" here – those are scattered across the globe. Most of the works on display are

▼ DALÍ SCULPTURE, SOUTH BANK

little-known bronze and glass sculptures, as well as drawings from the many illustrated books which he published, ranging from Ovid to the Marquis de Sade. Aside from these, there's one of the numerous Lobster Telephones, which Edward James commissioned for his London home, a copy of his famous Mae West lips sofa, and the oil painting from the dream sequence in Hitchcock's movie Spellbound.

Museum of Garden History

Lambeth Palace Rd ⓦwww .cix.co.uk/~museumgh. Daily 10.30am–5pm. Free, though £3 donation suggested. Housed in the deconsecrated Kentish ragstone church of **St Mary-at-Lambeth**, this unpretentious little museum puts particular emphasis on John Tradescant, gardener to James I and Charles I, who is buried here. The graveyard has been transformed into a small seventeenth-century garden, where two interesting sarcophagi lurk among the foliage: one belongs to Captain Bligh, the commander of the Bounty in 1787; the more unusual is Tradescant's memorial, depicting, among other things, a seven-headed griffin and several crocodiles.

Imperial War Museum

Lambeth Rd ⓦwww.iwm.org.uk. Daily 10am–6pm. Free. Housed in a domed building that was once the infamous "Bedlam" lunatic asylum, the Imperial War Museum holds by far the best collection of militaria in the capital. The treatment of the subject matter is impressively wide-ranging and fairly sober, with the main hall's militaristic display of guns, tanks and fighter planes offset by the lower-ground-floor array of documents and images attesting to the human damage of war. In addition to the static displays, there's a walk-through World War I trench and a re-creation of the Blitz. Entered from the third floor, the harrowing **Holocaust Exhibition** (not recommended for children under 14) pulls few punches, and has made a valiant attempt to avoid depicting the victims of the Holocaust as nameless masses by focusing on individual cases, interspersing the archive footage with eyewitness accounts from contemporary survivors.

Shops

Book Market

South Bank, beneath Waterloo Bridge. Sat & Sun 10am–5pm. Secondhand book market by the Thames, offering everything from current and recent fiction to obscure psychology textbooks, film theory, modern European poetry and pulp science fiction.

Radio Days

87 Lower Marsh. Mon–Sat 10am–6pm (Fri until 7pm). Fantastic collection of memorabilia and accessories from the 1930s to the 1970s, including shoes, shot-glass collections, cosmetics and vintage magazines. A huge stock of well-kept womens' and mens' clothing from the same period fills the back room.

Cafés

Konditor & Cook

22 Cornwall Rd ⓦwww .konditorandcook.com. Mon–Fri 7.30am–6.30pm, Sat 8.30am–2.30pm. Quality bakery making wonderful cakes and biscuits,

▲ KONDITOR & COOK

as well as offering a choice of sandwiches, coffee and tea. With only a few tables inside, most folk take away.

Marie's Café

90 Lower Marsh. Daily 5–10.30pm. As the name doesn't suggest, this is a Thai café – it's basic, cheap and friendly and dishes up tasty red and green curries. Bring your own booze; £1 corkage.

Masters Super Fish

191 Waterloo Rd. Tues–Sat noon–3pm & 5.30–10.30pm (Fri until 11pm). Good, old-fashioned, no-nonsense fish and chip pit stop, with complimentary prawns, pickled gherkins and onions.

Restaurants

RSJ

13a Coin St ☎020/7928 4554, ⓦwww.rsj.uk.com. Mon–Fri noon–2pm & 5.30–11pm, Sat 5.30–11pm. Regularly high standards of Anglo-French cooking make this a good spot for a meal before or after an evening at a South Bank theatre or concert hall. Mains range from pan-fried sea bass to risotto with goat's cheese. Set meals for £16–18.

Tas

33 The Cut ☎020/7928 1444, ⓦwww.tasrestaurant.com. Welcoming restaurant serving excellent, competitively priced Turkish food. The menu is a monster so most folk go for the set options, starting at three courses for under £10.

Pubs and bars

Anchor & Hope

36 The Cut. Mon 5–11pm, Tues–Sat 11am–11pm. Welcoming and unfussy gastropub, dishing up truly excellent grub. No bookings accepted, so if you want to eat, try not arrive here at peak times.

NFT Bar

South Bank. The National Film Theatre's bar is the only one on the South Bank riverfront between Westminster and Blackfriars bridges – worth checking out not only for the views, but also for the food and the congenial crowd.

Clubs and venues

BFI London IMAX Cinema
South Bank ☎020/7902 1234, ⊛www.bfi.org.uk/incinemas/imax. Remarkable glazed drum housing Europe's largest screen, showing 2D and 3D films, but like all IMAX cinemas, it suffers from the fact that very few movies are shot on 70mm film.

National Film Theatre
South Bank ☎020/7928 3232. ⊛www.nft.org.uk. Known for its attentive audiences and an exhaustive, eclectic programme that includes directors' seasons and thematic series. Around six films daily are shown in the vast NFT1 and the smaller NFT2 and 3.

National Theatre
South Bank ☎020/7452 3000. ⊛www .nt-online.org. See the country's top actors and directors in a programme ranging from Greek tragedies to Broadway musicals. Some productions sell out months in advance, but twenty to thirty of the cheapest tickets go on sale on the morning of each performance – get there by 8am for the popular shows.

Royal Festival Hall
South Bank ⊛www.rfh.org.uk. A gargantuan space with a programme of events from jazz festivals to dance and world music. It's tailor-made for large-scale choral and orchestral works, and plays host to some big-name soloists, though only a few can fill it.

Bankside and Southwark

In Tudor and Stuart London, the chief reason for crossing the Thames to Southwark was to visit the then-disreputable Bankside entertainment district around the south end of London Bridge. Four hundred years on, Londoners have rediscovered the area, thanks to wholesale regeneration that has engendered a wealth of new attractions along the riverside between Blackfriars and Tower bridges and beyond – with the charge led by the mighty Tate Modern art gallery. And with a traffic-free, riverside path connecting most of the sights, this is easily one of the most enjoyable areas of London in which to hang out.

Millennium Bridge

The first new bridge to be built across the Thames since Tower Bridge opened in 1894, the sleek, stainless-steel Millennium Bridge is London's sole pedestrian-only crossing. A suspension bridge of innovative design, it famously bounced up and down when it first opened and had to be closed immediately for another two years for repairs. It still wobbles a bit, but most people are too busy enjoying the spectacular views across to St Paul's Cathedral and Tate Modern to notice.

Tate Modern

Bankside ☎020/7887 8008, ⓦwww .tate.org.uk. Daily 10am–6pm (Fri & Sat until 10pm). Free. Bankside is dominated by the austere power station transformed by the Swiss duo Herzog & de Meuron into

▼ TATE MODERN

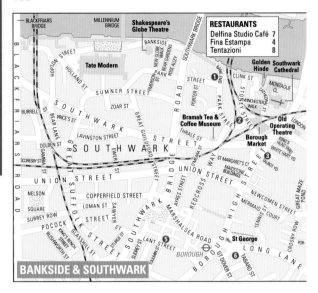

RESTAURANTS
Delfina Studio Café 7
Fina Estampa 4
Tentazioni 8

BANKSIDE & SOUTHWARK

Tate Modern. The masterful conversion has left plenty of the original industrial feel, while providing wonderfully light and spacious galleries to show off the Tate's vast collection of international twentieth-century art. The best way to enter is down the ramp from the west, so you get the full effect of the stupendously large **turbine hall**, usually used to display one huge, mind-blowing installation. Given that Tate Modern is the world's largest modern art gallery, you need to devote the best part of a day to do it justice – or be very selective. It's easy enough to find your way around the galleries: pick up a plan (and, for an extra £2, an audioguide), and take the escalator to level 3. This, and level 5, display the permanent collection; level 4 is used for fee-paying temporary exhibitions, and level 7 has a rooftop café with a great view over the Thames.

The curators have eschewed the usual chronological approach through the "-isms", preferring to group works together thematically: Landscape/Matter/Environment; Still Life/Object/Real Life; History/Memory/Society; and Nude/Action/Body. On the whole this works very well, though the early twentieth-century canvases, in their gilded frames, do struggle when made to compete with contemporary installations.

Although the displays change every six months or so, you're still pretty much guaranteed to see at least some works by **Monet** and Bonnard, Cubist pioneers **Picasso** and Braque, Surrealists such as **Dalí**, abstract artists like **Mondrian**, Bridget Riley and Pollock, and Pop supremos **Warhol** and Lichtenstein. There are seminal works such as a replica of **Duchamp**'s urinal, entitled

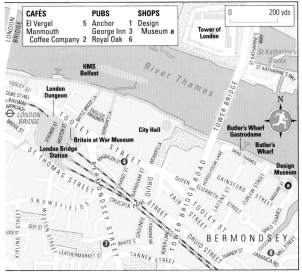

Fountain and signed "R. Mutt" and Yves Klein's totally blue paintings. And such is the space here that several artists get whole rooms to themselves, among them Joseph Beuys and his shamanistic wax and furs, and **Mark Rothko**, whose abstract *Seagram Murals*, originally destined for a posh restaurant in New York, have their own shrine-like room in the heart of the collection.

Shakespeare's Globe Theatre

21 New Globe Walk, Bankside
☎020/7902 1400 ⓦwww
.shakespeares-globe.org. Daily: May–Sept 9am–noon & 12.30–5pm; Oct–April 10am–5pm. Exhibition £9. Seriously dwarfed by the Tate Modern, the

Shakespeare's Globe Theatre is an equally spectacular reconstruction of the Elizabethan polygonal playhouse where most of the Bard's later works were first performed. Sporting the first new thatched roof in central London since the 1666 Great Fire, the theatre puts on plays (mid-Sept to mid-May only) by Shakespeare and his contemporaries. To get to see inside the building, you must either attend a performance, or visit the Globe's pricey but stylish exhibition. It begins by detailing the long campaign by the late American actor Sam Wanamaker to have the Globe rebuilt, but it's the imaginative hands-on exhibits that really hit the spot. You can have a virtual "play"

Tate to Tate

Tate to Tate boats (specially designed by Damien Hirst) shuttle between Tate Modern and Tate Britain via the London Eye every forty minutes; journey time is twenty minutes, and tickets cost £4.30 (£2.65 with a Travelcard).

on medieval instruments such as the crumhorn or sackbut, prepare your own edition of Shakespeare, and feel the thatch, hazelnut-shell and daub used to build the theatre. Visitors to the exhibition also get taken on an informative guided tour round the theatre itself, except in the afternoons during the summer season, when you can only visit the exhibition (for a reduced fee).

Golden Hinde

St Mary Overie Dock, Cathedral St ☎0870/011 8700, ⓦwww .goldenhinde.co.uk. Daily 10am–5.30pm. £5.50. An exact replica of the galleon in which Francis Drake sailed around the world from 1577 to 1580, the Golden Hinde was launched in 1973, and circumnavigated the world for some twenty years before eventually settling permanently in Southwark. The ship is surprisingly small, and its original crew of eighty-plus must have been cramped to say the least. There's a lack of interpretive panels, so it's worth phoning ahead and booking a guided tour from one of the folk in period garb.

Southwark Cathedral

London Bridge ⓦwww.dswark.org /cathedral. Mon–Fri 7.30am–6pm, Sat & Sun 8.30am–6pm. Free. Built as the medieval Augustinian priory church of St Mary Overie, Southwark Cathedral gained its cathedral status in 1905. Of the original thirteenth-century church, only the choir and retrochoir now remain, separated by a tall and beautiful stone Tudor screen; they're thought to be the oldest Gothic structures left in London. The nave was entirely rebuilt in the nineteenth century, but the cathedral contains numerous interesting monuments, from a thirteenth-century oak effigy of a knight to an early twentieth-century memorial to Shakespeare (his brother is buried here). Above the memorial is a stained-glass window featuring a whole cast of characters from the plays.

Borough Market

8 Southwark St ⓦwww .boroughmarket.org.uk. Fruit &

▼ SHAKESPEARE WINDOW, SOUTHWARK CATHERAL

veg daily until 9am; food stalls Fri noon–6pm, Sat 9am–4pm. There's been a thriving market in Southwark (also known as the Borough) since medieval times. Squeezed beneath the railway arches between the High Street and the cathedral, the present Borough Market is one of the few wholesale fruit and vegetable markets in London still trading under its original Victorian wrought-iron shed. On Fridays and Saturdays, though, it transforms itself into a small foodie haven, and the general public turn up in droves to sample the produce on the gourmet stalls and in the nearby shops.

Bramah Tea & Coffee Museum

40 Southwark St www .bramahmuseum.co.uk. Daily 10am–6pm. £4. Endearingly ramshackle and well worth a visit, the Tea and Coffee Museum was founded in 1992 by Edward Bramah, who began his career on an African tea garden in 1950. The museum's emphasis is firmly on tea, though the café also serves a seriously good cup of coffee. There's an impressive array of teapots from Meissen to the world's largest, plus plenty of novelty ones, and coffee machines spanning the twentieth century, from huge percolator siphons to espresso machines.

Old Operating Theatre, Museum and Herb Garret

9a St Thomas's St www.thegarret .org.uk. Daily 10.30am–5pm. £3.25. The Old Operating Theatre and Herb Garret is by far the most educational – and strangest – of Southwark's museums, and despite being entirely gore-free, it's as stomach-churning as the London Dungeon (see below). Visitors climb up to the attic of a former church tower, which houses an old hospital **apothecary** with displays explaining the painful truth about pre-anaesthetic operations. These took place in the adjacent women's **operating theatre**, designed in 1821 "in the round", literally like a theatre, so that students (and members of high society) could view the proceedings. The surgeons had to concentrate on speed and accuracy (most amputations took less than a minute), but there was still a thirty-percent mortality rate, with many patients simply dying of shock, and many more from bacterial infection, about which very little was known.

London Dungeon

28–34 Tooley St www.thedungeons .com. Daily: March to mid-July & Sep–Oct 10am–5.30pm; mid-July to Aug 9.30am–6pm; Nov–Feb 10.30am–5pm. £15.95. Young teenagers and the credulous probably get the most out of the life-sized waxwork tableaux of folk being hanged, drawn, quartered and tortured, the general hysteria being boosted by actors dressed as top-hatted Victorian vampires, executioners and monks pouncing out of the darkness. Visitors are led into the labyrinth, an old-fashioned mirror maze, before being herded through a series of live action scenarios, starting with an eighteenth-century courtroom, passing through the exploitative "Jack the Ripper Experience", and ending with a walk through a revolving tunnel of flames. Note that you can avoid the inevitable queues by pre-buying tickets online.

Britain at War Museum

64–66 Tooley St ⓦ www.britainatwar
.co.uk. Daily: April–Sept 10am–6pm;
Oct–March 10am–5pm. £9.50. For an
illuminating insight into London's
stiff-upper-lip mentality during
the World War II Blitz, head for
Winston Churchill's Britain at
War Exhibition, where you'll find
hundreds of fascinating wartime
artefacts, from ration books to
babies' gas masks. You can sit in
darkness in an Anderson shelter,
hear the chilling sound of the
V1 "doodlebugs" and tune in to
contemporary radio broadcasts.
The final set piece is a walk
through the chaos of a just-
bombed street.

HMS Belfast

Morgan's Lane, Tooley St ⓦ www.iwm
.org.uk. Daily: March–Oct 10am–6pm;
Nov–Feb 10am–5pm. £8.50. An
11,550-ton Royal Navy cruiser,
armed with six torpedoes and
six-inch guns with a range
of over fourteen miles, HMS
Belfast saw action both in the
Barents Sea during World War
II and in the Korean War, and
has been permanently moored
on the Thames since being
decommissioned in 1971. The
most enjoyable aspect of a visit
is exploring the *Belfast*'s maze
of cabins and scrambling up and
down the vertiginous ladders of
the ship's seven confusing decks,
which could accommodate a
crew of over nine hundred. If
you want to know more about
the ship's history, head for the
Exhibition Flat in Zone 5; in
the adjacent Life at Sea room,
you can practise your Morse
code and knots and listen to
accounts of naval life on board.

City Hall

The Queen's Walk ⓦ www.london
.gov.uk. Mon–Fri 8am–8pm,
plus occasional weekends.
Free. Bearing a striking
resemblance to a giant car
headlight, the centrepiece
of the redevelopment
near Tower Bridge is
Norman Foster's startling
glass-encased City Hall.
Headquarters for the
Greater London Authority
and the Mayor of London,
it's a "green" building
that uses a quarter of
the energy a high-
specification office would
normally use. Visitors are
welcome to stroll around
the building and watch
the London Assembly
proceedings from the
second floor. On certain
weekends, it's also possible
to visit "London's Living
Room" on the ninth floor,
from where there's a great
view over the Thames.

▼ HMS *BELFAST*

Design Museum

28 Shad Thames ⓦwww
.designmuseum.org. Daily
10am–5.45pm. £7. A
Bauhaus-like conversion
of an old 1950s riverside
warehouse, the stylish
white edifice of the
Design Museum is
the perfect showcase
for mass-produced
industrial design,
from classic cars to
Tupperware. The
museum has nothing on
permanent display, but
instead hosts a series of
temporary exhibitions
(up to four at any one
time) on important
designers, movements or
single products.

▲ DESIGN MUSEUM

Shops

Design Museum Shop

28 Shad Thames ☎020/7940 8753.
Daily 10am–5.45pm. This small
museum shop has all the latest
gadgets and gizmos, from
clocks and cups to posters
and stationery, beautifully
produced by the big names in
contemporary design.

Cafés

El Vergel

8 Lant St. Mon–Fri 8.30am–3pm,
Sat 10am–3pm. Small, very busy
café that does all the usual
lunchtime takeaways, but you're
really here to sample the Latin
American specialities such as
their empanadas, pasties filled
with meat and spices or spinach
and feta cheese.

Monmouth Coffee Company

2 Park St. ⓦwww.monmouthcoffee.
co.uk. Mon–Sat 7.30am–6pm. Perfect
pit stop in between perusing
the Borough Market stalls. This
place takes its coffee seriously,
as well as offering moist and
succulent cakes and pastries.

Restaurants

Delfina Studio Café

50 Bermondsey St ☎020/7357 0244,
ⓦwww.delfina.org.uk. Mon–Thurs
8am–5pm, Fri 8am–5pm & 7–10pm.
This light and spacious adjunct
to the Delfina art gallery is a
great place to go for lunch. The
cooking is "modern eclectic"
and the price is beyond café
norms, but the quality justifies a
bit of a splurge. Mains £10–14.

Fina Estampa

150 Tooley St ☎020/7403 1342. Mon–
Fri noon–10.30pm, Sat 6.30–10.30pm.
One of London's few Peruvian
restaurants, which happens to
be very good, bringing a little

of downtown Lima to London Bridge. The menu is traditional Peruvian; you can kick things off with a Pisco Sour cocktail. Mains £8–15.

Tentazioni

2 Mill St ☎020/7237 1100, ⓦwww. tentazioni.co.uk. Mon & Sat 7–10.45pm, Tues–Fri noon–2.30pm & 7–10.45pm. Smart, busy Italian restaurant serving high-quality peasant fare with strong, rich flavours. Mains are £17–19 or try the splendid three-course Tradizione Italiana (£28).

Pubs

Anchor

34 Park St. Mon–Sat 11am–11pm, Sun noon–10.30pm. While the rest of Bankside has changed almost beyond all recognition, this pub still looks much as it did when first built in 1770 (on the inside, at least). Good for alfresco drinking by the river.

George Inn

77 Borough High St. Mon–Sat 11am–11pm, Sun noon–10.30pm. London's only surviving coaching inn, dating from the seventeenth century and now owned by the National Trust; expect lots of wonky flooring, half-timbering and a good range of real ales.

Royal Oak

44 Tabard St. Mon–Fri 11.30am–11pm. Beautiful, lovingly restored Victorian pub that eschews jukeboxes and one-armed bandits, and opts simply for serving real ales from Lewes in Sussex.

Clubs and venues

Shakespeare's Globe Theatre

21 New Globe Walk ☎020/7902 1400, ⓦwww.shakespeares-globe.org. Mid-May to mid-Sept. This thatch-roofed replica Elizabethan theatre uses only natural light and the minimum of scenery, and currently puts on solid, fun Shakespearean shows with "groundling" tickets (standing-room only) for around a fiver.

Hyde Park and Kensington Gardens

Most visitors are amazed at how green and pleasant so much of London's centre is. Hyde Park, together with its westerly extension, Kensington Gardens, covers a distance of two miles from Oxford Street in the northeast to Kensington Palace in the southwest. In between, people jog, swim, fish, sunbathe or mess about in boats on the Serpentine, cross the park on horseback or mountain bike, or view the latest in modern art at the Serpentine Gallery. Kensington Palace, Princess Diana's home until her death, sits at the more fashionable end of the park, which gets mobbed on summer weekends with rollerbladers.

Wellington Arch

Hyde Park Corner ⓦ www.english-heritage.org.uk. Wed–Sun: April–Oct 10am–5pm; Nov–March 10am–4pm. £3.10. Standing in the midst of one of London's busiest traffic interchanges, Wellington Arch was erected in 1828 to commemorate Wellington's victories in the Napoleonic Wars. A standard Neoclassical triumphal arch, it was originally topped by an equestrian statue of the Duke himself, later replaced by Peace driving a four-horse chariot. Inside,

▼ WELLINGTON ARCH

PLACES

Hyde Park and Kensington Gardens

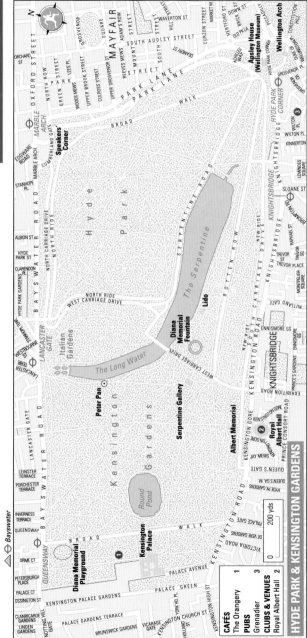

© Crown copyright

◁⊖◇ Bayswater

⊖◇ High Street Kensington

CAFÉS	
The Orangery	1
PUBS	
Grenadier	3
CLUBS & VENUES	
Royal Albert Hall	2

HYDE PARK & KENSINGTON GARDENS

you can view an informative exhibition on London's outdoor sculpture and take a lift to the top of the monument, where the exterior balconies offer a bird's-eye view of the swirling traffic.

Wellington Museum, Apsley House

149 Piccadilly ⓦwww.english-heritage.org.uk. Tues–Sun: April–Oct 10am–5pm; Nov–March 10am–4pm. £5.10. The former London residence of the "Iron Duke", Apsley House has housed the Wellington Museum since 1952. However unless you're a keen fan of the Duke (or the building's architect, Benjamin Wyatt), the highlight here is the **art collection**, much of which used to belong to the King of Spain. Among the best pieces, displayed in the Waterloo Gallery on the first floor, are works by de Hooch, van Dyck, Velázquez, Goya, Rubens and Murillo. The famous, more than twice life-size, nude statue of Napoleon by Antonio Canova stands at the foot of the main staircase. It was disliked by the sitter, not least for the figure of Victory in the emperor's hand, which appears to be trying to fly away.

Hyde Park

ⓦwww.royalparks.gov.uk. Daily 5am–midnight. Hangings, muggings, duels and the Great Exhibition of 1851 are just some of the public events that have been staged in Hyde Park, which was once a hunting ground for Henry VIII and remains a popular rallying point for political demonstrations. For most of the time, however, the park is simply a lazy leisure ground – a wonderful open space which allows you to lose

all sight of the city beyond a few persistent tower blocks.

At the treeless northeastern corner is **Marble Arch**, erected in 1828 as a triumphal entry to Buckingham Palace but now stranded on a ferociously busy traffic island at the west end of Oxford Street. This is the most historically charged spot in Hyde Park, as it marks the site of Tyburn gallows, the city's main public execution spot until 1783, when the action moved to Newgate. It's also the location of **Speakers' Corner**, a peculiarly English Sunday tradition, featuring an assembly of soap-box orators, religious extremists and hecklers.

A more immediately appealing approach is to enter from the southeast around Hyde Park Corner, from which paths lead past pretty flower gardens towards the curvaceous lake of the **Serpentine.** The lake's popular Lido (mid-June to mid-Sept daily 10am–6pm; £3.50) is situated on the south bank, alongside a café, and rowing boats and pedalos can be rented (March–Oct daily 10am–6.30pm or dusk; £4 per hour) from the boathouse on the north bank.

Diana Memorial Fountain

March & Oct 10am–6pm; April–Aug 10am–8pm; Sept 10am–7pm; Nov–Feb 10am–4pm. Less of a fountain, and more of an oval-shaped mini-moat, the memorial was designed in the shape of a giant oval ring by Kathryn Gustafson and constructed out of white Cornish granite. The intention was to allow children to play in the running water, but, after three people suffered minor injuries, the fountain has since been fenced off and supplied with security guards, making it rather less fun for kids, who are now only allowed to dabble their feet in the stream.

Kensington Gardens

ⓦwww.royalparks.gov.uk. Daily 6am–dusk. The more tranquil, leafier half of Hyde Park, Kensington Gardens is home to Long Water, the upper section of the Serpentine and by far the prettiest section of the lake. It narrows until it reaches a most unlikely sight in an English park: the **Italian Gardens**, a group of five fountains laid out symmetrically in front of a pumphouse disguised in the form of an Italianate loggia. The best-known of Kensington Gardens' outdoor monuments is **Peter Pan**, the fictional character who enters London along the Serpentine in the eponymous tale. The book's author, J.M. Barrie, used to walk his dog in Kensington Gardens, and it was here that he met the five pretty, upper-class Llewellyn Davies boys, who wore "blue blouses and bright red tam o'shanters", were the inspiration for the book's "Lost Boys", and

whose guardian he eventually became. Barrie himself paid for the statue, which was erected in secret during the night in 1912.

Serpentine Gallery

Kensington Gardens ⓦwww .serpentinegallery.org. Daily 10am–6pm. Free. The Serpentine Gallery was built as a tearoom in 1908 because the park authorities thought "poorer visitors" might cause trouble if left without refreshments. The building has served as an art gallery since the 1960s, with a reputation for lively, controversial exhibitions; it also annually commissions world-renowned architects to design a temporary pavilion for its summer-only teahouse extension. The results have been adventurous and exciting, ranging from Zaha Hadid's giant marquee to Toyo Ito's partially opaque enclosed box.

Albert Memorial

Kensington Gardens. Erected in 1876, the richly decorated, High Gothic Albert Memorial is as much a hymn to the glorious

▼ ROLLERBLADERS, KENSINGTON GARDENS

achievements of Britain as to its subject, Queen Victoria's husband (who died of typhoid in 1861). Recently restored to his former gilded glory, Albert occupies the central canopy, clutching a catalogue for the Great Exhibition that he helped to organize. If you want to learn more about the 169 life-sized depictions of long-gone artists (all men) around the pediment, and the various other allegorical sculptures dotted about the memorial, join one of the weekly guided tours (Sun 2 & 3pm; 45min; £4.50).

▲ PETER PAN STATUE, KENSINGTON GARDENS

Royal Albert Hall

Kensington Gore ⓦ www .royalalberthall.com. The profits of the Great Exhibition were used to buy a large tract of land south of the park, and to build the vast Royal Albert Hall, a splendid iron-and-glass-domed concert hall, with an exterior of red brick, terracotta and marble that became the hallmark of South Kensington architecture. As well as hosting a variety of events throughout the year, from pop concerts to sumo wrestling, the hall is the venue for Europe's most democratic music festival, the Henry Wood Promenade Concerts or **Proms**, which take place every night from July to September. The classical concerts are top-class and standing-room tickets go for as little as £4, but the Proms are best known for the flag-waving, patriotic last night.

Kensington Palace

Kensington Gardens ⓦ www.hrp.org .uk. March–Oct daily 10am–6pm; Nov–Feb 10am–5pm. £11.50. Bought by William and Mary in 1689, the modestly proportioned Jacobean brick mansion of Kensington Palace was the chief royal residence for the next fifty years. KP, as it's fondly known in royal circles, is best known today as the place where **Princess Diana** lived from her marriage until her death in 1997. It was, in fact, the official London residence of both Charles and Di until the couple formally separated and Charles moved to St James's Palace. In the weeks following Diana's death, literally millions of flowers, mementos, poems and gifts were deposited at the gates to the south of the palace.

Diana's former apartments, where various minor royals still live, are closed to the public. Instead, guided tours take in some of the frocks worn by Diana, as well as several of the Queen's, and then the sparsely furnished state apartments. The highlights are the trompe l'oeil ceiling paintings by William Kent, particularly those in the Cupola Room, and the

▲ ROYAL ALBERT HALL FACADE

paintings in the King's Gallery by, among others, Tintoretto. En route, you also get to see the tastelessly decorated rooms in which the future Queen Victoria spent her unhappy childhood.

Diana Memorial Playground

Kensington Gardens ⓦwww .royalparks.gov.uk. Daily 10am– 7.45pm. Free. As befits a play area dedicated to the memory of the Princess of Wales, this is no ordinary playground, and gets so popular that entry numbers have to be limited in the height of summer. The centrepiece is a sailing ship sunk into sand, which kids can clamber all over; elsewhere there's paving gongs and other groovy playthings.

Cafés

The Orangery

Kensington Palace, Kensington Gardens. Daily 10am–6pm; Nov–Feb closes 5pm. Very swish café in a brilliant-white orangery,

originally built for Queen Anne as a summer dining room, and offering great cakes as well as savoury tarts.

Pubs

Grenadier

18 Wilton Row. Mon–Sat noon–11pm, Sun noon–10.30pm. Wellington's local (his horse block is still outside) and his officers' mess; the original pewter bar survives, and the Bloody Marys are special. Classy but pricey bar food.

Clubs and venues

Royal Albert Hall

Kensington Gore. ☏020/7589 8212, ⓦwww.royalalberthall.com. Main venue for the annual BBC Proms festival (ⓦwww.bbc .co.uk/proms), of classical music, and also the place for a whole range of spectacular popular shows from opera to pop concerts.

South Kensington, Knightsbridge and Chelsea

London's wealthiest district, the Royal Borough of Kensington and Chelsea is particularly well-to-do in the area south of Hyde Park. Known popularly as the "Tiara Triangle", the moneyed feel here is evident in the flash shops and swanky bars as well as the plush houses and apartments. Aside from the shops around Harrods in Knightsbridge, however, the popular tourist attractions lie in South Kensington, where three of London's top museums stand side by side.

From the Swinging Sixties and even up to the Punk era, Chelsea had a slightly bohemian pedigree; then in the 1980s, it became the spiritual home of Sloanes, the sons and daughters of the wealthy, whose most famous specimen was Princess Diana herself; these days, it's just another wealthy west London suburb.

Natural History Museum

Cromwell Rd ⓦ www.nhm.ac.uk. Mon–Sat 10am–5.50pm, Sun 11am–5.50pm. Free. With its 675-foot terracotta facade, Alfred Waterhouse's purpose-built mock-Romanesque colossus ensures the Natural History Museum's status as London's most handsome museum. The contents, though, are a bit of a mishmash, with truly imaginative exhibits peppered amongst others little changed since the building opened in 1881. This disparity is the result of a genuine conundrum – the collections are as much an important resource for serious zoologists as they are a popular attraction.

The main entrance leads to the **Life Galleries**, whose vast Central Hall is dominated by an 85ft-long plaster cast of a Diplodocus skeleton. To one side, you'll find the Dinosaur gallery, where a team of animatronic deinonychi feast on a half-dead tenontosaurus. Other child-friendly sections

▼ DARWIN CENTRE, NATURAL HISTORY MUSEUM

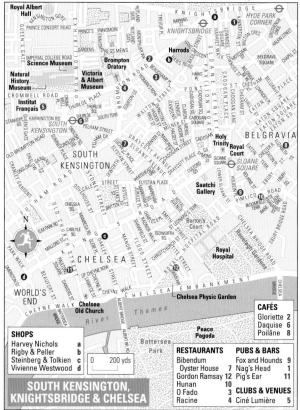

© Crown copyright

SHOPS
Harvey Nichols   a
Rigby & Peller   b
Steinberg & Tolkien   c
Vivienne Westwood   d

0   200 yds

CAFÉS
Gloriette   2
Daquise   6
Poilâne   8

RESTAURANTS
Bibendum
  Oyster House   7
Gordon Ramsay   12
Hunan   10
O Fado   3
Racine   4

PUBS & BARS
Fox and Hounds   9
Nag's Head   1
Pig's Ear   11

CLUBS & VENUES
Ciné Lumière   5

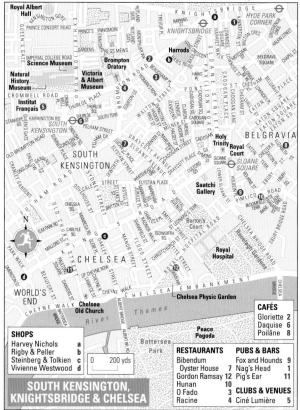

SOUTH KENSINGTON, KNIGHTSBRIDGE & CHELSEA

South Kensington, Knightsbridge and Chelsea   **PLACES**

include the Creepy-Crawlies Room, which features a live colony of leaf-cutter ants; the Mammals gallery with its life-size model of a blue whale; and the walk-through rainforest in the high-tech Ecology Gallery.

For a visually exciting romp through evolution, head for the **Earth Galleries**; popular sections include the slightly tasteless Kobe earthquake simulator, and the spectacular display of gems and crystals in the Earth's Treasury. Visitors can also sign up for a free half-hour guided tour (every 30min; book

ahead online or on ☎020/7942 6128) of the new **Darwin Centre**, which houses more of the museum's millions of zoological specimens, including a partially digested human head from a sperm whale's stomach. Tours allow visitors a closer look at the specimens, to see behind the scenes at the labs, and to talk to the museum's scientists.

Science Museum

Exhibition Rd ☎0870/870 4868, ⓦwww.sciencemuseum.org.uk. Daily 10am–6pm. Free. The Science Museum is undeniably impressive,

▲ STEPHENSON'S ROCKET, SCIENCE MUSEUM

filling seven floors with items drawn from every conceivable area of science, including space travel, telecommunications, time measurement, chemistry, computing, photography and medicine. Keen to dispel the enduring image of such museums as boring and full of dusty glass cabinets, the Science Museum has been busy updating its galleries with interactive displays, and puts on daily demonstrations to show that not all science teaching has to be deathly dry.

First off, ask at the information desk in the Power Hall for details of the day's (usually free) events and demonstrations. Most people will want to head for the four-floor **Wellcome Wing**, geared to appeal to even the most museum-phobic teenager with state-of-the-art interactive computers and an IMAX cinema (tickets £7.50). To get there, go past the info desk and through the Space gallery, with its full-size replica of the Apollo 11 landing craft, to the far side of the Making the Modern World, a display of iconic inventions from Robert Stephenson's *Rocket* steam train of 1829 to the Ford Model T, the world's first mass-produced car.

In the basement, the hands-on displays of the **Launch Pad**, aimed squarely at kids, remains as popular and enjoyable as ever, as do the Garden and Things galleries.

Victoria & Albert Museum

Cromwell Rd ⓦwww.vam.ac.uk. Daily 10am–5.45pm (Wed & last Fri of the month until 10pm). Free. In terms of sheer variety and scale, the Victoria and Albert (popularly known as the V&A) is the greatest museum of applied arts in the world. Beautifully but haphazardly displayed across a seven-mile, four-storey maze of halls and corridors, the V&A's treasures are impossible to survey in a single visit. Floor plans from the information desks can help you decide which areas to concentrate on.

The most celebrated of the V&A's exhibits are the **Raphael Cartoons**, seven vast biblical paintings that served as designs for a set of tapestries destined for the Sistine Chapel. Close by, you can view highlights from the UK's largest dress collection, and the world's biggest collection of Indian art outside India. In addition, there are galleries devoted to British, Chinese, Islamic, Japanese and Korean art, as well as costume jewellery, glassware, metalwork and photography. Wading through the huge collection of European sculpture, you

▲ WILLIAM MORRIS COLLECTION, V&A

come to the surreal **plaster casts** gallery, filled with copies of European art's greatest hits, from Michelangelo's *David* to Trajan's Column from the forum in Rome (sawn in half to make it fit). There's even a twentieth century gallery – everything from Bauhaus furniture to Swatch watches – to rival that of the Design Museum (see p.165).

As if all this were not enough, the V&A's temporary shows (for which you have to pay) are among the best in Britain, ranging over vast areas of art, craft and technology.

Brompton Oratory

Brompton Rd ⓦwww.bromptonoratory .com. London's most flamboyant Roman Catholic church, Brompton Oratory was completed in 1886 and modelled on the Gesù church in Rome. The ornate Italianate interior is filled with gilded mosaics and stuffed with sculpture, much of it genuine Italian Baroque, while the pulpit is a superb piece of Neo-Baroque from the 1930s; note the high cherub count on the tester. And true to its architecture, the church practises "smells and bells" Catholicism, with daily Mass in Latin.

Harrods

87–135 Brompton Rd ⓦwww .harrods.com. Mon–Sat 10am–7pm, Sun noon–6pm. London's most famous department store, Harrods started out as a family-run grocery shop in 1849 with a staff of two; the current 1905 terracotta building, owned by the *bête noire* of the Establishment, Mohammed Al Fayed, employs in excess of 3000 staff. Tourists flock here – it's thought to be one of the city's top-ranking tourist attractions – though if you can do without the Harrods carrier bag, you can buy most of what the shop stocks more cheaply elsewhere.

The store does, however, have a few sections that are architectural sights in their own right: on the ground floor, the **Food Hall**, with its exquisite Arts and Crafts tiling, and the pseudo-hieroglyphs and sphinxes of the Egyptian Hall are particularly striking, while the Egyptian Escalators whisk you to the first floor "luxury washrooms", where you can splash on free perfume.

At the base of the escalators is the Diana and Dodi fountain shrine. Here, to the strains of Mahler (and the like), you can contemplate photos of the ill-fated couple, and, preserved in a glass pyramid, a dirty wine-glass used on their last evening along with the engagement ring Dodi allegedly bought for Di the previous day.

Note that Harrods has a draconian dress code: no shorts or vest T-shirts, and backpacks must be carried in the hand.

Holy Trinity Church

Sloane Square. ⓦ www.holy trinitysloanestreet.org. Mon–Sat 8.30am–5.30pm, Sun 8.30am–1.30pm. Free. An architectural masterpiece created in 1890, Holy Trinity is probably the finest Arts and Crafts church in London. The east window is the most glorious of the furnishings, a vast, 48-panel extravaganza designed by Edward Burne-Jones, and the largest ever made by Morris & Co. Holy Trinity is very High Church, filled with the smell of incense and statues of Mary, and even offering confession.

King's Road

Chelsea's main artery, King's Road achieved household fame as the unofficial catwalk of the Swinging Sixties and of the hippie and punk eras. The "Saturday Parade" of fashion victims is not what it used to be, but posey cafés, boutiques (and antiques) are still what King's Road is all about. And the traditional "Chelsea Cruise", when every flash Harry in town parades his customized motor, still takes place at 8.30pm on the last Saturday of the month, though nowadays on the Battersea (south) side of the Chelsea Bridge.

Saatchi Gallery

King's Rd. ⓦ www.saatchi-gallery .co.uk. As of early 2007, the Saatchi Gallery of contemporary art will occupy the Neoclassical former Duke of York's barracks, former headquarters of the Territorial Army. Charles Saatchi, the collector behind the gallery, was the man whose clever advertising campaigns kept the Conservative government in power in the 1980s. Saatchi's extravagant wallet also helped promote the Young British Artists of the 1980s and 1990s, as he snapped up headline-grabbing works such as Damien Hirst's pickled shark and Tracey Emin's soiled and crumpled bed. The gallery puts on changing exhibitions drawn primarily from Saatchi's vast collection.

Chelsea Physic Garden

Royal Hospital Rd ⓦ www .chelseaphysicgarden.co.uk. April–Oct Wed noon–5pm, Sun 2–6pm. £6.50. Hidden from the road by a high wall, Chelsea Physic Garden is a charming little inner-city escape. Founded in 1673, it's the second oldest botanic garden in the country and remains an old-fashioned place, with terse Latinate labels and strictly regimented beds. Unfortunately, it's a rather small garden, and a little too close to Chelsea Embankment to be a peaceful oasis. It's really of most interest to very keen botanists – to learn more, take the free guided walk at 1.30pm.

Shops

Harvey Nichols

109–125 Knightsbridge ☎ 020/7235 5000, ⓦ www.harveynichols .co.uk. Mon–Sat 10am–8pm, Sun noon–6pm. Absolutely fabulous, darling, with all the latest designer collections on the first floor, where even the shop assistants look like models. The gorgeous cosmetics department is frequented by the famous and aspiring, while the fifth-floor food hall offers frivolous goodies at high prices.

Rigby & Peller

2 Hans Rd ☎020/7589 9293, ⓦwww .rigbyandpeller.com. Mon–Sat 9.30am–6pm (Wed until 7pm). Corsetières to HM the Queen, this old-fashioned store stocks a wide range of lingerie and swimwear for all shapes and sizes – take a ticket and wait for an assistant for a personal fitting.

Steinberg & Tolkien

193 King's Rd ☎020/7376 3660. Mon–Sat 11am–7pm, Sun noon–6pm. Claims to have London's largest collection of vintage and retro gear and accessories; clothing is displayed by designer, which says a lot for the quality of the stock.

Vivienne Westwood

430 King's Rd ☎020/7352 6551, ⓦwww.viviennewestwood.com. Mon–Sat 10am–6pm. Original outlet of the queen of punk fashion and most famous address on the King's Road. Her trademark style is madly eccentric English, but there's less flamboyant stuff, too.

Cafés

Daquise

20 Thurloe St. Daily 11.30am–11pm. This old-fashioned Polish café right by the tube is something of a South Ken institution, serving Polish home cooking or simple coffee, tea and cakes depending on the time of day.

Gloriette

128 Brompton Rd. Mon–Fri 7am–8pm, Sat 8am–8pm, Sun 9am–6pm. Long-established Viennese café serving coffee and outrageously tempting cakes as well as sandwiches, Wiener Schnitzel, pasta dishes, goulash, and fish and chips.

Poilâne

46 Elizabeth St. Mon–Fri 7.30am–7.30pm, Sat 7.30am–6pm. Tiny London outlet of the legendary French boulangerie, which produces the city's best Parisian bread, croissants and sourdough.

Restaurants

Bibendum Oyster House

Michelin House, 81 Fulham Rd ☎020/7589 1480, ⓦwww.bibendum .co.uk. Mon–Sat noon–10.30pm, Sun noon–10pm. A glorious tiled affair built in 1911, this former garage is the best place to eat shellfish in London. Grab some oysters at the bar or if you're really hungry, try the "Plateau de Fruits de Mer" for around £30, which has crab, clams, langoustine, oysters, prawns, shrimps, whelks and winkles.

Gordon Ramsay

68–69 Royal Hospital Rd ☎020/7352 4441, ⓦwww.gordonramsay.com. Mon–Fri noon–2pm & 6.45–11pm. Gordon Ramsay's Michelin-starred Chelsea restaurant is a class act through and through, though you have to book ahead to eat here. Set lunches start at £40; fixed-price à la carte menus from £70.

Hunan

51 Pimlico Rd ☎020/7730 5712. Mon–Sat noon–2.30pm & 6–11.30pm. Probably England's only restaurant serving Hunan food, a

relative of Sichuan cuisine. Most people opt for the "leave-it-to-us feast" for around £30, which lets the chef, Mr Peng, show what he can do.

O Fado

45–50 Beauchamp Place ☎ 020/7589 3002. Daily noon–3pm & 7pm–1am. This long-established Portuguese restaurant can get rowdy, what with the live *fado* ballads (Tues–Fri) and the family parties, but that's half the enjoyment. Book in advance. Mains £8–15.

Racine

239 Brompton Rd ☎ 020/7584 4477. Mon–Fri noon–3pm & 6–10.30pm, Sat noon–3.30pm & 6.30–10pm, Sun noon–3.30pm & 6–10pm. The food here is French – not just any old French, but familiar, delicious, nostalgic dishes from the glory days of French cooking, with friendly service. Booking is imperative. Mains £10–20.

Pubs

Fox and Hounds

27 Passmore St. Mon–Sat 11am–11pm, Sun noon–10.30pm. This Young's pub provides a perfect winter retreat. With an open fire, gleaming ranks of faux books and a flagstone floor, as well as plenty of hunting memorabilia, it feels as if you've stumbled into a country squire's manor.

Nag's Head

53 Kinnerton St. Mon–Sat 11am–11pm, Sun noon–10.30pm. A convivial, quirky and down-to-earth little pub in a posh cobbled mews, with dark wood-panelling, nineteenth-century china handpumps and old prints on a hunting, fishing and military theme. The unusual sunken backroom has a flagstone floor and fires in winter.

Pig's Ear

35 Old Church St. Mon–Sat noon–11pm, Sun noon–10.30pm. Sympathetically converted and stylish place. Enjoy a leisurely boardgame and a pint of Pig's Ear in the panelled downstairs bar, where classy pub grub is served, or head upstairs to the posh dining room.

Clubs and venues

Ciné Lumière

17 Queensberry Place. ⓦ www.institut-francais.org.uk. Predominantly, but by no means exclusively, French films, both old and new (sometimes with subtitles), put on by the Institut Français.

Royal Court

Sloane Square ☎ 020/7565 5000, ⓦ www.royalcourttheatre.com. Best place in London to catch radical new writing.

▼ BIBENDUM OYSTER HOUSE

PLACES South Kensington, Knightsbridge and Chelsea

High Street Kensington to Notting Hill

Kensington High Street – better known as High Street Ken – is a busy shopping district with all the major UK chains represented. Cultural diversion is at hand, though, in Holland Park and the exotically decorated Leighton House, tucked away in the peaceful surrounding streets of white stucco mansions. Notting Hill and adjoining Bayswater, to the north, were slum areas for many years, with a reputation as dens of vice and crime, but gentrification has changed them immeasurably over the last fifty years. Now the area is rammed solid with trendy – but wealthy – media folk, yet retains a strong Moroccan and Portuguese presence, as well as vestiges of the African-Caribbean community who initiated – and still run – Carnival, the city's (and Europe's) largest August Bank Holiday street party.

Leighton House

12 Holland Park Rd ⓦwww.rbkc .gov.uk/leightonhousemuseum. Daily except Tues 11am–5.30pm. £3. Leighton House was built by the architect George Aitchison for Frederic Leighton, President of the Royal Academy and the only artist ever to be made a peer (albeit on his deathbed). "It will be opulence, it will be sincerity", the artist opined before construction commenced in the 1860s. The big attraction is its domed Arab Hall. Based on the banqueting hall of a Moorish palace in Palermo, it has a central black marble fountain, and is decorated with Saracen tiles, gilded mosaics and latticework drawn from all over the Islamic world. The other rooms are less spectacular but, in compensation, are hung with excellent paintings by Lord Leighton and his Pre-Raphaelite friends Edward Burne-Jones, Lawrence Alma-Tadema and John Everett Millais.

Holland Park

The leafy former grounds of the Jacobean Holland House, now replete with woodland

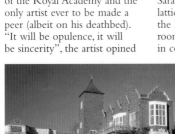

▲ HOLLAND HOUSE, HOLLAND PARK

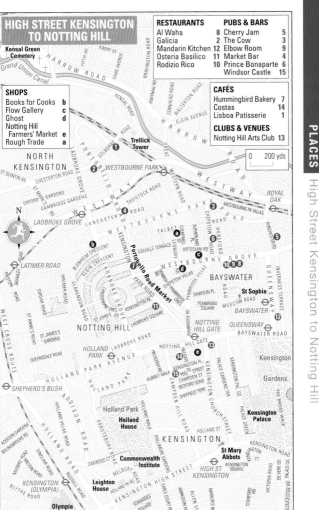

HIGH STREET KENSINGTON TO NOTTING HILL

SHOPS
Books for Cooks **b**
Flow Gallery **c**
Ghost **d**
Notting Hill
  Farmers' Market **e**
Rough Trade **a**

RESTAURANTS
Al Waha 8
Galicia 2
Mandarin Kitchen 12
Osteria Basilico 11
Rodizio Rico 10

PUBS & BARS
Cherry Jam 5
The Cow 3
Elbow Room 9
Market Bar 4
Prince Bonaparte 6
Windsor Castle 15

CAFÉS
Hummingbird Bakery 7
Costas 14
Lisboa Patisserie 1

CLUBS & VENUES
Notting Hill Arts Club 13

0   200 yds

© Crown copyright

and playing fields, Holland Park also boasts several formal areas, such as the Japanese-style Kyoto Garden laid out around the house (only the east wing of which survived World War II). Peppered with modern sculptures, the gardens drift down in terraces to the arcades, Garden Ballroom and Ice House, which have been converted into a café, a restaurant and a contemporary, small-scale art gallery.

Portobello Road Market

Main market Mon–Wed, Fri & Sat 8am–6.30pm, Thurs 8am–1pm;

▲ TERRACE PORTICOS, KENSINGTON

antiques Sat 6am–4pm. Situated in one of the wealthiest, celebrity-saturated parts of town, Portobello Road Market is probably London's trendiest, yet it's always a great spot for a browse and a bargain. Things kick off, at the intersection with Chepstow Villas, with junky antique stalls and classier, pricier antique shops. After a brief switch to fruit and veg around the Electric Cinema, the market gets a lot more fun and funky at Portobello Green under the Westway flyover, where the emphasis switches to retro clothes and jewellery, odd trinkets, records and books. The merchandise gets progressively cheaper as the market swings east into Golborne Road, which has its own constellation of bric-a-brac stalls.

Kensal Green Cemetery

Harrow Rd ☎ 020/8960 1030 ⓦ www .kensalgreen.co.uk. Opened in 1833, Kensal Green Cemetery was the first of the city's commercial graveyards, and immediately proved itself to be extremely popular – a whole host of luminaries are buried here under some of the most extravagant Gothic tombs in the whole of London. Hemmed in by railway, gasworks and canal, the cemetery is vast, so it makes a lot of sense to join one of the **guided tours** that take place every Sunday at 2pm (£5), and include a visit to the catacombs (bring a torch) on the first and third Sunday of the month. Graves of the more famous incumbents – Thackeray, Trollope, Siemens and the Brunels – are less interesting architecturally than those arranged on either side of the Centre Avenue, which leads from the easternmost entrance on Harrow Road. Worth looking out for are Major-General Casement's bier, held up by four grim-looking turbaned Indians; circus manager Andrew Ducrow's conglomeration of beehive, sphinx and angels; and artist William Mulready's neo-Renaissance extravaganza.

Shops

Books for Cooks

4 Blenheim Crescent ☎ 020/7221 1992, ⓦ www.booksforcooks.com. Tues–Sat 10am–6pm. Literature on anything and everything to do with food can be found on the shelves of this wonderful new and secondhand bookshop, which also has a tiny café offering cookery demonstrations, coffee for browsers and lunch (ring ahead to book).

Flow Gallery

1–5 Needham St ☎020/7243 0782, ⓦwww.flowgallery.co.uk. Mon–Sat 11am–6pm. Showing the work of mainly British artists, this enterprise excels in well-crafted goods, such as jewellery, fabrics and sculpture.

Ghost

36 Ledbury Rd ☎020/7229 1057, ⓦwww.ghost.co.uk. Mon–Fri 10.30am–6.30pm, Sat 10am–6pm. Romantic, floaty and hugely popular modern Victoriana in pastel shades. If you ever regretted chucking out your mum's dirndl skirt, this is where to replace it.

Notting Hill Farmers' Market

Kensington Palace car park. Sat 9am–1pm. Fresh fruit, veg, pastries and cakes brought in from farms around London.

Rough Trade

130 Talbot Rd ☎020/7229 8541, ⓦwww.roughtrade .com. Mon–Sat 10am–6.30pm, Sun 1–5pm. Indie music specialist with knowledgeable, friendly staff and a dizzying array of wares, from electronica to hardcore and beyond.

Cafés

Hummingbird Bakery

133 Portobello Rd. ⓦwww .hummingbirdbakery.com. Tues–Sat 10am–5.30pm, Sun 11am–5pm. A cute and kitsch place selling quality American homebaking, from prettily garish cupcakes to sumptuous Brooklyn Blackout Cake. Tables outside make for great people-watching.

Costas Fish Restaurant

18 Hillgate St. Tues–Sat noon–2.30pm & 5.30–10.30pm. One of the best fish-and-chips experiences in London can be had at this old-fashioned Greek-Cypriot caff.

Lisboa Patisserie

57 Golborne Rd. Daily 8am–8pm. Authentic Portuguese *pastelaria*, with the best *pasteis de nata* (custard tarts) this side of Lisbon – also coffee, cakes and a friendly atmosphere.

Restaurants

Al Waha

75 Westbourne Grove ☎020/7229 0806. Daily noon–midnight. Arguably London's best Lebanese

▼ N.H. FARMERS' MARKET

restaurant; meze-obsessed (£5 and under), but also painstaking in its preparation of the main-course dishes (£10–20).

Galicia

323 Portobello Rd ☎020/8969 3539. Tues–Sat noon–3pm & 7–11.30pm, Sun noon–3pm & 7–10.30pm. *Galicia* is a pleasant Spanish restaurant without pretensions. The tapas at the bar are straightforward and good, with a regular Spanish clientele. Most tapas are under £6. Mains £7–12.

Mandarin Kitchen

14–16 Queensway ☎020/7727 9012. Daily noon–11.30pm. Smart Chinese fish restaurant that purports to sell more lobsters than any other restaurant in Britain. Mains £7–25.

Osteria Basilico

29 Kensington Park Rd ☎020/7727 9372. Mon–Fri 12.30–3pm & 6.30–11pm, Sat 12.30–4pm & 6.30–11pm, Sun 12.30–3.30pm & 6.30–10.30pm. A pretty, traditional Italian restaurant that's a good place for the full Italian monty – antipasto, home-made pasta and then a fish or meat dish – or just for a pizza. Mains £7–17.

Rodizio Rico

111 Westbourne Grove ☎020/7792 4035. Mon–Fri 6pm–midnight, Sat noon–4pm & 6pm–midnight, Sun 12.30–11pm. Eat as much as you like for around £18 a head at this Brazilian *churrascaria*. Carvers come round and lop off chunks of freshly grilled smoky meats from whichever skewers they are holding, while you prime your plate from the salad bar and hot buffet.

Pubs and bars

Cherry Jam

52 Porchester Rd ⓦwww.cherryjam .net. Mon–Sat 6pm–2am, Sun 4pm–midnight. Co-owned by Ben Watt (house DJ and half of pop group Everything But The Girl), this smart, intimate basement place mixes a decadent cocktail bar with top-end West London DJs from the broken-beat and deep-house scenes.

The Cow

89 Westbourne Park Rd. Mon–Sat noon–11pm, Sun noon–10.30pm. Owned by Tom Conran, son of gastro-magnate Terence, this pub pulls in the beautiful W11 types,

▼ THE COW, WESTBOURNE PARK ROAD

thanks to its spectacular food, which includes a daily supply of fresh oysters.

Elbow Room

103 Westbourne Grove ⓦwww .elbowroom.co.uk. Mon–Sat noon– 11pm, Sun noon–10.30pm. With its designer decor, purple-felt American pool tables, and better-than-average grilled fast-food and beer, *Elbow Room* redefined the pool pub (and then opened several branches across the city).

Market Bar

240a Portobello Rd. Mon–Wed 11am– 11pm, Thurs–Sat 11am–midnight, Sun 11am–10.30pm. Relaxed boho pub with gilded mirrors and weird *objets* – all very Notting Hill.

Prince Bonaparte

80 Chepstow Rd. Mon–Sat noon–11pm, Sun noon–10.30pm. Very popular, trendy, minimalist pub, with acres of space for sitting and supping while enjoying the bar snacks or the excellent Brit or Med food in the restaurant area.

Windsor Castle

114 Campden Hill Rd. Mon–Sat 1am–11pm, Sun noon–10.30pm. Very pretty, very popular traditional English pub with a great courtyard, that would like to think it's out in the country rather than tucked away in the backstreets.

Clubs and venues

Notting Hill Arts Club

21 Notting Hill Gate ⓦwww .nottinghillartsclub.com. Mon–Sat 6pm–2am, Sun 6pm–1am. Free before 8pm then £5–8. Basement club that's popular for everything from Latin-inspired funk, jazz and disco through to soul, house and garage, and famed for its Sunday late afternoon into evening deep-house session and "concept visuals".

PLACES High Street Kensington to Notting Hill

Regent's Park and Camden

Framed by dazzling Nash-designed, magnolia-stuc-coed terraces, and home to London Zoo, Regent's Park is a very civilized and well-maintained spot. Nearby Camden, by contrast, has a scruffy feel to it, despite its many well-to-do residential streets. This is partly due to the chaos and fall-out from the area's perennially popular weekend market, centred around Camden Lock on the Regent's Canal. A warren of stalls with an alternative past still manifest in its quirky wares, street fashion, books, records and ethnic goods, the market remains one of the city's biggest off-beat attractions.

Regent's Park

Ⓦwww.royalparks.org.uk. According to John Nash's 1811 masterplan, drawn up for the Prince Regent (later George IV), Regent's Park was to be girded by a continuous belt of terraces, and

▼ CENTRAL LONDON MOSQUE

sprinkled with a total of 56 villas, including a magnificent pleasure palace for the Prince himself. The plan was never fully realized, but enough was built to create something of the idealized garden city that Nash and the Prince Regent envisaged. Pristine, mostly Neoclassical terraces form a near-unbroken horseshoe around the Outer Circle, which marks the park's perimeter along with a handful of handsome villas. Prominent on the skyline is the shiny copper dome and minaret of the **London Central Mosque** at 146 Park Road (Ⓦwww.iccuk .org), an entirely appropriate addition to the park given the Prince Regent's taste for the Orient. Non-Muslim visitors are welcome to look in at the information centre, and glimpse inside the hall of worship, which is packed out with a diversity of communities for the lunchtime Friday prayers.

By far the prettiest section of the park is Queen Mary's Gardens, which lie within the central Inner Circle. As well as a

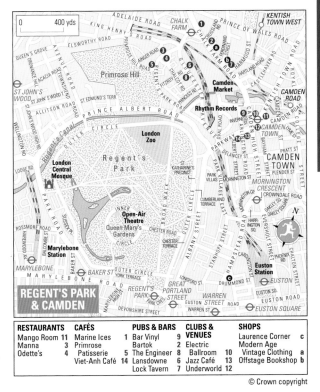

RESTAURANTS		CAFÉS		PUBS & BARS		CLUBS & VENUES		SHOPS	
Mango Room	11	Marine Ices	1	Bar Vinyl	9			Laurence Corner	c
Manna	3	Primrose		Bartok	2	Electric		Modern Age	
Odette's	4	Patisserie		The Engineer	8	Ballroom	10	Vintage Clothing	a
		Viet-Anh Café	14	Lansdowne	6	Jazz Café	13	Offstage Bookshop	b
				Lock Tavern	7	Underworld	12		

pond replete with exotic ducks, and a handsomely landscaped giant rockery, a large slice of the gardens is taken up with a glorious rose garden, featuring some 400 varieties surrounded by a ring of ramblers. Along the eastern edge of the park, the tree-lined Broad Walk forms a stately approach (much appreciated by rollerbladers) to the park's most popular attraction, London Zoo (see p.188).

Regent's Canal

Completed in 1820, Regent's Canal was constructed as part of a direct link from Birmingham to the newly built London Docks; its seemingly random meandering, from Paddington to the River Thames at Limehouse, traced the limit of London's northernmost suburbs at the time. Quickly superseded by the railway, the canal never really paid its way as its investors had hoped. By some miracle, however, it escaped being covered over or turned into a rail or road route, and its nine miles, 42 bridges, twelve locks and two tunnels stand as a reminder of London's industrial heyday, and provide an invaluable traffic-free towpath that's great for walking or cycling. The lockless run between **Little Venice**

▲ REGENT'S CANAL, LITTLE VENICE

and Camden Town is the most attractive stretch, tunnelling through to Lisson Grove, skirting Regent's Park, slicing London Zoo in two, and passing straight through the heart of Camden Market. It's also the one section that's served year-round by narrowboats offering pleasure cruises (see box below), which are without doubt the best way to take in the canal.

London Zoo

Outer Circle, Regent's Park ⊛ www. londonzoo.co.uk. Daily: March–Oct 10am–5.30pm; Nov–Feb 10am–4pm.

£14.50. Founded in 1826 with the remnants of the royal menagerie, the zoo has had to change with the times, and now bills itself as an eco-conscious place whose prime purpose is to save species under threat of extinction. It's still not the most uplifting spot for animal-lovers, though the enclosures are as humane as any inner-city zoo could make them, and kids usually love the place. The invertebrate house, now known as BUGS, and the new monkey walk-through forest are both guaranteed winners. Smaller ones are particularly taken with the children's enclosure, where they can handle the animals, and the regular "Animals in Action" live shows where the keepers bring some of their charges out into the open – owls swoop over the audience's heads and lemurs climb up the furniture, but there's no demeaning "performing" involved. The zoo boasts some striking architectural features, too, most notably the modernist, spiral-ramped 1930s concrete penguin pool.

Regent's Canal by boat

Three companies run boat services on the Regent's Canal between Camden and Little Venice, passing through the Maida Hill tunnel and stopping off at London Zoo on the way. The narrowboat Jenny Wren (☎020/7485 4433) starts off at Camden goes through a canal lock (the only company to do so) and heads for Little Venice, while Jason's narrowboats (☎020/7286 3428, ⊛www.jasons.co.uk) start off at Little Venice; the London Waterbus Company (☎020/7482 2660, ⊛www.london-waterbus.com) sets off from both places. Whichever you choose, you can board at either end; tickets cost around £5–6 one-way (and only a little more return) and journey is 50 minutes one-way.

Camden Market

Ⓦ www.camdenlock.net. Camden. Most stalls open daily 9.30am–5.30pm.

For all its tourist popularity, Camden Market (in actual fact, a conglomeration of markets) remains a genuinely offbeat place. The tiny crafts market which began in the cobbled courtyard by the lock has since mushroomed out of all proportion, with everyone trying to grab a piece of the action on both sides of Camden High Street and Chalk Farm Road. More than 150,000 shoppers turn up here each weekend, and some stalls now stay open all week long, alongside a crop of shops, cafés and bistros. The overabundance of cheap leather, hippy chic, naff jewellery and out-and-out kitsch is compensated for by the sheer variety of what's on offer: everything from bootleg tapes to furniture and mountain bikes, alongside a mass of clubwear and street-fashion stalls, and takeaway food outlets ready to fuel hungry shoppers with wok-fried noodles, bowls of paella, burgers, kebabs, cakes and smoothies.

Shops

Laurence Corner

62–64 Hampstead Rd ☎020/7813 1010. Mon–Sat 9.30am–6pm. London's oldest and most eccentric army surplus shop, which also stocks catering uniforms, thermals, heavy-duty waterproofs and many kinds of hats.

Modern Age Vintage Clothing

65 Chalk Farm Rd ☎020/7482 3787 Ⓦ www.modern-age.co.uk. Daily 10.30–6pm. Splendid outlet (mostly menswear) for lovers of 1940s and 1950s American-style gear. The best bargains are on the rails outside: inside, the very lovely cashmere and leather coats are a bit pricier.

Offstage Theatre and Cinema Bookshop

37 Chalk Farm Rd ☎020/7485 4996. Mon–Fri 9.30am–5pm, Sat & Sun noon–6pm. Excellent, well-stocked shop covering all aspects of stage and screen craft, plus theory, criticism, scripts and biographies.

Cafés

Marine Ices

8 Haverstock Hill. Mon–Sat 10.30am–11pm, Sun 11am–10pm. Splendid and justly famous old-fashioned

▼ CHESTER TERRACE ARCHES, REGENT'S PARK

Italian ice-cream parlour; pizza and pasta are served in the adjacent restaurant.

Primrose Patisserie

136 Regent's Park Rd. Daily 8.15am–6.30pm. Very popular pastel-pink and sky-blue patisserie in fashionable Primrose Hill, offering superb East European cakes and pastries.

Viet-Anh Cafe

41 Parkway ☎020/7284 4082. Daily noon–4pm & 5.30–11pm. Authentic, bright, cheerful café run by a friendly and welcoming young Vietnamese couple. Try the prawn sugar-cane sticks, the slurpy noodle soups or the hot lemongrass chicken.

Restaurants

Mango Room

10 Kentish Town Rd ☎020/7482 5065. ⓦwww.mangoroom.co.uk. Tues–Sat noon–3pm & 6pm–midnight, Sun noon–11pm. An engaging, laid-back, Camden-cool Caribbean place whose cooking is consistent and whose presentation is first class. Mains such as Creole snapper with mango from £10–13.

Manna

4 Erskine Rd ☎020/7722 8028, ⓦwww.manna-veg.com. Mon–Fri 6.30–10.30pm, Sat & Sun 12.30–3pm. Old-fashioned, casual vegetarian restaurant with 1970s decor, serving large portions of very good food. Mains £10–13.

Odette's

130 Regent's Park Rd ☎020/7586 5486. Mon–Fri 12.30–2.30pm & 7–11pm, Sat 7–11pm, Sun 12.30–2.45pm. Charming, picturesque local restaurant idyllically set in pretty Primrose Hill, serving well-judged Modern British food accompanied by warm and delicious olive and walnut bread. Set lunches £17; mains £15–24.

▼ CAMDEN MARKET

Pubs and bars

Bar Vinyl

6 Inverness St. Mon–Sat 11am–11pm, Sun noon–10.30pm. Small, funky glass-bricked place with a record shop downstairs (open noon–8pm) and DJs providing a break-beat, funky house or electro vibe.

Bartok

78–79 Chalk Farm Rd. Mon–Thurs 5pm–1am, Fri 5pm–2am, Sat noon–2am, Sun noon–midnight. Stylish bar where punters can sink into a sofa and listen to a varied programme of classical music.

The Engineer

65 Gloucester Ave. Mon–Sat 9am–11pm, Sun 9am–10.30pm. Smart, popular Victorian pub and restaurant with excellent though pricey food – get here early to eat in the pub, or book a table in the restaurant or lovely garden out back.

Lansdowne

90 Gloucester Ave. Mon–Sat noon–11pm, Sun noon–10.30pm. Big, bare-boards minimalist pub with comfy sofas, in elegant Primrose Hill. Pricey, tasty food that's a far cry from most pub grub.

Lock Tavern

35 Chalk Farm Rd. Mon–Sat 11am–11pm, Sun 11am–10.30pm. Rambling refurbished pub with large battered wooden tables, comfy sofas, a leafy upstairs terrace and beer garden down below, as well as posh pub grub and DJs playing anything from punk funk and electro to rock. Effortlessly cool.

Clubs and venues

Electric Ballroom

184 Camden High St ⓦwww .electricballroom.co.uk. Fri & Sat 10.30pm–3am, plus other nights. £7–10. Long-running and large club that hosts rock and metal (Fri) and disco (Sat) nights, as well as being an occasional venue for live music.

Jazz Café

5 Parkway ⓦwww.meanfiddler.com. Daily 7pm–2am. Entry from £10. Excellent, chilled-out venue with an adventurous booking policy exploring Latin, rap, funk, hip-hop and musical fusions. Restaurant upstairs with a few prime tables overlooking the stage (book ahead if you want one).

Open Air Theatre

Regent's Park, Inner Circle ☎020/7486 2431, ⓦwww.openairtheatre.org. Summer programme of Shakespeare, musicals, plays and concerts.

Underworld

174 Camden High St ⓦwww .theunderworldcamden.co.uk. Doors 11pm–late. Popular grungy venue under the *World's End* pub, that's a great place to check out metal, hard core, ska punk and heavy rock bands.

Hampstead and Highgate

The high points of North London, both geographically and aesthetically, the elegant, largely eighteenth-century developments of Hampstead and Highgate have managed to cling on to their village origins. Of the two, Highgate is slightly sleepier and more aloof, Hampstead busier and buzzier, with high-profile intelligentsia and discerning pop stars among its residents. Both benefit from direct access to one of London's wildest patches of greenery, Hampstead Heath, where you can enjoy stupendous views over London, kite-flying and nude bathing, as well as outdoor concerts and high art in and around the Neoclassical country mansion of Kenwood House.

Fenton House

Windmill Hill ☎020/7435 3471, ⓦwww.nationaltrust.org.uk. March Sat & Sun 2–5pm; April–Oct Wed–Fri 2–5pm, Sat & Sun 11am–5pm. £4.90. Set grandly behind wrought-iron gates, Fenton House is decorated in impeccable eighteenth-century taste, and

▲ FENTON HOUSE

houses a collection of European and Oriental ceramics as well as a superb assortment of early musical instruments, bequeathed by the building's last private owner, Lady Binning. Among the spinets, virginals and clavichords, look out especially for the early English grand piano, an Unverdorben lute from 1580 (one of only three in the world) and, on the ground floor, a harpsichord from 1612, on which Handel is thought to have played. Experienced keyboard players are sometimes let loose on the instruments during the day. There's very little information in the house, so it's worth buying the briefer of the guides on sale at the entrance, and hiring a tape of music played on the above instruments (£1), to listen to while you walk round. You should also take a stroll in the beautiful formal garden (garden only; £2), which features some top-class herbaceous borders.

Freud Museum

20 Maresfield Gardens
℡ 020/7435 2002, ⊕ www.
freud.org.uk. Wed–Sun
noon–5pm. £5. Hidden
away in the leafy streets
of south Hampstead, the
Freud Museum is one
of the most poignant
of London's museums.
Having lived in Vienna
for his entire adult life,
Sigmund Freud was
forced to flee the Nazis,
and arrived in London
during the summer of
1938 as a semi-invalid
(he died within a year).
The ground-floor study
and library look exactly
as they did when Freud
lived here – the collection
of erotic antiquities and the
famous couch, sumptuously
draped in Persian carpets, were
all brought here from Vienna.
Upstairs, home movies of
family life in Vienna are shown
continually, and a small room is
dedicated to his daughter, Anna,
herself an influential child
analyst, who lived in the house
until her death in 1982.

▲ HAMPSTEAD HEATH

is that the rooms are packed
with **works of art by** the likes
of Max Ernst, Duchamp, Henry
Moore and Man Ray.

Before 3pm, visits are by
hour-long guided tour only
(noon, 1 & 2pm), for which
you must book in advance; after
3pm, the public has unguided,
unrestricted access. Incidentally,
James Bond's adversary is
indeed named after Ernö – Ian
Fleming lived close by and had
a deep personal dislike of both
Goldfinger and his modernist
abode.

2 Willow Road

℡ 020/7435 6166, ⊕ www
.nationaltrust.org.uk. March & Nov
Sat noon–5pm; April–Oct Thurs–Sat
noon–5pm. £4.70. An unassuming
red-brick terraced house
built in the 1930s by the
Hungarian-born architect Ernö
Goldfinger, 2 Willow Road
gives a fascinating insight into
the modernist mindset. This
was a state-of-the-art pad when
Goldfinger moved in, and as
he changed little during the
following sixty years, what you
see today is a 1930s avant-garde
dwelling preserved in aspic, a
house at once both modern and
old-fashioned. An added bonus

Keats House

Keats Grove ⊕ www.keatshouse.org.
uk. Tues–Sun noon–5pm. £3.50. An
elegant, whitewashed Regency
double villa, Keats House is a
shrine to Hampstead's most
lustrous figure. Inspired by the
tranquillity of the area and by
his passion for girl-next-door
Fanny Brawne (whose house is
also part of the museum), Keats
wrote some of his most famous
works here before leaving
for Rome, where he died of
consumption in 1821 aged just

Hampstead Garden Suburb

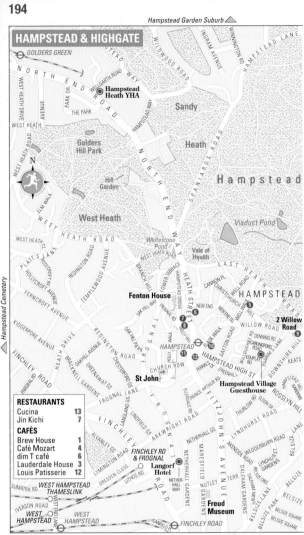

HAMPSTEAD & HIGHGATE

GOLDERS GREEN

Hampstead Heath YHA

Sandy

Golders Hill Park

Hill Garden

Heath

Hampstead

West Heath

Viaduct Pond

Whitestone Pond

Vale of Health

Fenton House

HAMPSTEAD

New End

2 Willow Road

Hampstead

St John

Hampstead Village Guesthouse

RESTAURANTS

| Cucina | 13 |
| Jin Kichi | 7 |

CAFÉS

Brew House	1
Café Mozart	4
dim T café	6
Lauderdale House	3
Louis Patisserie	12

FINCHLEY RD & FROGNAL

Langorf Hotel

WEST HAMPSTEAD THAMESLINK

WEST HAMPSTEAD

WEST HAMPSTEAD

Freud Museum

FINCHLEY ROAD

Swiss Cottage

25. The neat, rather staid interior contains books and letters, Fanny's engagement ring and the four-poster bed in which the poet first coughed up blood, confiding to his companion, Charles Brown, "that drop of blood is my death warrant".

Hampstead Heath

North London's "green lung" Hampstead Heath is the city's most enjoyable public park, and though little of its original heathland remains, there's still a wonderful variety of bucolic scenery in its 800 acres. At

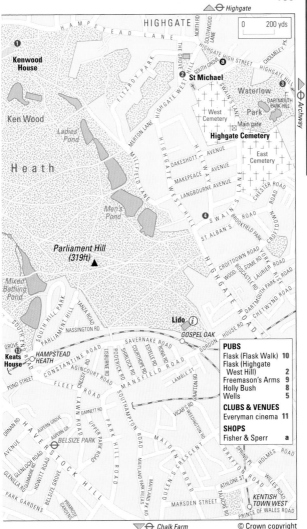

△ ⊖ Highgate

HIGHGATE

0   200 yds

H A M P S T E A D   L A N E

❶ Kenwood House

Ken Wood

Ladies' Pond

H e a t h

Men's Pond

Parliament Hill (319ft) ▲

Mixed Bathing Pond

Keats House

❷ St Michael

Waterlow Park

West Cemetery

Highgate Cemetery

East Cemetery

❸

⊖ Archway

Lido (i)

GOSPEL OAK

HAMPSTEAD HEATH

△ ⊖ Chalk Farm

KENTISH TOWN WEST

© Crown copyright

PLACES Hampstead and Highgate

PUBS

Flask (Flask Walk)	10
Flask (Highgate West Hill)	2
Freemason's Arms	9
Holly Bush	8
Wells	5

CLUBS & VENUES

Everyman cinema	11

SHOPS

Fisher & Sperr	a

the park's southern end are the rolling green pastures of **Parliament Hill**, north London's premier spot for kite-flying. On either side are numerous ponds, three of which – one for men, one for women and one mixed – you can swim in for free (daily 7am–9pm or dusk). The thickest woodland is to be found in the West Heath, beyond Whitestone Pond, also the site of the most formal section, **Hill Garden**, a secretive and romantic little gem with eccentric balustraded terraces and a ruined pergola. Beyond lies **Golders Hill Park**, where you can gaze at pygmy goats and fallow deer, and inspect the impeccably maintained aviaries, home to flamingos, cranes and other exotic birds.

Kenwood House

Hampstead Heath ⓦwww.english-heritage.org.uk. Daily: April–Oct 11am–5pm; Nov–March 11am–4pm. Free. The Heath's most celebrated sight is the whitewashed Neoclassical mansion Kenwood House, set in its own magnificently landscaped grounds at the high point of the park. The house is home to the **Iveagh Bequest**, a superlative collection of seventeenth- and eighteenth-century art, including a handful of real masterpieces by Vermeer, Rembrandt, Boucher, Gainsborough and Reynolds. Of the period interiors, the most spectacular is Robert Adam's sky-blue and gold library, its book-filled apses separated from the central entertaining area by paired columns. Upstairs, you can also view the **Suffolk Collection**, whose highlights include William Larkin's full-length portraits of a Jacobean wedding party.

To the south of the house, a grassy amphitheatre slopes down to a lake, where outdoor classical concerts are held on summer evenings (more info on ☎020/7973 3427, or visit ⓦwww.picnicconcerts.com).

Highgate Cemetery

Swain's Lane ⓦwww.highgate-cemetery.org. Receiving far more visitors than Highgate itself, Highgate Cemetery is London's most famous graveyard. The most illustrious incumbent of the **East Cemetery** (April–Oct Mon–Fri 10am–4.30pm; Sat & Sun 11am–4.30pm; Nov–March closes 3.30pm; £2) is **Karl Marx**. Erected by the Communist movement in 1954, his vulgar bronze bust surmounting a granite plinth is a far cry from the unfussy memorial he had requested; close by lies the much simpler grave of the author George Eliot.

The East Cemetery's lack of atmosphere is in part compensated for by the fact that you can wander at will through its maze of circuitous paths. On the other side of Swain's Lane, the overgrown **West Cemetery,** with its spooky Egyptian Avenue and **terraced catacombs**, is the ultimate Hammer-horror graveyard. Visitors

▼ HIGHGATE CEMETERY

can only enter by way of a guided tour (March–Nov Mon–Fri 2pm, Sat & Sun hourly 11am–4pm; Dec–Feb Sat & Sun hourly 11am–3pm; £5) – get there early on summer Sundays. Among the prominent graves usually visited are those of artist Dante Gabriel Rossetti, and of lesbian novelist Radclyffe Hall.

Shops

Fisher & Sperr
46 Highgate High St ☎020/8340 7244. Mon–Sat 10.30am–5pm. Bookshop with several rooms, one entirely dedicated to books about London, plus a few expensive antiquarian jewels and a wide range of titles covering travel, literature, history and philosophy.

Cafés

Brew House
Kenwood House, Hampstead Heath, Daily 9am–6pm. Full English breakfasts, lunches, cakes and teas served in the old laundry, in the courtyard or on the terrace overlooking the lake.

Café Mozart
17 Swain's Lane. Mon–Fri 8am–10pm, Sat & Sun 9am–10pm. Conveniently located on the southeast side of Hampstead Heath, with a wicked Viennese cake selection and soothing classical music.

dim T café
3 Heath St. Daily noon–11pm. Narrow Thai café serving dim sum and noodle dishes, washed down with Chinese tea.

Lauderdale House
Waterlow Park, Highgate Hill. Tues–Sun 8am–6pm. Lovely café with a terrace overlooking the park, offering full meals and, on summer weekends, delicious strawberry-and-cream scones.

Louis Patisserie
32 Heath St. Daily 9am–6pm. Popular and engagingly old-fashioned Hungarian tearoom serving fantastic sticky cakes to a mix of Heath-bound hordes and elderly locals.

Restaurants

Cucina
45a South End Rd ☎020/7435 7814. Mon–Sat noon–2.30pm & 7–11pm, Sun noon–3pm. Brightly painted, fashionable first-floor restaurant serving excellent modern Italian food. Set meals £17–20.

Jin Kichi
73 Heath St ☎020/7794 6158. Tues–Fri 6–11pm, Sat 12.30–2pm & 6–11pm, Sun 12.30–2pm & 6–10pm. Eschewing the slick minimalism and sushi-led cuisine of most Japanese restaurants, *Jin Kichi* is cramped, homely and very busy (so book ahead) and specializes in grilled skewers of meat. Mains £6–12.

Pubs

Flask
14 Flask Walk. Mon–Sat 11am–11pm, Sun noon–10.30pm. Located on one of Hampstead's more atmospheric lanes, this convivial local has retained much of its original Victorian interior.

Flask
77 Highgate West Hill. Mon–Sat noon–11pm, Sun noon–10.30pm. Ideally situated at the heart of Highgate village green, with a rambling, low-ceilinged interior and a

▲ *FLASK* PUB, FLASK WALK

summer terrace – as a result, it's very popular.

Freemason's Arms

32 Downshire Hill. Mon–Sat noon–11pm, Sun noon–10.30pm. Big, smart pub close to the Heath, of interest primarily for its large beer garden and its basement skittle alley.

Holly Bush

22 Holly Mount. Mon–Sat noon–11pm, Sun noon–10.30pm. A lovely old pub, with a real fire in winter, tucked away in the steep backstreets of Hampstead village, which can get a bit too mobbed at weekends.

Wells

30 Well Walk. Mon–Sat noon–11pm, Sun noon–10.30pm. Gastropub keeping punters happy with chess, scrabble and backgammon, top notch modern British bar meals, and a more formal restaurant upstairs.

Clubs and venues

Everyman

Hollybush Vale. ⓦwww .everymancinema.com. The city's oldest rep cinema, and still one of its best, with a strong programme of classics, cultish crowd-magnets and directors' seasons.

Greenwich

Greenwich is one of London's most beguiling spots. Its nautical associations are trumpeted by the likes of the magnificent Cutty Sark tea clipper and the National Maritime Museum; its architecture, especially the Old Royal Naval College and the Queen's House, is some of the finest on the river; and its Observatory is renowned throughout the world. With the added attractions of riverside pubs and walks, a large and well-maintained park with superb views across the river and to Dock-lands, plus a popular weekend market, you can see why Greenwich is the one place in southeast London that draws large numbers of visitors.

Cutty Sark

King William Walk ☎020/858 3445, ⊛www.cuttysark.org.uk. Daily 10am–5pm. Tours £5. The *Cutty Sark* cuts an impressive figure on the riverfront, its three square-rigged masts towering over the centre of Greenwich. The world's last surviving tea clipper, built in 1869, it in fact lasted just eight years in the China tea trade, and it was as a wool clipper that it made its name, returning from Australia in a record-breaking 72 days. Undergoing major maintenance work until 2009, hard-hat tours from spring 2007 will give people the opportunity to see the conservation work in progress and find out more about the ship's fascinating history, from its inception to its arrival in Greenwich in 1954.

Greenwich Market

⊛www.greenwich-market.co.uk. At the weekend (particularly on Sundays), Greenwich Market pulls in as many visitors as the rest of the area's attractions combined. Like Camden (see p.189), it's a sprawling, slightly disparate affair, with three main areas to head for. In the original covered Victorian section is the Crafts Market, which sells twentieth-century **antiques** (Thurs & Fri 7.30am–5.30pm), assorted arts and crafts (Thurs–Sun 9.30am–5.30pm), from spoon mobiles to mounted exotic butterflies, and deli food. Nearby Stockwell Street holds the Central Market (Sat & Sun 7am–5pm), with a two-floor, indoor secondhand books section, plus outdoor

▲ CUTTY SARK

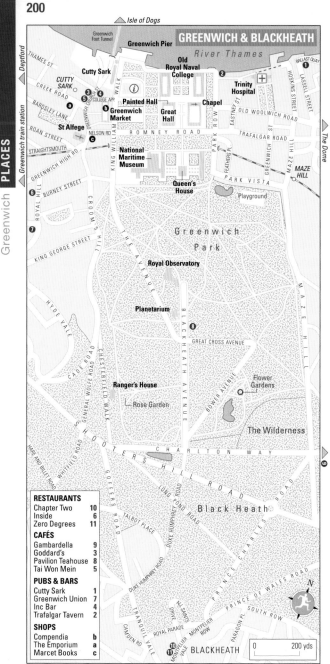

GREENWICH & BLACKHEATH

Isle of Dogs

Greenwich Foot Tunnel

Greenwich Pier

River Thames

BALLAST QUAY ❶

THAMES ST

Deptford

CUTTY SARK

CREEK ROAD

Cutty Sark

Old Royal Naval College

❷

Trinity Hospital

HOSKINS STREET

LASSELL STREET

BARDSLEY LANE

Greenwich train station

ROAN STREET

ⓐ

ⓑ

❸
❹
❺

COLLEGE APP

Painted Hall

Greenwich Market

Great Hall

Chapel

PARK ROW

OLD WOOLWICH ROAD

EASTNEY ST

St Alfege

NELSON RD

WALK

KING WILLIAM

ROMNEY ROAD

TRAFALGAR ROAD

GREENWICH ST

The Dome

MAZE HILL

GREENWICH HIGH RD

STRAIGHTSMOUTH

ⓒ

National Maritime Museum

PARK VISTA

FEATHER R.

MAZE HILL

❻

BURNEY STREET

ROYAL HILL

Queen's House

Playground

❼

KING GEORGE STREET

Greenwich Park

HYDE VALE

CROOM'S

Royal Observatory

THE AVENUE

Planetarium

BLACKHEATH AVENUE

❽

GREAT CROSS AVENUE

CADE ROAD

CHESTERFIELD WALK

GENERAL WOLFE ROAD

Ranger's House

Rose Garden

BOWER AVENUE

Flower Gardens

MAZE HILL

The Wilderness

HARE AND BILLET RD

WHITFIELD ROAD

HOOTER'S

CHARLTON WAY

HILL

❾

GOFFERS ROAD

TALBOT PLACE

ROAD

LONG POND ROAD

DUKE HUMPHREY ROAD

Black Heath

PRINCE CHARLES ROAD

PRINCE OF WALES ROAD

SOUTH ROW

PARAGON PL.

N

CAMDEN RD

TRANQUIL VALE

ROYAL PARADE

DUKE HUMPHREY ROAD

ALL SAINTS DRIVE

MONTPELIER VALE

MONTPELIER ROW

❿
⓫

BLACKHEATH

0   200 yds

Blackheath train station

© Crown copyright

Getting to Greenwich

Greenwich is most quickly reached from central London by train from Charing Cross, Waterloo East or London Bridge (every 30min), although taking a boat from one of the piers between Westminster and Tower Bridge is more scenic and leisurely (and more expensive). Another possibility is to take the Docklands Light Railway (DLR; see p.145) from Bank or Tower Gateway direct to Cutty Sark. For the best view of the Wren buildings, get out at Island Gardens, and then take the Greenwich Foot Tunnel under the Thames.

stalls and the indoor Village Market, stuffed with bric-a-brac and clothes – there's even an adjacent organic food market on Saturdays. Finally, there's the Antiques Market (Sat & Sun 9am–5pm), off Greenwich High Road, which is really more about collectibles – old comics, pop and sports memorabilia – and junk.

Old Royal Naval College

Romney Rd ⓦ www. greenwichfoundation.org.uk. Daily 10am–5pm. Free. It's entirely appropriate that the Old Royal Naval College is the one London building that makes the most of its riverbank location. Initially intended as a royal palace, Wren's beautifully symmetrical Baroque ensemble was eventually converted into a hospital for disabled seamen in the eighteenth century. From 1873 until 1998 it was home to the Royal Naval College, but now houses the University of Greenwich and the Trinity College of Music.

The two grandest rooms, situated underneath Wren's twin domes, are magnificently opulent and well worth visiting. The **Chapel**'s exquisite pastel-shaded plasterwork and spectacular decorative detailing on the ceiling were designed by James

"Athenian" Stuart, after a fire in 1799 destroyed the original interior. The magnificent Painted Hall features trompe l'oeil fluted pilasters, and James Thornhill's gargantuan allegorical ceiling painting depicting William and Mary handing down Peace and Liberty to Europe, with a vanquished Louis XIV clutching a broken sword below them.

National Maritime Museum and Queen's House

Romney Rd ⓦ www.nmm.ac.uk. Daily 10am–5pm; June–Aug closes 6pm. Free.
The excellent National Maritime Museum houses a vast collection of boats and nauticalia, imaginatively displayed in modern, interactive galleries designed to appeal to visitors of all ages. The spectacular glass-roofed, central courtyard houses the museum's largest artefacts, among them the splendid 63ft-long gilded

▼ GREENWICH MARKET

▲ TULIP STAIRCASE, QUEEN'S HOUSE

Royal Barge, designed in Rococo style by William Kent for Prince Frederick, the much unloved eldest son of George II.

The themed galleries of the museum proper are superbly designed to appeal to visitors of all ages. **Explorers**, on Level 1, takes you from the Vikings to Franklin's attempt to discover the Northwest Passage; on display are the relics recovered from the Arctic by John Rae in 1854, many of which had to be bought from the local Inuit. On Level 2, there's a large maritime art gallery, a contemporary section on the future of the sea, and a gallery devoted to the legacy of the British Empire, warts and all.

Level 3 boasts two hands-on galleries: "The Bridge", where you can navigate a catamaran, a paddle steamer and a rowing boat to shore; and "All Hands", where children can have a go at radio transmission, loading miniature cargo, firing a cannon and so forth. Also on this level is the **Oceans of Discovery** gallery, where Cook's K1 marine chronometer is displayed and a replica of the *James Caird*, in which Shackleton made the 300-mile journey from Elephant Island to South Georgia. Finally,

you reach the Nelson Gallery, which contains the museum's vast collection of Nelson-related memorabilia, including Turner's *Battle of Trafalgar, 21st October, 1805*, his largest work and only royal commission.

The **Queen's House** is the focal point of Greenwich's riverside architectural ensemble and an integral part of the Maritime Museum. A bright white Palladian villa flanked by colonnades, it's modest for a royal residence, but as the first Neoclassical building in the country it has enormous significance. Inside, one or two features survive (or have been reinstated) from Stuart times, most notably the cuboid Great Hall, with its Gentileschi fresco, and the beautiful Tulip Staircase, Britain's earliest cantilevered spiral staircase – its name derives from the floral patterning in the wrought-iron balustrade.

Greenwich Park

www.royalparks.gov.uk. Daily dawn–dusk. A welcome escape from the traffic and crowds, Greenwich Park is a great place to have a picnic or collapse under the shade of one of the giant plane trees. The chief delight, though, is the superb view from the steep hill crowned by the Royal Observatory (see below), from which Canary Wharf looms large over Docklands and the Dome. The park is also celebrated for its rare and ancient trees, its royal deer enclosure in "The Wilderness" and its semicircular rose garden.

Royal Observatory

Greenwich Park ⊛www.rog.nmm. ac.uk. Daily 10am–5pm; July & Aug closes 6pm. Free. Perched on the crest of Greenwich Park's highest hill, the Royal Observatory is housed in a rather dinky Wren-built red-brick building, whose northeastern turret sports a bright-red time-ball that climbs the mast at 12.58pm and drops at 1pm GMT precisely; it was added in 1833 to allow ships on the Thames to set their clocks.

Greenwich's greatest claim to fame, of course, is as the home of **Greenwich Mean Time** (GMT) and the Prime Meridian. Since 1884, Greenwich has occupied zero longitude – hence the world

sets its clocks by GMT. The observatory itself was established in 1675 by Charles II to house the first Astronomer Royal, John Flamsteed, whose chief task was to study the night sky in order to discover an astronomical method of finding the longitude of a ship at sea, the lack of which was causing enormous problems for the emerging British Empire. Astronomers continued to work here until the postwar smog forced them to decamp; the old observatory, meanwhile, is now a very popular museum.

The oldest part of the complex is the aforementioned Wren-built Flamsteed House, containing Flamsteed's restored apartments and the Octagon Room, where the king used to show off to his guests. The Chronometer Gallery beyond focuses on the search for the precise measurement of longitude, and displays four of the marine clocks designed by **John Harrison**, including "H4", which helped win the Longitude Prize in 1763.

▼ ROSE GARDEN, GREENWICH PARK

In the Meridian Building, you get to see several meridians, including the present-day Greenwich Meridian fixed by the cross hairs in Airy's "Transit Circle", the astronomical instrument that dominates the last room. Things end on a soothing note in the Telescope Dome of the octagonal Great Equatorial Building, home to Britain's largest telescope. In addition, there are regular presentations in the **Planetarium** (daily 2.30 & 3.30pm; £4), housed in the adjoining South Building.

Ranger's House

Chesterfield Walk ⓦ www.english -heritage.org.uk. Wed–Sun: April–Sept 10am–5pm. £5.50. An imposing red-brick Georgian villa, the Ranger's House shelters an art collection amassed by Julius Wernher, the German-born millionaire who made his money by exploiting South Africa's diamond deposits. His taste was eclectic, ranging from medieval ivory miniatures to Iznik pottery, though he was definitely a man who placed technical virtuosity above artistic merit. Upstairs, the high points of the collection are Memlinc's *Virgin and Child*, a pair of sixteenth-century majolica dishes decorated with mythological scenes for Isabella d'Este; downstairs, take note of the Reynolds portraits and de Hooch interior.

Shops

Compendia

10 Greenwich Market ☎ 020/8293 6616, ⓦ www.compendia.co.uk. Daily 11am–5.30pm. Old-fashioned games shop, selling traditional board games from all over the globe, as well as pub favourites like bagatelle, shove ha'penny and skittles.

The Emporium

330–332 Creek Rd ☎ 020/8305 1670. Tues–Sun 10.30am–6pm. Elegant retro store specializing in 1940s to 1960s clothes for men and women, and featuring kitsch and well-preserved bras, stockings, compacts and cigarette-holders in its beautiful glass-fronted cases.

Marcet Books

23 Nelson Rd ☎ 020/8853 5408, ⓦ www.marcetbooks.co.uk. Daily 10am–5.30pm. As befits Greenwich, this is one of a number of bookshops specializing in nautical titles. Good selection of old prints and maps, too, as well as crime novels.

Cafés

Gambardella

48 Vanbrugh Park. Mon–Fri 7.30am–5.30pm, Sat 7.30am–2.30pm. Good old caff to the southeast of Greenwich Park, serving filling comfort food in a beautiful Art Deco interior with lots of chrome and formica.

Goddard's

45 Greenwich Church St. Mon–Fri 10am–6.30pm, Sat & Sun 10am–7.30pm. Since 1890 this place has been serving traditional pies (including veggie ones), eels and mash in an emerald green-tiled interior, with crumble and custard for afters.

Pavilion Teahouse

Greenwich Park. Mon–Fri 9am–6pm, Sat & Sun 9am–7pm. The park's teahouse, which serves everything from breakfasts to cream teas, has been nicely refurbished and is now the perfect pit stop after a visit to the observatory.

Tai Won Mein

39 Greenwich Church St. Daily 11.30am–11.30pm. Good-quality noodle bar that gets very busy at weekends. Choose between rice, soup or various fried noodles all for under a fiver.

Restaurants

Chapter Two

43–45 Montpelier Vale ☎020/8333 2666, ⊛www.chaptersrestaurants .com. Mon–Thurs noon–2.30pm & 6.30–10.30pm, Sat 12.30–2.30pm & 6.30–11pm, Sun noon–3.30pm & 7–9.30pm. Sleek, modern and professionally run, this is a decent local restaurant serving classic, well-thought-out Mediterranean dishes. Dishes such as roast duck or organic salmon with pumpkin gnocchi £16.

Inside

19 Greenwich South St ☎020/8265 5060, ⊛www.insiderestaurant. co.uk. Tues 6.30–11pm, Wed–Fri noon–2.30pm & 6.30–11pm, Sat 11am–2.30pm & 6.30–11pm, Sun noon–3pm. Swish haven of a restaurant that serves up wonderfully aromatic modern European dishes. Mains £11–17.

Zero Degrees

29–31 Montpelier Vale ☎020/8852 5619, ⊛www.zerodegrees -microbrewery.co.uk. Mon–Sat

noon–midnight, Sun noon–11pm. Micro-brewery beers and gourmet pizzas cooked in a wood-fired oven are the rewards at this modern pizzeria.

Pubs and bars

Cutty Sark

Ballast Quay, off Lassell St. Mon–Sat 11am–11pm, Sun noon–10.30pm. The best riverside pub in Greenwich, with friendly staff, an appropriately nautical flavour, a good range of real ales and pub grub served all day.

Greenwich Union

56 Royal Hill. Mon–Sat 11am–11pm; Sat & Sun noon–6pm. A modern laid-back place with a youthful feel, good gastro grub and a nice garden. Go for free samples of the unusual lagers and pale ale on offer before buying your pint.

Inc Bar

7 College Approach. Mon–Thurs & Sun 5pm–midnight; Fri & Sat 5pm–1am. Unbelievably over-the-top bar, designed with the help of Lawrence Llewelyn-Bowen, that's serves up good cocktails and bar snacks.

Trafalgar Tavern

5 Park Row. Mon–Sat 11.30am– 11pm, Sun noon–10.30pm. A great riverside position and a mention in Dickens' *Our Mutual Friend* have made this Regency-style inn a firm favourite. Good whitebait and other pub snacks.

Kew and Richmond

The wealthy suburbs of Kew and Richmond like to think of themselves as aloof from the rest of London, and in many ways they are. Both have a distinctly rural feel: Kew, thanks to its outstanding botanic gardens; Richmond, owing to its picturesque riverside setting. Taking the leafy towpath from Richmond Bridge to one of the nearby stately homes, or soaking in the view from Richmond Park, you'd be forgiven for thinking you were in the countryside. Both Kew and Richmond are an easy tube ride from the centre, but the most pleasant way to reach them is to take one of the boats that plough up the Thames from Westminster.

Syon House and gardens

Twickenham Rd ⓦ www.syonpark .co.uk. House April–Oct Wed, Thurs & Sun 11am–5pm. Gardens March–Oct 10.30am–5pm, Nov–Feb Sat & Sun 10.30am–4pm. Gardens £3.75. House and gardens £7.50. From its rather plain, castellated exterior, you'd never guess that Syon House boasts London's most opulent eighteenth-century interior. The splendour of Robert Adam's refurbishment is immediately revealed in the pristine Great Hall, an apsed double cube with a screen of Doric columns at one end and classical statuary dotted around the edges. There are several more Adam-designed rooms to admire, and a smattering of works by van Dyck, Lely, Gainsborough and Reynolds adorn the walls.

While Adam beautified Syon House, Capability Brown laid out its gardens around an artificial lake, surrounding the water with oaks, beeches, limes and cedars.

▼ SYON PARK GATES

Tropical Forest

Syon Park, Twickenham Rd ⓦ www.aquatic-experience.org. Daily: April–Sept 10am–6pm; Oct–March 10am–5pm. £5. This purpose-built vivarium displays a mixed range of creatures from the mysterious basilisk, which can walk on water, to the perennially popular piranhas. There are

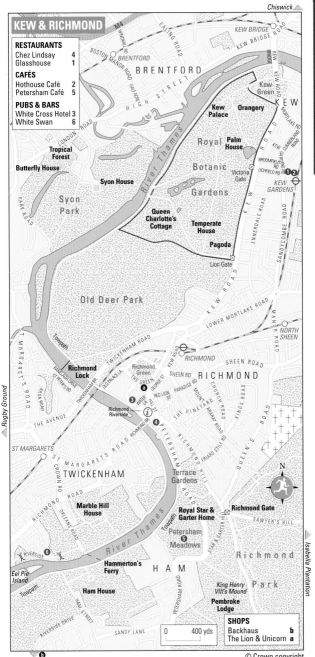

KEW & RICHMOND

RESTAURANTS
Chez Lindsay   4
Glasshouse   1

CAFÉS
Hothouse Café   2
Petersham Café   5

PUBS & BARS
White Cross Hotel   3
White Swan   6

SHOPS
Backhaus   **b**
The Lion & Unicorn   **a**

BRENTFORD

Kew Palace

Orangery

KEW

Kew Green

Royal

Palm House

Botanic

Victoria Gate

KEW GARDENS

Tropical Forest

Butterfly House

Syon House

Gardens

Syon Park

Queen Charlotte's Cottage

Temperate House

Pagoda

Lion Gate

Old Deer Park

LOWER MORTLAKE ROAD

NORTH SHEEN

Richmond Lock

TWICKENHAM ROAD

RICHMOND

SHEEN ROAD

Richmond Green

RICHMOND

Richmond Riverside

THE AVENUE

ST MARGARETS

Terrace Gardens

TWICKENHAM

Marble Hill House

Royal Star & Garter Home

Richmond Gate

SAWYER'S HILL

Petersham Meadows

Hammerton's Ferry

Eel Pie Island

Ham House

HAM

River Thames

Richmond

Park

King Henry VIII's Mound

Pembroke Lodge

SANDY LANE

0   400 yds

PLACES   Kew and Richmond

Rugby Ground

Isabella Plantation

© Crown copyright

plenty of other life-threatening creatures, too, such as crocodiles, pythons, boas and even poison-arrow frogs. Look out also for the bird collection, which includes macaws, parrots, weaver birds and some very colourful starlings.

Kew Gardens

ⓦwww.kew.org. April–Aug Mon–Fri 9.30am–6pm, Sat & Sun 9.30am–7pm; Sept–March closes at dusk. £11.75.

Established in 1759, Kew's Royal Botanic Gardens have grown from their original eight acres into a 300-acre site in which more than 33,000 species are grown in plantations and glasshouses, a display that attracts over a million visitors every year, who come simply to enjoy the beautiful landscaped parkland and steamy palmhouses. There's always something to see, whatever the season, but to get the most out of the place, come sometime between spring and autumn, bring a picnic and stay for the day.

There are four entry points to the gardens, but the majority of people arrive at Kew Gardens tube and train station, a few minutes' walk east of the Victoria Gate. Immediately opposite the Victoria Gate, the **Palm House** is by far the most celebrated of the gardens' glasshouses, a curvaceous mound of glass and wrought-iron designed by Decimus Burton in the 1840s. Its drippingly humid atmosphere nurtures most of the known palm species, while there's a small but excellent tropical aquarium in the basement. South of here is the largest of the glasshouses, the Temperate House, which contains plants from every continent, including the sixty-foot Chilean Wine Palm, one of the largest indoor palms in the world.

Elsewhere in the park, Kew's origins as an eighteenth-century royal pleasure garden are evident in the diminutive royal residence, Kew Palace (bought by George II as a nursery for his umpteen children), the numerous follies dotted about the gardens, the most conspicuous of which is the ten-storey, 163-foot-high **Pagoda**, visible to the south of the Temperate House. A sure way to lose the crowds is to head for the thickly wooded, southwestern section of the park around **Queen Charlotte's Cottage** (July & Aug Sat & Sun 10am–4pm; free), a tiny thatched summerhouse built in the 1770s as a royal picnic spot for George III's queen.

Richmond Riverside

Pedestrianized, terraced and redeveloped in the late 1980s,

▼ PAGODA, KEW GARDENS

▲ DEER IN RICHMOND PARK

Richmond's riverside is a neo-Georgian pastiche for the most part, and a popular one at that. The real joy of the waterfront, though, is **Richmond Bridge**, an elegant span of five arches made from Purbeck stone in 1777 and cleverly widened in the 1930s, thus preserving what is London's oldest extant Thames bridge. From April to October you can rent rowing boats from the nearby jetties, or take a boat trip to Hampton Court or Westminster. Alternatively, you can simply head south down the towpath, past the terraced gardens which give out great views over the river. Quite quickly, the towpath leaves the rest of London far behind. On either side are the wooded banks of the Thames; to the left cows graze on Petersham Meadows; beyond lies Ham House (see opposite).

Richmond Park

ⓦwww.royalparks.gov.uk. Daily: March–Sept 7am–dusk; Oct–Feb 7.30am–dusk. Richmond's greatest attraction is its enormous park, at the top of Richmond Hill – 2500 acres of undulating grassland and bracken, dotted with coppiced ancient woodland. Eight miles across at its widest point, this is Europe's largest city park, famed for its red and fallow deer, which roam freely, and for its venerable oaks. For the most part untamed, the park does have a couple of deliberately landscaped areas which feature splendid springtime azaleas and rhododendrons; the Isabella Plantation is particularly attractive. For refreshment, head for Pembroke Lodge, a teahouse near King Henry VIII's Mount; this is the park's highest point, affording wonderful views right out to Windsor and back into central London. Tradition has it the king waited here for the flare that signalled the execution of his second wife, Anne Boleyn.

Ham House

Ham St ⓦwww.nationaltrust.org.uk/hamhouse. April–Oct Mon–Wed, Sat & Sun 1–5pm. £8. Expensively furnished in the seventeenth century but little altered since then, Ham House boasts one of the finest Stuart interiors in the country, from the stupendously ornate Great Staircase to the Long Gallery, featuring six "Court Beauties" by Peter Lely. Elsewhere, there are several fine Verrio ceiling paintings, some exquisite parquet flooring, lavish plasterwork and silverwork as well as paintings by van Dyck and Reynolds. Another bonus are the formal seventeenth-century gardens (all year

▲ RICHMOND HILL, RICHMOND PARK

Mon–Wed, Sat & Sun 11am–6pm; £3), especially the Cherry Garden, with a pungent lavender parterre surrounded by yew hedges and pleached hornbeam arbours. The Orangery, overlooking the original kitchen garden, currently serves as a tearoom.

Marble Hill House

Marble Hill Park, Richmond Rd Ⓦ www.english-heritage.org.uk. April–Sept Sun 10am–5pm. £4. This stuccoed Palladian villa, set in rolling green parkland, was built in 1729 for the Countess of Suffolk, mistress of George II for some twenty years and, conveniently, also a lady-in-waiting to his wife, Queen Caroline (apparently "they hated one another very civilly"). Nothing remains of the original furnishings, and though some period furniture has taken its place the house can feel barren – it's a good idea to get some background via a free audioguide. The principal space is the Great Room, a perfect cube whose coved ceiling carries on up into the top-floor apartments. Copies of van Dyck decorate the walls as they did in Lady Suffolk's day, and a further splash of colour is provided by Panini's Roman landscapes above each of the doors. The other highlight is Lady Suffolk's Bedchamber, which features an Ionic columned recess – a classic Palladian device. You can play minigolf in the grounds, and there are open-air concerts on occasional summer evenings (visit Ⓦ www.picnicconcerts .com for more info).

Shops

Backhaus

175 Ashburnham Rd, Richmond ☎ 020/8948 6040, Ⓦ www.backhaus .co.uk. Mon–Fri 8am–4.30pm, Sat 8am–4pm. Top German bakery making authentic cheesecakes, Stollen and to-die-for rye breads, with an adjacent deli selling sausages and cheese.

The Lion & Unicorn

19 King St, Richmond ☎ 020/8940 0483, Ⓦ www.lionunicornbooks .co.uk. Mon–Fri 9.30am–5.30pm, Sat 9.30am–6pm, Sun noon–5pm. Wonderful, busy children's bookshop that regularly organizes visits by popular children's writers on Saturdays.

Cafés

Hothouse Café

9 Station Parade, Kew. Daily 10am–
7pm. This stylish, inexpensive
and congenial café is a great
place to fuel up before hitting
the botanic gardens. Full English
breakfasts, sandwiches and
pastries, and an unusually large
variety of breads, coffees, teas
and juices.

Petersham Café

off Petersham Rd, nr Richmond. Mon
& Sun 11.30am–4.30pm, Tues–Sat
9.30am–4pm. A real charmer of a
place for lunch or afternoon tea
– wooden tables and chairs hide
behind exotic ferns, profuse
vines and Indian antiques. The
food is mainly organic and a
little on the pricey side, but well
worth the trek.

Restaurants

Chez Lindsay

11 Hill Rise, Richmond ☎ 020/8948
7473. Mon–Sat 11am–11pm,
Sun noon–10pm. Small, bright,
authentic Breton creperie, with
a loyal local following. Choose
between traditional buckwheat

pancakes (£3–9) or more
formal French main courses
(£10–16), and lots of fresh fish
and shellfish.

Glasshouse

14 Station Parade, Kew ☎ 020/8940
6777. Mon–Sat noon–2.30pm &
7–10.30pm, Sun 12.30–2.45pm &
7.30–10pm. Clean-cut, modern
Kew restaurant, with masterful
service and sophisticated but
classic French cuisine. Set menus
£19–35.

Pubs

White Cross Hotel

Water Lane, Richmond. Mon–Sat
11am–11pm, Sun noon–10.30pm.
With a longer pedigree
and more character than its
rivals, the *White Cross* has a
very popular, large garden
overlooking the river.

White Swan

Riverside, Twickenham. Mon–Sat 11am–
11pm, Sun noon–10.30pm. Filling
pub food, draught beer and a
quiet riverside location – except
on rugby match days – make
this a good halt on any towpath
ramble. The excellent summer
Sunday BBQs are a big draw.

Hampton Court

Hampton Court Palace is the finest of England's royal abodes and well worth the trip out from central London. A wonderfully imposing, sprawling red-brick ensemble on the banks of the Thames, it was built in 1516 by the upwardly mobile Cardinal Wolsey, Henry VIII's Lord Chancellor, only to be purloined by Henry himself after Wolsey fell from favour. Charles II laid out the gardens, inspired by what he had seen at Versailles, while King William III and Queen Mary II had large sections of the palace remodelled by Wren. With so much to see, both inside and outside the palace, you'd be best off devoting the best part of a day to the place, taking a picnic with you to have in the grounds.

Royal Apartments

@www.hrp.org.uk. April–Oct daily 10am–6pm; Nov–March closes 4.30pm. £12.30. Arriving by train or boat, you approach the Tudor Great Gatehouse, no longer moated but still very mighty, prickling with turrets, castellations, chimneypots and pinnacles. King Henry lavished more money on Hampton Court than any other palace, yet the only major survival from Tudor times in Henry VIII's State Apartments is his Great Hall, which features a glorious double hammerbeam ceiling. The other highlight is the superbly ornate **Chapel Royal**, one of the most memorable sights in the whole palace, with its colourful plasterwork vaulting, heavy

with pendants of gilded music-making cherubs. The Queen's Apartments (intended for Queen Mary) boast wonderful trompe l'oeil frescoes on the grandiose Queen's Staircase and in the Queen's Drawing Room, where Anne's husband is depicted riding naked and wigless on the back of a "dolphin". The gem of the Georgian Rooms is in fact the Wolsey Closet, a tiny Tudor room that gives a tantalizing glimpse of the splendour of the original palace. The King's Apartments, built at the same time as the Queen's, are even more grand, particularly the militaristic trompe l'oeil paintings on the King's Staircase and the Great Bedchamber, which boasts a superb vertical Gibbons frieze and ceiling paintings by Verrio. The Renaissance Picture Gallery is chock-full of treasures from the vast Royal Collection including paintings by Tintoretto, Lotto,

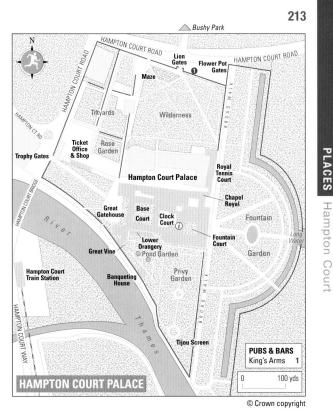

© Crown copyright

Titian, Cranach, Bruegel and Holbein. Last, but not least, are the earthy and evocative Tudor Kitchens, large sections of which have survived to this day and have been restored and embellished with historical reconstructions. To make the

Getting to and around the palace

Trains from Waterloo take around half an hour to reach Hampton Court train station which is just across the river from the palace.

The Royal Apartments are divided into six thematic walking tours, which are numbered and colour-coded. There's not a lot of information in any of the rooms, but guided tours (book at the info desk in Clock Court), each lasting half an hour or so, are available at no extra charge for the state apartments; all are led by period-costumed historians, who do a fine job of bringing the place to life. In addition, the King Henry VIII's Apartments, the Tudor Kitchens, the King's Apartments and the Georgian Rooms are served by an audioguide, available (again at no extra charge) from the information centre on the east side of Clock Court. If your energy is lacking – and Hampton Court is a huge complex – the most rewarding sections are Henry VIII's State Apartments (aka the Tudor Rooms), the King's Apartments (remodelled by William III) and the Tudor Kitchens. And be sure not to miss out on the Maze.

most of this route, you really do need to use the **audioguide**, which helps to evoke the scene with contemporary accounts.

The Gardens and the Maze

If you're coming from the Royal Apartments, you'll probably emerge onto the magnificent Broad Walk, which runs along Wren's austere east front and is lined with superbly maintained herbaceous borders. Halfway along is the indoor Royal Tennis Court, established here by Henry VIII – if you're lucky, you might catch a game of this arcane precursor of modern tennis.

Fanning out from the Broad Walk is the Fountain Garden, a grand, semicircular parterre featuring conical dwarf yew trees. To the south of the palace is the more formal Privy Garden (£4; free with palace ticket) which features magnificent wrought-iron riverside railings by Jean Tijou. The Pond Gardens, originally constructed as ornamental fish ponds stocked with freshwater fish for the kitchens, feature some of the gardens' most spectacularly colourful flowerbeds. Further along, protected by glass, is the palace's celebrated Great Vine, grown from a cutting in 1768 by Capability Brown and averaging about seven hundred bunches of Black Hamburg grapes per year.

Close by stands the Wren-built Lower Orangery, now a dimly lit gallery for **Andrea Mantegna**'s luminous richly coloured masterpiece, *The Triumphs of Caesar*. Painted around 1486 for the Ducal Palace in Mantua, Mantegna's home town, these heroic paintings are among his best works, characterized by an accomplished use of perspective and an obsessive interest in archeological and historical accuracy.

The most famous feature of the palace gardens, however, is the yew hedge **Maze** (£3.50; free with palace ticket), laid out in 1714. It's a deceptively tricky labyrinth that's a winner with kids and adults alike.

Bushy Park

Bushy Park is the perfect place to escape the crowds and head off into the semi-wilderness, home to copious herds of fallow and red deer. Wren's mile-long royal road, Chestnut Avenue, cuts through the park and is at its best in May when the horse chestnuts are in blossom. Off to the west of Chestnut Avenue, it's worth heading to the Waterhouse Woodland Gardens, created in 1949, and at their most colourful each spring when the rhododendrons, azaleas and camellias are in bloom.

Pubs

King's Arms

2 Lion Gate, Hampton Court Road. Mon–Sat 11am–11pm, Sun noon–10.30pm. Bare bricks, wood panelling and mosaic floor tiles combine to recreate the feel of a Georgian coaching inn. Popular pub food and Badger beers.

▼ SWANS IN BUSHY PARK

Accommodation

Hotels, B&Bs and hostels

Compared with most European cities, accommodation in London is expensive. The cheapest option is a dorm bed at one of the numerous independent hostels, followed closely behind by the official YHA (@www.yha.org.uk) places. Even the most basic B&Bs struggle to bring their tariffs below £50 for a double with shared facilities, and you're more likely to find yourself paying £60 to £70 or more. For a decent hotel room, you shouldn't expect much change out of £100 a night. In upmarket hotels – particularly those in or near the City – prices are significantly higher during the week. Unless otherwise stated, all accommodation is marked on the maps in this chapter.

Westminster

B&B Belgravia 64–66 Ebury St ☎020/7823 4928, @www.bb-belgravia.com. A real rarity in this neck of the woods – a B&B with flair, very close to Victoria train and coach station. Rooms are of boutique-hotel quality, with original features and stylish modern touches – all have flatscreen TVs and funky bathrooms with mosaic tiling. Communal spaces are light and similarly well designed, and staff are welcoming and enthusiastic. Doubles from £100.
James & Cartref House 108 Ebury St ☎020/7730 7338 & 129 Ebury St, SW1 ☎020/7730 6167, @www.jamesandcartref.co.uk. Two clean Georgian B&Bs situated opposite one another, and run by the same owners. Fresh and bright en-suite rooms and ones with shared facilities available. Doubles from £70.
Morgan House 120 Ebury St ☎020/7730 2384, @www.morganhouse.co.uk. An

Booking a room

London doesn't really have a low season, though things do slacken off a little in the months just after Christmas. It's wise, therefore, to try and book your accommodation in advance, particularly if you want to stay in one of the more popular places. If you book by phone, many places will ask for a credit card number, others for written or faxed confirmation, while a few may even ask for a deposit.

If you're stuck, all London tourist offices (see p.232) operate a room-booking service, for which around £5 is levied. You can also book for free online at @www.londontown.com; payment is made directly to the hotel on checking out and they can offer discounts of up to fifty percent. Other useful websites include @www.lastminute.com, @www.hotelsengland.com and @www.laterooms.com which has great deals if you book right at the last moment.

In addition, there are British Hotel Reservation Centre (BHRC; @www.bhrc.co.uk) desks at Heathrow (☎020/8564 8808 or 8564 8211) and Gatwick Airport (☎01293/502 433); there are also four desks in and around Victoria: at the train station (☎020/7828 1027), coach station (☎020/7824 8232), underground (☎020/7828 2262) and at 13 Grosvenor Gardens, SW1 (☎020/7828 2425). Most offices are open daily from 6am till midnight, and there's no booking fee.

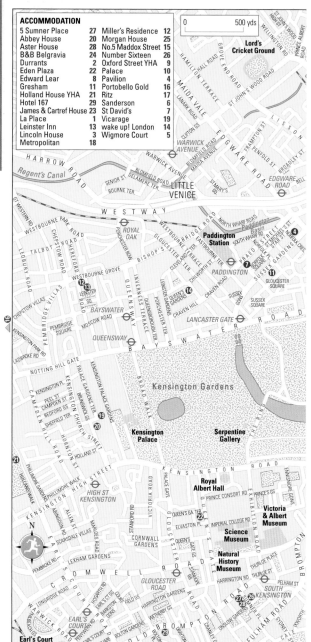

ACCOMMODATION

5 Sumner Place	27	Miller's Residence	12
Abbey House	20	Morgan House	25
Aster House	28	No.5 Maddox Street	15
B&B Belgravia	24	Number Sixteen	26
Durrants	2	Oxford Street YHA	9
Eden Plaza	22	Palace	10
Edward Lear	8	Pavilion	4
Gresham	11	Portobello Gold	16
Holland House YHA	21	Ritz	17
Hotel 167	29	Sanderson	6
James & Cartref House	23	St David's	7
La Place	1	Vicarage	19
Leinster Inn	13	wake up! London	14
Lincoln House	3	Wigmore Court	5
Metropolitan	18		

0   500 yds

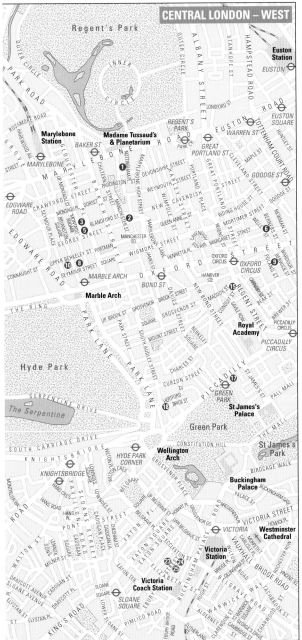

CENTRAL LONDON – WEST

© Crown copyright

above average B&B, run by a vivacious couple. Great breakfasts, patio garden, and a fridge for guests to use. Most rooms are en suite. Doubles from £66.

Sanctuary House Hotel 33 Tothill St ☎020/7799 4044, ⓦwww.fullershotels .co.uk. Situated above a Fuller's pub, and decked out like one, too, in smart, pseudo-Victoriana. Breakfast is extra. Doubles from £100 (weekends); £150 (weedays).

Piccadilly and Mayfair

The Metropolitan Old Park Lane ☎020/7447 1000, ⓦwww.metropolitan .co.uk. This terrifyingly trendy hotel near the Hilton adheres to the current fad for pared-down minimalism. The Japanese restaurant, *Nobu*, is outstanding, and the famous *Met* bar is open to members- and residents-only in the evenings. Doubles from around £300.

No. 5 Maddox Street 5 Maddox St ☎020/7647 0200, ⓦwww.5maddoxstreet.com. With a very discreet entrance, this complex of apartments is all bamboo flooring and trendy minimalist decor. Suites have open fireplaces, workstations, TVs, kitchens and decked balconies, and Muji foldaway bikes are available for guests' use, too. Suites from £350.

The Ritz 150 Piccadilly ⓦ020/7300 2308, ⓦwww.theritzhotel.co.uk. In a class of its own among London's hotels, with its extravagant Louis XVI interiors and overall air of decadent luxury. Rooms maintain the opulent French theme, with the west-facing accommodation, overlooking Green Park, in greatest demand. Doubles from around £350.

Marylebone

Durrants Hotel George St ☎020/7935 8131, ⓦwww.durrantshotel.co.uk. Just round the corner from the Wallace Collection and Oxford Street, this Georgian terrace hotel first opened in 1790, and has been run by the same family since 1921. Inside, it's a great exercise in period-piece nostalgia, with doormen, lots of wood panelling and old prints. Doubles from £170.

Edward Lear Hotel 28–30 Seymour St ☎020/7402 5401, ⓦwww.edlear.com. Lear's former home enjoys a great location close to Oxford Street and Hyde Park, lovely flower boxes and a plush foyer. Rooms themselves need a bit of a makeover, but the low prices reflect both this and the fact that most only have shared facilities. Doubles from £65.

Hotel La Place 17 Nottingham Place ☎020/7486 2323, ⓦwww.hotellaplace .com. Just off busy Marylebone Road, this is a small, good-value if rather old-fashioned place; rooms are en suite and comfortably furnished. Doubles from £120.

Lincoln House Hotel 33 Gloucester Place ☎020/7486 7630, ⓦwww .lincoln-house-hotel.co.uk. Dark wood panelling gives this Georgian B&B in Marylebone a ship's-cabin feel, while all the rooms are en suite and well equipped. Rates vary according to the size of the bed and length of stay. Doubles from £80.

Palace Hotel 31 Great Cumberland Place ☎020/7262 5585. Small but luxurious hotel close to Marble Arch which oozes class, from the hand-painted friezes on the staircase to the four-poster beds in many of the rooms. Continental breakfast included. Doubles from £90.

Wigmore Court Hotel 23 Gloucester Place ☎020/7935 0928, ⓦwww .wigmore-court-hotel.co.uk. The ruched curtains and floral decor may not be to everyone's taste, but this Georgian townhouse has comfortable rooms with en-suite facilities, plus two doubles with shared facilities. Unusually, there's also a laundry and basic kitchen for guests' use. Doubles from £80.

Soho

Hazlitt's 6 Frith St ☎020/7434 1771, ⓦwww.hazlittshotel.com. Early eighteenth-century hotel of real character and charm, offering en-suite rooms decorated as close to period style as convenience and comfort allow. Continental breakfast (served in the rooms) is extra. Doubles from £250.

Manzi's 1–2 Leicester St ☎020/7734 0224, ⓦwww.manzis.co.uk. Set over the Italian and seafood restaurant of the same name, *Manzi's* is one of the very few West End hotels in this price range, although noise might prove to be a nuisance. Continental breakfast is included in the price. Doubles from £85.

Oxford Street YHA 14 Noel St ⊕020/7734 1618, ⓔoxfordst@yha.org .uk. The West End location and modest size (75 beds in rooms of 2, 3 and 4 beds) mean that this hostel tends to be full year round. No children under 6, no groups, no café, but a large kitchen. Beds from £25.

St Martin's Lane 45 St Martin's Lane ⊕020/7300 5500, ⓦwww .morganshotelgroup.com. This self-consciously chic boutique hotel with a bafflingly anonymous glassed facade is a big hit with the media crowd. The *Light Bar* is the most startling of the hotel's eating and drinking outlets. Rates come down at the weekend. Doubles from £250.

Soho Hotel 4 Richmond Mews ⊕020/7559 3000, ⓦwww.sohohotel .com. An ex-carpark made over by designer Kit Kemp. No two areas are the same and the result is eclecticism bordering on schizophrenia, from the Oriental lobby to the camp fuchsia boudoirs and a screening room done out in fake fur and scarlet leather. Facilities are, as you'd expect, top-notch. Doubles from £275.

Bloomsbury

The Academy 21 Gower St ⊕020/7631 4115, ⓦwww.theetoncollection.com. Smart if rather chintzy place popular with business folk. Service is excellent, all rooms are air-conditioned, with luxurious bathrooms, and there are two lovely patio gardens to enjoy. Doubles from £165.

Ashlee House 261–265 Gray's Inn Rd ⊕020/7833 9400, ⓦwww.ashleehouse .co.uk. Clean and friendly hostel in a converted office block near King's Cross Station. Internet access, laundry and kitchen facilities are provided. Breakfast is included. Dorms from £16, twins £50.

Crescent Hotel 49–50 Cartwright Gardens ⊕020/7387 1515, ⓦwww .crescenthoteloflondon.com. Comfortable and clean B&B, with pink furnishings. All doubles are en suite, but there are a few

bargain singles with shared facilities. Doubles from £95.

Generator Compton Place, off Tavistock Place ⊕020/7388 7666, ⓦwww .generatorhostels.com. A huge, funky hostel, with over 800-beds. The neon and UV lighting and post-industrial decor may not be to everyone's taste, but with such keen prices, this is without doubt the best bargain in this part of town. Facilities include Internet access, games rooms, movie nights, a bar open to residents only (till 2am) and a canteen serving buffet Continental breakfast included in the room rate. Dorms from £12.50, doubles £50.

Harlingford Hotel 61–63 Cartwright Gardens ⊕020/7387 1551, ⓦwww .harlingfordhotel.com. Another good option in this fine Georgian crescent. All rooms are en suite with TV, the lounge has a real fire, and the breakfast room is bright and cheery. Doubles from £100.

Museum Inn 27 Montague St ⊕020/7580 5360, ⓦwww.astorhostels .com. In a lovely Georgian house by the British Museum, this is the quietest of the Astor hostels. There's no bar, though it's still a sociable, laid-back place, and well situated. Decent-sized kitchen and TV lounge, also laundry and Internet access. Breakfast included. Dorms from £16; doubles from £50.

Ridgemount Hotel 65–67 Gower St ⊕020/7636 1141, ⓦwww .ridgemounthotel.co.uk. Old fashioned, very friendly, family-run place, with small rooms, half with shared facilities, a garden, free hot-drinks machine and a laundry service. A reliable, basic bargain for Bloomsbury. Doubles from £50.

Hotel Russell Russell Square ⊕020/7837 6470, ⓦwww.principal -hotels.com. From its grand 1898 exterior to its opulent interiors of marble, wood and crystal, this late-Victorian landmark fully retains its period atmosphere in all its public areas. The rooms live up to the grandeur of the lobby, if not necessarily to its style. Expensive, but various deals are available; check their website. Breakfast is not included. Doubles from £230.

St Pancras YHA 79–81 Euston Rd ⊕020/ 7388 9998, ⓔstpancras@yha.org.uk.

Hostel on the busy Euston Road; rooms are very clean, bright, triple-glazed and air-conditioned – some even have en-suite facilities. All doubles are en suite and family rooms are available, all with TVs. Dorms from £25; doubles from £50.

Thanet Hotel 8 Bedford Place ☎020/7636 2869, ⊛www.thanethotel .co.uk. Small, friendly, family-run B&B close to the British Museum. Rooms are clean, bright and freshly decorated, all with en-suite showers and tea/coffee-making facilities. Doubles from £100.

Covent Garden

The Fielding Hotel 4 Broad Court, Bow Street ☎020/7836 8305, ⊛www.the -fielding-hotel.co.uk. Quietly and perfectly situated on a traffic-free and gas-lit court, this excellent hotel is one of Covent Garden's hidden gems. Its en-suite rooms are a firm favourite with visiting performers, since it's just a few yards from the Royal Opera House. Breakfast is extra. Doubles from £100.

Sanderson 50 Berners St, W1 ☎020/7300 1400, ⊛www.sanderson hotel.com. The usual assemblage of objets d'art peppers the white-and-magnolia lobby of this converted 1960s office block and the *Long Bar* is all translucent backlit onyx but, like the restaurant, is ludicrously overpriced. 3D "space" lifts take you to the equally bright white rooms. There's a large gym, steam room, sauna and health club on site. Doubles from £240.

Seven Dials Hotel 7 Monmouth St ☎020/7681 0791, ⊛www.smooth hound.co.uk/hotels/sevendials. Pleasant family-run hotel in the heart of theatreland. All rooms are en suite and have TV, tea/coffee-making facilities and direct-dial phones. Doubles from £65.

Clerkenwell

Malmaison Charterhouse Square ☎020/7012 3700, ⊛www.malmaison -london.com. The Victorian red-brick facade gives way to modern, understated decor in muted tones; well-equipped rooms have enormous beds and the restaurant is very good. Doubles from £195.

The Rookery 12 Peter's Lane, Cowcross Street ☎020/7336 0931, ⊛www .rookeryhotel.com. Rambling Georgian town-house on the edge of the City that makes a fantastically discreet little hideaway. Each room has been individually designed in a deliciously camp, modern take on the Baroque period, and all have super bathrooms with lots of character. Doubles from £245.

Zetter Hotel 86–88 Clerkenwell Rd ☎020/7324 4444, ⊛www.thezetter.com. A warehouse converted with real style and a dash of Sixties glamour. Rooms are simple and minimalist, with fun touches such as lights which change colour and decorative floral panels; ask for a room at the back, overlooking quiet cobbled St John's Square. The attached restaurant serves good modern Italian food, and water for guests is supplied from the Zetter's own well, beneath the building. Doubles from £160.

The City

City of London YHA 36 Carter Lane ☎020/7236 4965, ℮city@yha.org.uk. Large 200-bed hostel in a superb location opposite St Paul's Cathedral. There's no kitchen, but a café serves lunch and dinner. No groups. Dorms from £18; twins from £50.

Great Eastern Hotel Liverpool St ☎020/7618 5010, ⊛www.great -eastern-hotel.co.uk. This venerable late-nineteenth-century station hotel had a complete Conran makeover, yet manages to retain much of its old-world clubby flavour. The George pub boasts a superb mock-Tudor ceiling; the rooms themselves are tastefully furnished; and the fabulous old lobby is now the Aurora restaurant. Doubles from £320 (£160 at the weekend).

The King's Wardrobe 6 Wardrobe Place, Carter Lane ☎020/7792 2222, ⊛www .bridgestreet.com. In a quiet courtyard just behind St Paul's Cathedral, the apartments (1- to 3-bed) offer fully equipped kitchens and workstations, a concierge service and housekeeping. Though housed in a fourteenth-century building that once contained Edward III's royal regalia, the interior is unrelentingly modern. Apartments from £130–160.

Threadneedles 5 Threadneedle St ☎020/7657 8080, ⊛www .theetoncollection.com. Magnificent former Midland Bank in the heart of the financial district, now converted into the City's first boutique hotel, with every mod con from plasma TV screens to cordless digital telephones. Doubles from £300 (£200 at the weekend).

Hoxton and Spitalfields

City Hotel 12 Osborn St ☎020/7247 3313, ⊛www.cityhotellondon.co.uk. Spacious and clean, this modern hotel stands on the eastern edge of the City, in the heart of the Bengali East End at the bottom of Brick Lane. The plainly decorated rooms are all en suite, and many have kitchens, too; four-person rooms are a bargain for families or small groups. Doubles from £70.

Docklands

Four Seasons Hotel Canary Wharf 46 Westferry Circus ☎020/7510 1999, ⊛www.fourseasons.com. See map on p.197. A spectacular riverfront setting, with ultra-modern interiors and good links to the City. Pool, fitness centre, spa and tennis courts. Several rooms have superb Thames views. There's also the option of taking a boat into town. Doubles from £330 (£200 at weekends).

South Bank

London County Hall Travel Inn Belvedere Rd ☎0870/238 3300, ⊛www .travelinn.co.uk. Don't expect river views at these prices, but the location in County Hall itself is pretty good if you're up for a bit of sightseeing. Decor and ambience are functional, but for those with kids, the flat-rate rooms are a bargain. Rooms from £90.

Mad Hatter 3–7 Stamford St ☎020/7401 9222, ⊛www.fullershotels.co.uk. Situated above a Fuller's pub on the corner of Blackfriars Road, and run by the Fuller's Brewery. Breakfast is extra on weekdays,

and is served in the pub, but this is a great location, a short walk from Tate Modern and the South Bank. Doubles from £125 (weekends £95).

Marriott London County Hall Hotel County Hall ☎020/7928 5200, ⊛www .marriott.com. Historic County Hall stands right on the river with over three quarters of its rooms offering river views, many with small balconies. It's all suitably pompous inside, and there's a full-sized indoor pool and well-equipped gym. Doubles from £280.

Bankside and Southwark

London Bridge Hotel 8–18 London Bridge St ☎020/7855 2200, ⊛www .london-bridge-hotel.co.uk. Perfectly placed for Southwark and Bankside or the City, this is a tastefully smart hotel right by the station. As it attracts a mainly business clientele, rates go down considerably at the weekend. Doubles from £160.

St Christopher's Village 161–165 Borough High St ☎020/7407 1856, ⊛www .st-christophers.co.uk. Flagship of a chain of independent hostels, with no fewer than three properties on Borough High Street (and branches elsewhere in London). The decor is upbeat and cheerful, the place is efficiently run and there's a party-animal ambience, fuelled by the neighbouring bar and the rooftop hot tub and sauna. Dorms £13–22, twins £44.

Southwark Rose Hotel 43–47 Southwark Bridge Rd ☎020/7015 1480, ⊛www.southwarkrosehotel.co.uk. A budget boutique-style hotel with some nice design touches that raise the rooms several notches above the bland chain hotels in the area. The penthouse restaurant offers breakfast with a rooftop view and free Internet access. Doubles from £120.

Hyde Park and Kensington Gardens

Leinster Inn 7–12 Leinster Square ☎020/7229 9641, ⊛www.astorhostels .com. With 360 beds, this is the biggest and liveliest of the Astor hostels, with a

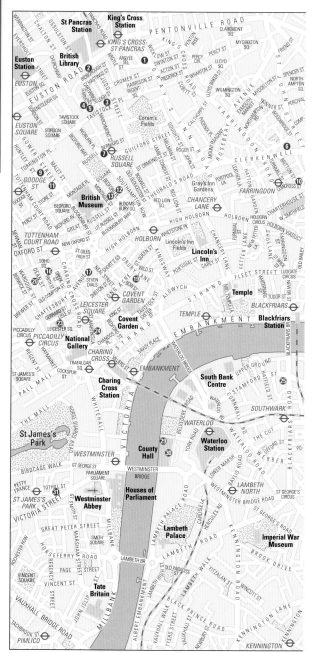

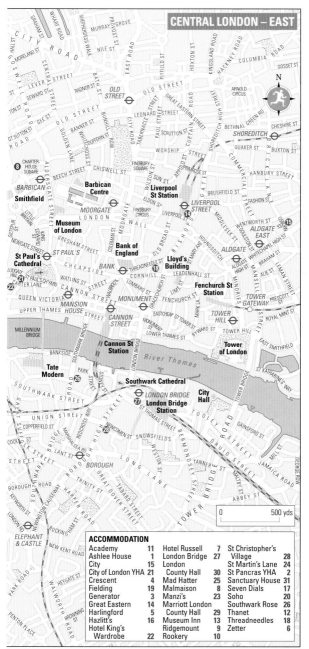

CENTRAL LONDON – EAST

ACCOMMODATION					
Academy	11	Hotel Russell	7	St Christopher's	
Ashlee House	1	London Bridge	27	Village	28
City	15	London		St Martin's Lane	24
City of London YHA	21	County Hall	30	St Pancras YHA	2
Crescent	4	Mad Hatter	25	Sanctuary House	31
Fielding	19	Malmaison	8	Seven Dials	17
Generator	3	Manzi's	23	Soho	20
Great Eastern	14	Marriott London		Southwark Rose	26
Harlingford	5	County Hall	29	Thanet	12
Hazlitt's	16	Museum Inn	13	Threadneedles	18
Hotel King's		Ridgemount	9	Zetter	6
Wardrobe	22	Rookery	10		

party atmosphere, and two bars open until the small hours. Some rooms in all categories have their own shower. Dorm beds £14–18 per person, doubles from £45.

South Kensington, Knightsbridge and Chelsea

5 Sumner Place 5 Sumner Place ☎020/7584 7586, ⓦwww .sumnerplace.com. Discreetly luxurious B&B in a pretty white-stuccoed terrace; all rooms are en suite and breakfast is served in the lovely conservatory. Doubles from £130.

Aster House 3 Sumner Place ☎020/7581 5888, ⓦwww.asterhouse .com. Pleasant, non-smoking and award-winning B&B in a luxurious white-stuccoed street; there's a lovely garden at the back and a large conservatory, where breakfast is served. Doubles from £140.

Eden Plaza Hotel 68–69 Queen's Gate ☎020/7370 6111, ⓦwww.edenplaza kensington.co.uk. Part of a fast-growing budget-hotel chain catering for business and leisure clients. Rooms (sleeping up to four) are small, modern, en suite and brightly furnished, and there's a bistro and bar on the ground floor; breakfast is included. Doubles from £85.

Hotel 167 167 Old Brompton Rd ☎020/7373 3221, ⓦwww.hotel167 .com. Small, stylishly furnished B&B with en-suite facilities, double glazing and a fridge in all rooms. Continental buffet-style breakfast is served in the attractive morning room/reception. Doubles from £100.

Number Sixteen 16 Sumner Place, SW7 ☎020/7584 5232, ⓦwww.number sixteenhotel.co.uk. A plush but relaxed boutique hotel, prettily furnished in shades of blue, lilac and grey. Food is served in the light, modern conservatory, which looks on to a secluded garden, where you can dine on wrought-iron chairs under the trees. Doubles from £170.

High Street Kensington to Notting Hill

Abbey House 11 Vicarage Gate ☎020/7727 2594, ⓦwww.abbeyhouse kensington.com. Inexpensive Victorian B&B in a quiet street just north of Kensington High Street, maintained to a very high standard by its attentive owners. Rooms are large and bright – prices are kept down by sharing facilities. Full English breakfast, with free tea and coffee available all day. Cash only. Doubles from £75.

The Gresham Hotel 116 Sussex Gardens, W2 ☎020/7402 2920, ⓦwww .gresham@renbec.com. B&B with a touch more class than many in the area. Rooms are small but tastefully kitted out, and all have TV. Continental breakfast included. Doubles from £85.

Holland House YHA Holland Walk ☎020/7937 0748, ⓔhollandhouse@yha .org.uk. Idyllically situated in the wooded expanse of Holland Park and fairly convenient for the centre, this extensive hostel offers a decent kitchen and an inexpensive café, but tends to be popular with school groups. Dorms from around £22.

Miller's Residence 111a Westbourne Grove ☎020/7243 1024, ⓦwww.miller suk.com. The address is deceptive – this grandiose and eccentric B&B is accessed from Hereford Road. Every inch is littered with nineteenth-century antiques, from the sumptuous Baronial drawing room to the bedrooms. Some of the rooms are a little small and dark for the price, but the welcome is warm and the ambience unique. Doubles from £150.

The Pavilion Hotel 34–36 Sussex Gardens ☎020/7262 0905, ⓦwww .pavilionhoteluk.com. A decadent rock star's home from home, with outrageously over-the-top decor and every room individually themed, from "honky tonk Afro" to "Highland Fling". Doubles from £100.

Portobello Gold 95–97 Portobello Rd, W1 ☎020/7460 4900, ⓦwww.portobello gold.com. A fun and friendly option – six rooms and an apartment above a cheery modern pub. Rooms are plain and some are tiny, with miniature en-suite bathrooms, but all are fairly priced. Doubles from £70.

St David's Hotels 14–20 Norfolk Square, W2 ☎020/7723 3856, ⊛www .stdavidshotels.com. A friendly welcome is assured at this inexpensive B&B, famed for its substantial English breakfast. Most rooms share facilities. The large rooms make it a good option for families on a budget. Doubles from £60.

Vicarage Hotel 10 Vicarage Gate ☎020/7229 4030, ⊛www.london vicaragehotel.com. Ideally located B&B a step away from Hyde Park. Clean and smart floral rooms with shared facilities, and a full English breakfast included in the rates. Cash or travellers' cheques only. Doubles from £80.

wake up! London 1 Queens Gardens ☎020/7262 4471, ⊛www .wakeuplondon.co.uk. Funky hostel with single-sex 4- to 8-bed dorms, singles and doubles, and great facilities, including an information desk, 24hr reception and a basement bar (with a pool table) that's open daily till 3am. Dorms from £15.

Hampstead and Highgate

The places listed below appear on the map on pp.194–195.

Hampstead Heath YHA 4 Wellgarth Rd ☎020/8458 9054, ⊕hampstead @yha.org.uk. One of the biggest and best-appointed YHA hostels, with its own garden and the wilds of Hampstead Heath nearby. Dorms from around £21; twins from £45.

Hampstead Village Guesthouse 2 Kemplay Rd ☎020/7435 8679, ⊛www .hampsteadguesthouse.com. Lovely B&B in a freestanding Victorian house on a quiet backstreet near the Heath. Rooms (most en suite, all non-smoking) are wonderfully characterful, crammed with books, pictures and handmade and antique furniture. Doubles from £75.

Langorf Hotel 20 Frognal ☎020/7794 4483, ⊛www.langorfhotel.com. Pristinely maintained if rather old-fashioned hotel in a trio of red-brick Victorian mansions, with a walled garden. There are also apartments, sleeping four or five available. Doubles from £100.

Essentials

Arrival

London's international airports are all less than an hour from the city centre, and the city's **train** and **bus** terminals are all pretty central, and have **tube** stations close at hand.

By plane

Heathrow Airport (℡ 0870/000 0123, ⓦ www.heathrowairport.com), fifteen miles west of central London, has four terminals and is served by two train/tube stations: one for terminals 1, 2 and 3, and another for terminal 4. The **Heathrow Express** (℡ 0845/600 1515, ⓦ www .heathrowexpress.com) travels non-stop to Paddington Station (every 15min; 15–20min) for £14.50 each way or £27 return (£2 more if you buy your ticket on board). Cheaper but slower is the Piccadilly **Underground** line into central London (every 5min; 50min) for £4 one-way. If you plan to make several journeys on your arrival day, buy a One-Day Travelcard (see p.233). National Express (℡ 0870/580 8080, ⓦ www.nationalexpress.com) operate **bus services** between 5am to 9.30pm from Heathrow's central bus station direct to central London's Victoria Coach Station (every 20–30min; 40min–1hr; £10). From midnight, you'll have to take **night bus** #N9 to Trafalgar Square (every 30min; 1hr) for a bargain fare of £1.50. A **taxi** will cost between £40 and £70 to central London, and take an hour (longer in the rush hour).

Gatwick (℡ 0870/000 2468, ⓦ www .gatwickairport.com), thirty miles to the south of London, has two terminals, North and South, connected by a monorail. The **Gatwick Express** (℡ 0870/ 530 1530, ⓦ www.gatwickexpress. co.uk) train runs non-stop between the South Terminal and Victoria Station (every 15–30min; 30min) for £14 single, £25 return. A cheaper option is to take a **Southern train** service to Victoria, which costs £9 single, departs every fifteen minutes or so, and takes around forty minutes. A **taxi** ride into central London will set you back £90 or more, and take at least an hour.

Stansted (℡ 0870/000 0303, ⓦ www .stanstedairport.com) lies 35 miles north-east of the capital, and is served by the **Stansted Express** (℡ 0870/530 1530, ⓦ www.stanstedexpress.com) to Liverpool Street (every 15–30min; 45min), which costs £15 single, £25 return. **Airbus** #6 also runs 24 hours a day to Victoria Coach Station (every 30min; 1hr 30min), and costs £10 single, £15 return. A **taxi** into central London will cost around £75, and take at least an hour.

Luton airport (℡ 01582/405100, ⓦ www.london-luton.com) is roughly thirty miles north of London, and mostly handles charter flights. A free shuttle-bus takes five minutes to transport passengers to Luton Airport Parkway station, connected by **Thameslink** trains to King's Cross and other stations (every 15min; 30–40min) for £11 single, £22 return. Alternatively, **Green Line** buses (℡ 0870/608 7261, ⓦ www.greenline .co.uk) run from Luton to Victoria Station (every 30min; 1hr 15min), costing £10.50 single, £15 return. A **taxi** will cost around £70 and take at least an hour to reach central London.

City airport (℡ 020/7646 0000, ⓦ www.londoncityairport.com), the capital's smallest, is situated ten nine miles east of central London in the Docklands area. It handles European flights only, and is connected by the **Docklands Light Railway** (DLR) which will take you straight to Bank in the City in around 25 minutes; tickets cost around £3. A **taxi** into the city's financial sector will cost around £20 and take half an hour or so.

By train and coach

Eurostar (℡ 0870/160 6600, ⓦ www .eurostar.com) trains arrive at Waterloo

International station in central London (at St Pancras from 2008 onwards). Trains from the Channel ports arrive at the equally central Charing Cross or Victoria, while boat trains from Harwich arrive at Liverpool Street, just east of the centre and linked to the tube network. Arriving by **train** (☎0845/748 4950, Ⓦ www.nationalrail.co.uk) from elsewhere in Britain, you'll come into one of London's numerous mainline stations, all of which have adjacent Underground stations linking into the city centre's tube network. Coming into London by **coach** (☎0870/580 8080, Ⓦ www .nationalexpress.com), you're most likely to arrive at Victoria Coach Station, a couple of hundred yards south down Buckingham Palace Road from Victoria train station and tube.

Information

The main tourist office is the **London Visitor Centre**, near Piccadilly Circus at 1 Regent St (Ⓦ www.visitbritain .com; Mon 9.30am–6.30pm, Tues–Fri 9am–6.30pm, Sat & Sun 10am–4pm; June–Sept same times except Sat 9am–5pm). There's also a tiny information window in the **tkts kiosk** on Leicester Square (Ⓦ www.visitlondon.com; Mon–Fri 8am–11pm, Sat & Sun 10am–6pm). Individual London boroughs also run **tourist offices**, the most useful of which are: on the south side of St Paul's Cathedral (☎020/7332 1456; May–Sept daily 9.30am–5pm; Oct–April Mon–Fri 9.30am–5pm); in Greenwich's old Royal Naval College (☎0870/608 2000; daily 10am–5pm); and inside Richmond's Old Town Hall (☎020/8940 9125; Mon–Sat 10am–5pm).

For "what's on" information, buy the weekly listings magazine **Time Out** (£2.50), published every Tuesday afternoon. In it you'll find details of all the latest exhibitions, shows, films, music, sport, guided walks and events in and around the capital.

Websites

Ⓦ **www.24hourmuseum.co.uk** Up-to-date information on virtually every single museum, large or small, in London.
Ⓦ **www.londonnet.co.uk** A virtual guide to London with useful up-to-date listings on eating, drinking and nightlife.
Ⓦ **www.myvillage.com** Huge site that covers every district/borough in London, giving club, music, cinema and theatre listings, restaurant reviews, plus local gossip and messageboards.
Ⓦ **www.streetmap.co.uk** Type in the London address you want and this site will locate it for you in seconds.
Ⓦ **www.thisislondon.com** Website of The *Evening Standard*, London's only daily newspaper, with constantly updated news and listings.

City transport

Thanks to London's mayor, Ken Livingstone, the city's highly complex transport system is finally receiving the attention and investment it badly needs. The controversial congestion charge has reduced traffic by thirty percent within central London, and much of the money has been ploughed into improving the buses. Nevertheless, London still has one of the most expensive transport systems in the world. You can get a free transport map from any tube station, or from one of the more comprehensive Transport for London (TfL) **travel information offices**, at Piccadilly Circus tube station (Mon–Sat 7.15am–9pm, Sun 8.15am–8pm); there are other desks at the arrivals at Heathrow (terminals 1, 2, & 3), Oxford Circus and St James's Park (Mon–Fri only) tubes, Victoria Coach Station, and Euston, King's Cross, Liverpool Street, Paddington and Victoria train stations. There's also a 24-hour phone line and a website for transport information (☎ 020/7222 1234, ⓦ www.tfl.gov .uk). If you can, avoid travelling during the **rush hour** (Mon–Fri 8–9.30am & 5–7pm) when tubes become unbearably crowded, and occasionally buses get so full they won't let you on.

Travelcards

To get the best value out of London's public transport system, buy a Travelcard. Available from machines and booths at all tube and train stations, and at some newsagents (look for the sign), these are valid for the bus, tube, DLR, Tramlink and suburban rail networks. **Day Travelcards** come in two varieties: Off-Peak – which are valid after 9.30am on weekdays and all day during the weekend – and Peak. A Day Travelcard (Off-Peak) costs £4.70 for unlimited travel in central zones 1 and 2, rising to £6 for zones 1–6 (including Heathrow); the Day Travelcard (Peak) starts at £5.10 for zones 1 and 2. A **Three-Day Travelcard** costs £15 for zones 1 and 2, but is obviously only worth it if you need to travel during peak hours. Weekly Travelcards begin at £18.50 for zone 1. Travelcards also give you discounts on boat services (see p.234).

The tube

Except for very small journeys, the Underground – or tube – is by far the quickest way to get about. Each line has its own colour and name – all you need to know is which direction you're travelling in: northbound, eastbound, southbound or westbound. Services operate from around 5am until 12.30am Monday to Saturday, and from 7.30am until 11.30pm on Sundays; you rarely have to wait more than five minutes for a train from central stations.

Tickets must be bought in advance from the machines or booths in station entrance halls; if you cannot produce a valid ticket, you will be charged an on-the-spot **Penalty Fare** of £20. A single journey in the central zone costs an unbelievable £3, so a Travelcard is your best bet.

The driverless **Docklands Light Railway** (see p.145), which connects the City with Docklands, Greenwich and parts of the East End, is an integral part of the tube system. Travelcards are valid on the DLR, which also has its own selection of tickets and passes.

Buses

In central London, and on all the extra-long "bendy buses", you must buy your **ticket** before boarding from one of the machines at the bus stop, unless of course you already have a Travelcard. Tickets for bus journeys within London cost £1.50. Note that at request stops (easily recognizable by their red sign) you must stick your arm out to hail the bus you want (or ring the bell if you want to get off). In addition to the Travelcards mentioned opposite, a **One-Day Bus Pass** (zones 1–4) is also available for £3 and can be used before 9.30am.

Some buses run a 24-hour service, but most run between about 5am and midnight, with a network of **night buses** (prefixed with the letter "N") operating outside this period. Night bus routes radiate out from Trafalgar Square at approximately twenty- to thirty-minute intervals, more frequently on some routes and on Friday and Saturday nights. Travelcards are valid. At all stops you must wave to get the bus to stop, and when on the bus, press the bell in order to get off.

Taxis

Compared to most capital cities, London's metered **black cabs** are an expensive option unless there are three or more of you – a ride from Euston to Victoria, for example, costs around £12–15 (Mon–Fri 6am–8pm). After 8pm on weekdays and all day during the weekend, a higher tariff applies, and after 10pm, a much higher one. A yellow light over the windscreen tells you if the cab is available – just stick your arm out to hail it. To order a black cab in advance, phone ☎0871/871 8710, and be prepared to pay an extra £2. Note that a tip is customary.

Minicabs look just like regular cars and are considerably cheaper than black cabs, but they cannot be hailed from the street. All minicabs should be licensed and able to produce a Public Carriage Office licence on demand. The best way to pick a company is to take the advice of the place you're at, unless you want to be certain of a woman driver, in which case call Ladycabs (☎020/7254 3501), or a gay/lesbian-friendly driver, in which case call Freedom Cars (☎020/7734 1313). Green Tomato Cars (☎020/8748 8881, ⓦwww.greentomatocars.com) operates a fleet of eco-friendly cabs mainly within west London. Last, and definitely least, there are usually plenty of **bicycle taxis** available for hire in the West End. The oldest and biggest of the bunch are Bugbugs (☎020/7620 0500, ⓦwww.bugbugs.co.uk), who have over fifty rickshaws operating Monday to Saturday from 7pm until the early hours of the morning. The rickshaws take up to three passengers and fares are negotiable, though they should work out at around £5 per person per mile.

Boats

Boat services on the Thames are much improved, but they still do not form part of an integrated public transport system. As a result fares are quite expensive, with Travelcards currently only giving the holders a 33 percent discount on tickets.

All services are keenly affected by demand, tides and the weather, and tend to be drastically scaled down in the winter months. Timetables and services are complex, and there are numerous companies and small charter operators – for a full list pick up the Thames River Services booklet from an TfL information office (see p.233), or phone ☎020/7222 1234 or visit ⓦwww.tfl.gov.uk/river.

The busiest part of the river is the central section between Westminster and the Tower of London, but boats run direct as far as Greenwich, downstream, and Hampton Court upstream. Look out, too, for the MV Balmoral and paddle steamer Waverley, which make regular visits to Tower Pier over the summer and autumn (☎0845/130 4647, ⓦwww .waverleyexcursions.co.uk). From April to September, you can also take a boat

---

The London Pass

If you're thinking of visiting a lot of fee-paying attractions in a short space of time, it's worth considering buying a **London Pass** (ⓦwww.londonpass.com), which gives you free entry to a mixed bag of attractions including Hampton Court Palace, Kensington Palace, Kew Gardens, London Aquarium, St Paul's Cathedral, the Tower of London and Windsor Castle, plus a whole host of lesser attractions, and various discounts at selected outlets. You can choose to buy the card with or without an All-Zone Travelcard thrown in; the saving is relatively small, but it does include free travel out to Windsor. The pass costs around £27 for one day (£18 for kids), rising to £72 for six days (£48 for kids); or £32 with a Travelcard (£20 for kids) rising to £110 (£61 for kids). The London Pass can be bought online or in person from tourist offices and London's mainline train or chief underground stations.

Congestion charge

The latest attempt to cut down on car usage in London is the congestion charge, pioneered by the Mayor of London, Ken Livingstone. All vehicles entering central London on weekdays between 7am and 6.30pm are liable to a congestion charge of £8 per vehicle. Drivers can pay for the charge online, over the phone and at garages and shops, and must do so before 10pm the same day or incur a surcharge. The congestion charging zone is bounded by Marylebone and Euston roads in the north, Commercial Street and Tower Bridge in the east, Kennington Lane and Elephant & Castle in the south, and Edgware Road and Park Lane in the west – though, beware, as there are plans to extend the zone westwards. For the latest visit ⓦ www.cclondon.com.

from Westminster via Kew and Richmond to Hampton Court (3hr one-way; £13.50 single, £19.50 return.

Sightseeing tours and guided walks

Sightseeing **bus tours** are run by several rival companies, their open-top double-deckers setting off every fifteen minutes from Victoria station, Trafalgar Square, Piccadilly, and other tourist spots. Tours take roughly two hours (though you can hop on and off as often as you like) and cost around £17. A money-saving option is to skip the commentary and hop on an old London double-decker Routemaster – they run every fifteen minutes on the **#9** between Knightsbridge and the Strand and on the **#15** between Trafalgar Square and the Tower.

Alternatively, you can climb aboard one of the bright yellow World War II amphibious vehicles used by London Duck Tours (☎ 020/7928 3132, ⓦ www.londonduck tours.co.uk), which offers a combined **bus and boat tour** (daily 9.30am–6pm or dusk; £17.50). After departing from behind County Hall, near the London Eye, you spend forty-five minutes driving round the usual sights, before plunging into the river for a half-hour cruise. At the weekend and in the school holidays, it's as well to book ahead.

Walking tours are infinitely more appealing, mixing solid historical facts with juicy anecdotes in the company of a local specialist. Organized walks range from literary pub crawls round Bloomsbury to tours of places associated with the Beatles. They tend to cost around £5 and usually take two hours. To find out what's on offer, check the "Around Town" section of *Time Out*. The widest range of walks are offered by Original London Walks (☎ 020/7624 3978, ⓦ www.walks.com).

Festivals and events

January 1
London Parade A procession of floats, marching bands, clowns, American cheerleaders and classic cars wends its way at noon from Parliament Square to Berkeley Square. ☎ 020/8566 8586, ⓦ www.londonparade.co.uk.

Late January/Early February
Chinese New Year Celebrations Chinatown explodes in a riot of dancing dragons, firecrackers and heaving crowds. ⓦ www.chinatown-online.org.uk.

Late March/Early April

Oxford and Cambridge Boat Race Since 1845, Oxford and Cambridge university rowers have battled it out on a four-mile, upstream course on the Thames from Putney to Mortlake. 🌐 www.theboatrace.org.

Third Sunday in April

London Marathon The world's most popular city marathon, with over 40,000 runners sweating the 26.2 miles from Greenwich Park to Westminster Bridge. 🌐 www.london-marathon.co.uk.

May Bank Holiday Weekend

IWA Canalway Cavalcade Lively celebration of the city's inland waterways held at Little Venice (near Warwick Avenue): decorated narrowboats, Morris dancers and children's activities. 🌐 www.waterways.org.uk.

Third or Fourth Week in May

Chelsea Flower Show The world's finest horticultural event, with the public admitted only for the closing stages (the last two days). Tickets must be bought in advance: ☎ 0870/906 3781, 🌐 www.rhs.org.uk.

Late May/Early June

Beating Retreat Annual military display held on Horse Guards' Parade over three evenings, marking the old custom of drumming the troops back to base at dusk, followed by a floodlit performance by the Massed Bands of the Queen's Household Cavalry. ☎ 020/7414 2271, 🌐 www.army.mod.uk/ceremonialandheritage.

Second Saturday in June

Trooping the Colour The Queen's official birthday celebrations, featuring massed bands, gun salutes and fly-pasts. Tickets for the ceremony itself must be applied for before the end of February, but there are free rehearsals (minus Her Majesty) on the two preceding Saturdays.

Last Week of June and First Week of July

Wimbledon Lawn Tennis Championships This Grand Slam tournament is one of the highlights of the sporting and social calendar. ☎ 020/8946 2244, 🌐 www.wimbledon.org.

Early July

Pride London Colourful, whistle-blowing lesbian and gay march through the city streets followed by a rally in Trafalgar Square. 🌐 www.pridelondon.org.

Mid-July to Mid-September

BBC Henry Wood Promenade Concerts "The Proms" are a series of outstanding nightly classical concerts at the Royal Albert Hall, with standing-room tickets from as little as £4. ☎ 020/7589 8212, 🌐 www.bbc.co.uk/proms. See p.171.

Last bank holiday weekend in August

Notting Hill Carnival The two-day free festival is the longest-running, best-known and biggest street party in Europe, a tumult of imaginatively decorated floats, eye-catching costumes, thumping sound systems, irresistible food and huge crowds. 🌐 www.lnhc.org.uk.

Third Weekend in September

Open House Peek inside hundreds of buildings around London, many of which are normally closed to the public. 🌐 www.londonopenhouse.org.

September–November

Dance Umbrella Six-week season of often groundbreaking new dance work at various venues across town. ☎ 020/8741 4040, 🌐 www.danceumbrella.co.uk.

Late October/Early November

State Opening of Parliament The Queen arrives by horse-drawn coach at the Houses of Parliament at 11am, accompanied by the Household Cavalry and gun salutes. ☎ 020/7219 4272, 🌐 www.parliament.uk.

November

London Film Festival Three-week cinematic season, with scores of new international films screened at the National Film Theatre and other central venues. ☎ 020/7928 3232, 🌐 www.bfi.org.uk or (nearer the time) 🌐 www.rlff.org.uk.

Early November

London Jazz Festival Ten-day international jazz fest held in all London's jazz venues, large and small, in association with BBC Radio 3. ℡020/7405 9900, 🌐www.bbc.co.uk/radio3.

November 5

Bonfire Night In memory of Guy Fawkes – who tried to blow up King James I and the Houses of Parliament in 1605 – effigies are burned on bonfires all over London, and numerous council-run fires and fireworks displays are staged. ℡020/8365 2121.

Second Saturday in November

Lord Mayor's Show The newly appointed Lord Mayor sets off at 11.10am, in the 1756-built State Coach at the head of a vast ceremonial procession from the Guildhall to the Strand and back. Later, there's a big fireworks display on the Thames. ℡020/7606 3030, 🌐www.cityoflondon.gov.uk.

Christmas (6–24 December)

Trafalgar Square carols In gratitude for British help in liberating the country from the Nazis, Norway supplies a mighty spruce tree for Trafalgar Square. Decorated with lights, it becomes the focus for carol singing versus traffic noise each evening (from 5pm) until Christmas Eve.

New Year's Eve

The New Year is welcomed en masse in Trafalgar Square as thousands of inebriated revellers stagger about and slur to Auld Lang Syne at midnight. London Transport runs free public transport to get you home.

Directory

Banks You"ll find a branch of at least one of the big four high-street banks (NatWest, Barclays, Lloyds TSB and HSBC) in every area; opening hours are generally Mon–Fri 9.30am–4.30pm. Outside banking hours go to a bureau de change; these can be found at train stations and airports and in most areas of the city centre.

Bike rental London Bicycle Tour Company, 1a Gabriel's Wharf SE1 ℡020/7928 6838, 🌐www.londonbicycle.com. Waterloo or Southwark tube; On Your Bike, 52–54 Tooley St SE1 ℡020/7378 6669, 🌐www.onyourbike.net. London Bridge tube.

Car rental For the most competitive rates, ring round a few local firms from the Yellow Pages (🌐www.yell.com) before you try your luck with the usual suspects.

Consulates and embassies Australia, Australia House, Strand, WC2 ℡020/7379 4334, 🌐www.australia.org.uk; **Canada**, Canada House, Trafalgar Square, WC2 ℡020/7528 6533 🌐www.dfait-maeci.gc.ca; **Ireland**, 17 Grosvenor Place, SW1 ℡020/7235 2171, 🌐www.irlgov.ie; **New Zealand**, New Zealand House, 80 Haymarket, SW1 ℡020/7930 8422, 🌐www.nzembassy.com; **South Africa**, South Africa House, Trafalgar Square, WC2 ℡020/7451 7299, 🌐www.southafricahouse.com; **USA**, 24 Grosvenor Square, W1 ℡020/7499 9000, 🌐www.usembassy.org.uk.

Cricket Two Test matches are played in London each summer: one at Lord's (℡020/7432 1000, 🌐www.lords.org), the home of English cricket, in St John's Wood; the other at The Oval (℡020/7582 6660, 🌐www.surreycricket.com), in Kennington. In tandem with the full-blown five-day Tests, there's also a series of one-day internationals, two of which are usually held in London.

Cultural institutes Austrian Cultural Forum, 28 Rutland Gate SW7 ℡020/7584 8653, 🌐www.austria.org.uk; **Czech Centre**, 13 Harley St, W1 ℡020/7307 5180, 🌐www.czechcentres.cz/london; **French Institute**, 17 Queensberry Place, SW7 ℡020/7073 1350, 🌐www.institut-francais.org.uk; **Goethe Institute**, 50 Princes Gate, Exhibition Road, SW7 ℡020/7596 4000, 🌐www.goethe.de; **Hungarian Cultural Centre**, 10 Maiden Lane, WC2 ℡020/7240 6162, 🌐www.hungary.org.uk; **Instituto Cervantes**, 102 Eaton Square SW1 ℡020/7235 0353, 🌐londres.cervantes.es; **Italian**

Cultural Institute, 39 Belgrave Square, SW1 ☎020/7235 1461, ⊛www.italcultur .org.uk.

Dentists Emergency treatment: Guy's Hospital, St Thomas Street SE1 ☎020/7188 0511 (Mon–Fri 9am–5pm); London Bridge tube.

Doctors Walk-in consultation: Great Chapel Street Medical Centre, Great Chapel Street, W1 ☎020/7437 9360 (phone for surgery times).

Electricity Electricity supply in London conforms to the EU standard of approximately 230V.

Emergencies For police, fire and ambulance services, call ☎999.

Football Chelsea (☎0870/300 1212, ⊛www.chelseafc.com) lifted the Premiership title for the first time in fifty years in the 2004–05 season, but with the money of Russian oil tycoon, Roman Abramovich, at their disposal, they look set to dominate the Premiership for some time to come. However, for the last decade or so Arsenal (☎020/7704 4000, ⊛www.arsenal.com) have been London's most successful club; their closest rivals (geographically) are Tottenham Hotspur (☎0870/420 5000, ⊛www.spurs.co.uk). Tickets for most Premiership games start at £20–25 and are virtually impossible to get hold of on a casual basis: you need to book in advance, or try and see one of the European or knock-out cup fixtures.

Gay & lesbian London Lesbian & Gay Switchboard ☎020/7837 7324, ⊛www.queery.org.uk. Huge database on everything you might ever want to know, plus legal advice and counselling. Lines are 24hr: keep trying if you can't get through.

Hospitals For 24hr accident and emergency: Charing Cross Hospital, Fulham Palace Road, W6 ☎020/8846 1234; Chelsea & Westminster Hospital, 369 Fulham Rd, SW10 ☎020/8746 8000; Royal Free Hospital, Pond Street, NW3 ☎020/7794 0500; Royal London Hospital, Whitechapel Road, E1 ☎020/7377 7000; St Mary's Hospital, Praed Street, W2 ☎020/7886 6666; University College London Hospital, Grafton Way, WC1 ☎020/7387 9300; Whittington Hospital, Highgate Hill, N19 ☎020/7272 3070.

Ice skating Leisurebox, 17 Queensway (☎020/7229 0172), is a centrally located year-round ice rink. From October to March, there's the Broadgate outdoor ice rink (☎020/7505 4068, ⊛www. broad-gateice.co.uk); in the Christmas and New Year period there are outdoor rinks at Somerset House (⊛www.somerset-house .org.uk) and several other places around London.

Internet Most hotels, B&Bs hostels and libraries will have Internet access; there are also Internet cafés (£2–5 per hour) dotted around the city; ⊛www.easyEvery thing.com is the biggest chain, with eight branches, including a 24hr branch at 456 Strand, off Trafalgar Square (Charing Cross tube).

Left luggage Airports Gatwick: North Terminal ☎01293/502 013 (daily 5am–9pm); South Terminal ☎01293/502 014 (24hr). Heathrow: Terminal 1 ☎020/8745 5301 (daily 6am–11pm); Terminal 2 ☎020/8745 4599 (daily 5.30am–11pm); Terminal 3 ☎020/8759 3344 (daily 5am–11pm); Terminal 4 ☎020/8897 6874 (daily 5.30am–11pm). London City ☎020/7646 0000 (daily 6am–9pm). Stansted ☎0870/000 0303 (24hr). Luton has 24hr lockers (no phone). **Train stations** Charing Cross (daily 7am–11pm); Euston (Mon–Sat 6.45am–11.15pm, Sun 7.15am–11pm); Victoria (daily 7am–10.15pm); Waterloo International (daily 7am–10pm).

Lost property Airports Gatwick ☎01293/503 162 (Mon–Sat 8am–7pm, Sun 8am–4pm); Heathrow ☎020/8745 7727 (daily 8am–4pm); London City ☎020/7646 0000 (Mon–Sat 5.30am–9pm, Sun 10am–9pm); Stansted ☎0870/000 0303 (daily 6am–midnight). **Buses**: ☎020/7222 1234(24hr) ⊛www .londontransport.co.uk; Heathrow Express ☎0845/600 1515 (daily 8am–4pm), ⊛www.heathrowexpress.co.uk. **Taxis** (black cabs only) ☎020/7918 2000 (Mon–Fri 9am–4pm). **Train stations** Euston ☎020/7387 8699 (Mon–Fri 9am–5.30pm); King's Cross ☎020/7278 3310 (Mon–Sat 9am–5pm); Liverpool Street ☎020/7247 4297 (Mon–Fri 9am–5.30pm); Paddington ☎020/7313 1514 (Mon–Fri 9am–5.30pm); Victoria ☎020/7963 0957 (daily 7am–11pm); Waterloo ☎020/7401 8444 (Mon–Fri 7am–11pm). **Tube trains** Transport for London ☎020/7486 2496, ⊛www.tfl.gov.uk.

Markets Brick Lane Brick Lane, Cygnet St, Sclater St; Bacon St, Cheshire St, Chilton St. Sun 8am–2pm. Fruit and

239

veg, cheap goods, bric-a-brac. **Brixton** Electric Avenue, Pope's Rd, Brixton Station Rd, Atlantic Rd. Mon, Tues & Thurs–Sat 8am–6pm, Wed 8am–1pm. African and Caribbean foods, hair and beauty products, records, clothes. **Camden** Camden High St to Chalk Farm Rd. Daily 9.30am–5.30pm (outdoor stalls Sat & Sun 10am–6pm). A conglomeration of markets, selling food, clothes, jewellery, gifts, records, arts and crafts. **Columbia Road** Columbia Rd. Sun 8am–1pm. Flowers and plants. **Covent Garden** The Piazza, and Jubilee Market, off Southampton St. Daily 10.30am–6.30pm. Crafts, gifts, clothes and (on Mon only) antiques. **Greenwich** Greenwich High Rd, Stockwell St, and College Approach. Thurs–Sun 10am–5pm. Antiques (Thurs & Fri), arts & crafts (Fri–Sun). **Portobello** Portobello Rd and Golborne Rd. Main market Mon–Wed, Fri & Sat 8am–6.30pm, Thurs 8am–1pm. Antiques (Sat 6am–4pm)), fruit and veg, clothes, furniture and bric-a-brac. **Old Spitalfields** Commercial St, between Brushfield St and Lamb Streets. Mon–Fri 10am–4pm, Sun 9am–5pm. Organic food, crafts and clothes.

Money The basic unit of currency is the pound sterling (£), divided into 100 pence (p). Coins come in denominations of 1p, 2p, 5p, 10p, 20p, 50p, £1 and £2; notes come in denominations of £5, £10, £20 and £50.

Motorbike rental Raceways, 201–203 Lower Rd, SE16 ☏020/7237 6494 (Surrey Quays tube) and 17 The Vale, Uxbridge Road, W3 ☏020/8749 8181 (Shepherds Bush tube), ☮www.raceways.net. Mon–Sat 9am–5pm.

Police Central police stations include: Charing Cross, Agar Street, WC2 ☏020/7240 1212; Holborn, 10 Lambs Conduit St, WC1 ☏020/7704 1212; Marylebone, 1–9 Seymour St W1 ☏020/7486 1212; West End Central, 27 Savile Row, W1 ☏020/7437 1212, ☮www.met.police.uk; City of London Police, Bishopsgate, EC2 ☏020/7601 2222 ☮www.cityoflondon.police.uk.

Post offices The only (vaguely) late-opening post office is the Trafalgar Square branch at 24–28 William IV St, WC2 4DL ☏020/7930 9580 (Mon–Sat 8am–6.30pm); it's also the city's poste restante collection point. For general postal enquiries phone ☏0845/7740 740 (Mon–Fri 8am–7.30pm, Sat 8am–2pm), or visit the website ☮www.royalmail.com.

Public holidays On the following days, all banks and offices are closed, while everyone else pretty much runs to a Sunday schedule: New Year's Day (January 1); Good Friday (early April); Easter Monday (early April); Spring Bank Holiday (first Monday in May); May Bank Holiday (last Monday in May); August Bank Holiday (last Monday in August); Christmas Day (December 25); Boxing Day (December 26). Note that if January 1, December 25 or December 26 falls on a Saturday or Sunday, the holiday falls on the following weekday.

Rape crisis ☏020/8683 3300, ☮www.rapecrisis.co.uk; Mon–Fri noon–2.30pm & 7–9.30pm, Sat & Sun 2.30–5pm.

Samaritans Drop-in at 46 Marshall St, W1 (daily 9am–9pm); ☏020/7734 2800 (24hr) or ☏08457/909090, ☮www.samaritans.org.

Saunas Turkish baths: Ironmonger Row Baths, Ironmonger Row (☏020/7253 4011) and Porchester Spa, 226 Queensway ☏020/7792 3980. **Women-only:** The Sanctuary, 12 Floral St ☏0870/770 3350, ☮www.thesanctuary.co.uk. **Gay:** Chariots 1, 201–207 Shoreditch High St; ☏020/7247 5333, ☮www.gaysauna.co.uk.

Swimming Outdoor and indoor pools at Covent Garden's Oasis Sports Centre, 32 Endell St ☏020/7831 1804. Outdoor swimming at the Serpentine Lido in Hyde Park (mid-June to mid-Sept daily 10am–6pm; £3.50), or the open-air pools on Hampstead Heath (daily 7am–9pm or dusk).

Telephones There should be a public payphone within five minutes' walk of wherever you're standing. Most take all coins from 10p upwards, though some take only phonecards (available from post offices and newsagents).

Time Greenwich Mean Time (GMT) is used from October to March; for the rest of the year the country switches to British Summer Time (BST), one hour ahead of GMT.

Tipping Porters, bellboys and table waiters rely on being tipped to bump up their often dismal wages. It's not normal, however, to leave tips in pubs, although bar staff are sometimes offered drinks, which they may accept in the form of money. Taxi drivers expect tips – add about ten percent to the fare – as will traditional barbers.

ESSENTIALS Directory

Fly Less – Stay Longer!

Rough Guides believes in the good that travel does, but we are deeply aware of the impact of fuel emissions on climate change. We recommend taking fewer trips and staying for longer. If you can avoid travelling by air, please use an alternative, especially for journeys of under 1000km/600miles. And always offset your travel at Ⓦ www.roughguides.com/climatechange.

Toilets There are surprisingly few public toilets in London. All mainline train stations have toilets as do major tube stations. Department stores and free museums and galleries are another good option.

Train enquiries For national rail enquiries, call ☎ 0845/748 4950 or visit Ⓦ www .nationalrail.co.uk.

Travel agents STA Travel, 33 Bedford St, WC2, ☎ 020/7240 9821, Ⓦ www .statravel.co.uk; Trailfinders, Lower Ground Floor, Waterstone's, 203–205 Piccadilly, W1 ☎ 020/7292 1888, Ⓦ www .trailfinders.co.uk.

Chronology

Chronology

43 AD ▶ Romans invade and establish a permanent military camp by the Thames called Londinium.

410 ▶ The Romans abandon Londinium and leave the place at the mercy of marauding Saxon pirates.

871–1066 ▶ The Danes and Norwegians fight it out with the kings of Wessex over who should control London.

1066 ▶ Following the defeat of the English King Harold at the Battle of Hastings, William the Conqueror, Duke of Normandy is crowned king in Westminster Abbey.

1348 ▶ The Black Death wipes out some two-thirds of London's population of 75,000.

1381 ▶ During the Peasants' Revolt, London is overrun by the rebels who lynch the archbishop, plus countless rich merchants and clerics.

1532–35 ▶ The Reformation: King Henry VIII breaks with the Roman Catholic church, establishes the Church of England, dissolves the monasteries and executes religious dissenters.

1553–58 ▶ The religious pendulum swings the other way as Elizabeth's fervently Catholic sister, forever known as "Bloody Mary", takes to the throne and it's the Protestants' turn to be martyred.

1558–1603 ▶ During the reign of Elizabeth I, London enjoys an economic boom and witnesses the English Renaissance, epitomised by the theatre of William Shakespeare.

1603 ▶ James VI of Scotland becomes James I of England, thereby uniting the two crowns and marking the beginning of the Stuart dynasty in England.

1605 ▶ The Gunpowder Plot to blow up the Houses of Parliament (and King James I along with it) is foiled and Guy Fawkes and his Catholic conspirators executed.

1642–49 ▶ English Civil War between the Parliamentarians and Royalists ends with the victory of the former under the leadership of Oliver Cromwell. King Charles I (1625–49) is tried and beheaded in Westminster.

1660 ▶ The Restoration: Charles I's son, Charles II (1660–1685), returns from exile to restore the monarchy and as the "Merry Monarch" actively encourages the development of the arts and sciences.

1665 ▶ The Great Plague kills some 100,000 Londoners, around half the population.

1666 The Great Fire rages for four days, kills just seven people but destroys four-fifths of the city.

1714–1830 ▶ The Georgian period: From the reign of George I to George IV, London's population doubles to one million, making it Europe's largest city. The period is one of boom and bust, gin drinking, rioting and hanging.

1837–1901 ▶ During the reign of Queen Victoria, London becomes the capital of an empire that stretches across the globe. Its population increases to nearly seven million, making it the largest city in the world. Industrialization brings pollution, overcrowding and extreme poverty.

1851 ▶ The Great Exhibition is held in a giant glasshouse known as the "Crystal Palace", erected on Hyde Park.

1914–1918 ▶ During World War I, London experiences its first aerial attacks, with Zeppelin raids leaving some 650 dead – a minor skirmish in the context of a war that takes the lives of millions.

1939–1945 ▶ During the course of World War II, London suffers a lot of bomb damage, with 60,000 killed and many thousands more made homeless.

1948 ▶ The SS *Windrush* brings the first postwar immigrants to London from the West Indies; over the next two decades, thousands more follow suit, not just from the Caribbean, but also from the former colonies of Pakistan, Bangladesh and Hong Kong.

1951 ▶ The Festival of Britain is held on the south bank of the Thames, in an attempt to dispel the postwar gloom. The Royal Festival Hall is its one lasting legacy.

1960s ▶ Pop music and fashion helps turn London into the epicentre of the "Swinging Sixties", with King's Road and Carnaby Street the hippest places to shop and be seen.

1980s ▶ Under the right-wing Thatcher government, the gap between rich and poor grows. Homelessness returns to London in a big way and London's governing body, the GLC, is abolished, leaving London as the only European city without a directly elected body to represent it.

2000 ▶ London gets to vote for its own Mayor and its own elected assembly, London's national museums introduce free entry, the London Eye enhances the city's skyline and the Millennium Dome opens for one year, and proves a critical and financial flop.

2005 ▶ London wins the right to hold the 2012 Olympic Games. Two days later on July 7, the city is hit by four suicide bombers who kill themselves and over fifty commuters in four separate explosions.

small print & Index

A Rough Guide to Rough Guides

In 1981, Mark Ellingham, a recent graduate in English from Bristol University, was travelling in Greece on a tiny budget and couldn't find the right guidebook. With a group of friends he wrote his own guide, combining a contemporary, journalistic style with a practical approach to travellers' needs. That first Rough Guide was a student scheme that became a publishing phenomenon. Today, Rough Guides include recommendations from shoestring to luxury and cover hundreds of destinations around the globe, including almost every country in the Americas and Europe, more than half of Africa and most of Asia and Australasia. Millions of readers relish Rough Guides' wit and inquisitiveness as much as their enthusiastic, critical approach and value-for-money ethos. The guides' ever-growing team of authors and photographers is spread all over the world.

In the early 1990s, Rough Guides branched out of travel, with the publication of Rough Guides to World Music, Classical Music and the Internet. All three have become benchmark titles in their fields, spearheading the publication of a range of more than 350 titles under the Rough Guide name, including phrasebooks, waterproof maps, music guides from Opera to Heavy Metal, reference works as diverse as Conspiracy Theories and Shakespeare, and popular culture books from iPods to Poker. Rough Guides also produce a series of more than 120 World Music CDs in partnership with World Music Network.

Visit www.roughguides.com to see our latest publications.

Rough Guide travel images are available for commercial licensing at www.roughguidespictures.com

Publishing information

This second edition published March 2007 by Rough Guides Ltd, 80 Strand, London WC2R ORL. 345 Hudson St, 4th Floor, New York, NY 10014, USA.

Distributed by the Penguin Group
Penguin Books Ltd, 80 Strand, London WC2R ORL
Penguin Group (USA), 375 Hudson Street, NY 10014, USA
14 Local Shopping Centre, Panchsheel Park, New Delhi 110017, India
Penguin Group (Australia), 250 Camberwell Road, Camberwell, Victoria 3124, Australia
Penguin Group (Canada), 10 Alcorn Avenue, Toronto, ON M4V 1E4, Canada
Penguin Group (NZ), 67 Apollo Drive, Mairangi Bay, Auckland 1310, New Zealand
Typeset in Bembo and Helvetica to an original design by Henry Iles.
Cover concept by Peter Dyer.

Printed and bound in China
© Rob Humphreys, March 2007
No part of this book may be reproduced in any form without permission from the publisher except for the quotation of brief passages in reviews.
256pp includes index
A catalogue record for this book is available from the British Library
ISBN 10: 1-84353-758-3
ISBN 13: 9-781-84353-758-8

The publishers and authors have done their best to ensure the accuracy and currency of all the information in London DIRECTIONS, however, they can accept no responsibility for any loss, injury, or inconvenience sustained by any traveller as a result of information or advice contained in the guide.

1 3 5 7 9 8 6 4 2

Help us update

We've gone to a lot of effort to ensure that the second edition of London DIRECTIONS is accurate and up-to-date. However, things change – places get "discovered", opening hours are notoriously fickle, restaurants and rooms raise prices or lower standards. If you feel we've got it wrong or left something out, we'd like to know, and if you can remember the address, the price, the phone number, so much the better.

We'll credit all contributions, and send a copy of the next edition (or any other DIRECTIONS guide or Rough Guide if you prefer) for the best letters. Everyone who writes to us and isn't already a subscriber will receive a copy of our full-colour thrice-yearly newsletter. Please mark letters: "London DIRECTIONS Update" and send to: Rough Guides, 80 Strand, London WC2R ORL, or Rough Guides, 4th Floor, 345 Hudson St, New York, NY 10014. Or send an email to mail@roughguides.com

Have your questions answered and tell others about your trip at www.roughguides.atinfopop.com

Rough Guide credits

Text editor: Karoline Densley
Layout: Ajay Verma
Photography: Suzanne Porter, Victor Borg and
Mark Thomas
Cartography: Maxine Repath

Picture editor: Jj Luck
Proofreaders: Serena Stephenson, Stewart Wild
Production: Katherine Owers
Cover design: Chlöe Roberts

Acknowledgements

Rob: thanks to Val and Gordon for the odd foray, to Josh for company and to the wonderful Karoline.

Readers' letters

Dr Leon Allen, Laura Boggs, A. Brodie, Megan
Bollman, Sergio Burns, Charlotte Stewart Clark,
John Collins, Russ & Jane Davison, Paul Deneve,
Ming Wei Hui, John Fisher, Dean Fox, Ron Fry,
Angela Greenfield, Chihiro Goddard, Jan Hamilton,
Amy Jackson, Andrew Kleissner, Maria Kleissner,
Nathaniel Koschmann, Jim Lyons, Miss C A
Mumford, Paul Nicol, Joan Nikelsky, Harley Nott,
Christelle Passuello, Candice Pettifer, Debbie Porter,
Lorraine Rainbow, Irmgard Rathmacher, H H Saffery,
Sasha from E13, Caroline Schubert, Pete Tenerelli,
Mr A C Wells, Jim Young, Ellen Zimmerman

Photo credits

All images © Rough Guides except the following:

Front cover picture: St Paul's Cathedral © Getty
Back cover picture: British Museum © Mark Thomas
p.1 Waterloo Bridge © Mark Thomas
p.2 Big Ben from Trafalgar Square © Jon Arnold Images
p.3 Thames view © Mark Thomas
p.6 Door knocker © Brigitte Bott/Alamy
p.8 *Golden Hinde*, near Southwark Cathedral © Travelshots.com/Alamy
p.8 Hampstead Heath © Mark Thomas
p.10 *The Marriage of Giovanni Arnolfini and Giovanna Cenam* by Jan van Eyck © Corbis
p.11 Tate Modern © Pawel Libera
p.12 Somerset House ice rink © Mark Thomas
p.25 G-A-Y © Mean Fiddler
p.26 Brixton undercover market © Janine Wiedel Photolibrary /Alamy
p.27 London Central Mosque © Mark Thomas
p.27 Chinatown at night © Alex Segre/Alamy
p.28 Tate Modern © Mark Thomas
p.28 Iveagh Bequest, Kenwood House © Bill Batten/English Heritage
p.29 *A Bar at the Folies-Bergère* by Edouard Manet © The Samuel Courtauld Trust, Courtauld Institute of Art Gallery, London
p.29 *Venus and Mars* by Sandro Botticelli © The National Gallery, London
p.30 Lewis chessmen, British Museum © British Museum
p.30 Thomas Chippendale: The V&A's British Galleries © Derry Moore/ Victoria and Albert Museum
p.31 Atrium in Sir John Soane's Museum © Massimo Listri/Corbis
p.33 St. Paul's Cathedral © Mark Thomas
p.35 The Imperial Crown of India © Tim Graham/Corbis
p.37 Shakespeare's Globe Theatre © Duncan Soar/Alamy
p.40 Millennium Bridge © Rachel Royse/Corbis
p.44 Courtesy *The Rookery Hotel*
p.45 Courtesy The Sanctuary
p.45 Courtesy *Light Bar, St Martins Lane Hotel*
p.46 Diana Memorial Playground © Graham Tim/Corbis Sygma
p.47 Child and monkey © Natural History Museum
p.48 Shakespeare Globe Theatre © Adrian Chinery/Alamy
p.50 Evensong at St. Paul's Cathedral © www.britainonview.com
p.51 Kenwood House © Mark Thomas
p.51 Impressionist art sale, Sotheby's Auction House © Ian Shaw/Alamy
p.54 Chamber of Horrors © Madame Tussaud's

p.55 London Dungeon © Cordaiy Photo Library Ltd./Corbis

p.55 Courtesy the Hunterian Museum

p.55 Old Operating Theatre © Michael Jenner/Collections

p.57 The Globe © Julian Nieman/Collections

p.57 The Place © Dennis Gilbert

p.57 Donmar Warehouse © Robbie Jack/Corbis

p.57 National Theatre © Hideo Kurihara/Collections

p.58 Live band at the Astoria © Mark Thomas

p.58 Courtesy Jazz Café

p.59 Courtesy Ronnie Scott's

p.60 Courtesy Handel House Museum

p.60 2 Willow Road © National Trust

p.61 British Museum Egypt Antiquity © Peter Horree/Alamy

p.62 Courtesy Dance Umbrella

p.62 Last Night at the Proms © Robbie Jack/Corbis

p.63 Notting Hill Carnival © James McCormick/ArenaPAL

p.63 The Durbar Court of the Foreign Office © Peter Aprahamian/ Corbis

p.63 Canalway Cavalcade, Little Venice © Michael Freeman/Corbis

p.63 Wimbledon Lawn Tennis Championships © Nils Jorgensen/Rex Features

p.64 Hungerford footbridge © Mark Thomas

p.66 The National Gallery © Mark Thomas

p.69 *Battle of San Romano* by Paolo Uccello © Corbis

p.70 Portrait of Isambard Kingdom Brunel © Hulton-Deutsch Collection/Corbis

p.71 St. Martins © Mark Thomas

p.77 *Newton* by William Blake, 1795 © Bettmann/Corbis

p.79 St James's Park © Mark Thomas

p.83 Courtesy Berry Bros. & Rudd

p.114 Somerset House fountains © Mark Thomas

p.127 Busts of Lenin in the Marx Memorial Library © Mark Thomas

p.135 The Monument, City of London © Mark Thomas

p.143 Courtesy the *Loungelover*

p.154 Royal Festival Hall © Jeremy Horner/Corbis

p.159 Exhibition at The Tate Gallery © Timothy Allen/Axiom

p.167 Wellington Arch at Hyde Park © nagele-stock.com/Alamy

p.176 William Morris: The V&A's New British Galleries © Victoria and Albert Museum

p.183 Farmer's market, Notting Hill Gate © Ferruccio/Alamy

p.202 Tulip staircase © Mark Thomas

Index

Maps are marked in colour